SPENSER'S 'FIERCE WARRES AND FAITHFULL LOVES'

Martial and Chivalric Symbolism in *The Faerie Queene*

For Alice
in lieu of many ornaments

Spenser's 'Fierce Warres and Faithfull Loves'

Martial and Chivalric Symbolism in *The Faerie Queene*

Michael Leslie

D. S. BREWER · BARNES & NOBLE

First published in 1983
by D.S. Brewer, 240 Hills Road, Cambridge
an imprint of Boydell & Brewer Ltd
PO Box 9, Woodbridge, Suffolk IP12 3DF
and by Barnes & Noble Books
81 Adams Drive, Totowa, NJ 07512, U.S.A.

ISBN 0 85991 150 0

British Library Cataloguing in Publication Data

Leslie, Michael
    Spenser's 'Fierce warres and faithfull loves'.
    1. Spenser, Edmund. Faerie Queene
    I. Title
    821'.3   PR2358

Library of Congress Cataloging in Publication Data

Leslie, Michael.
    Spenser's 'fierce warres and faithfull loves'.

    Bibliography: p.196
    Includes index.
    1. Spenser, Edmund, 1552?-1599. Faerie Queene.
    2. Spenser, Edmund, 1552?-1599 — Allegory
       and symbolism.
    3. Chivalry in literature.
    4. War in literature.
    I. Spenser, Edmund, 1552?-1599. Faerie Queene.
    II. Title.
    PR2358.L4   1983   823'.3   83-14929

    US ISBN 0 389 20465 X

Printed by Nene Litho
Bound by Woolnough Bookbinding
Both of Wellingborough, Northamptonshire

CONTENTS

ILLUSTRATIONS

PREFACE

Unless otherwise stated, the spelling and punctuation in all quotations are as in the editions cited, with the exceptions that 'u/v' and 'i/j' have been normalized and that common contractions have been silently expanded.

Translations are my own unless otherwise stated. In the case of Virgil I have based my translations on the Loeb Classics edition, but have emended silently to achieve particular fidelity to the original where I have thought this necessary.

In writing this book I have received the help and encouragement of many people. Specific debts are recorded in the notes, but I should like to thank particularly Dr Peter Armour of London University for discussing some Italian material; Dr Douglas Brooks-Davies of Manchester University for comments on Chapters One and Four; and Professor John Dixon Hunt of the Sir Thomas Browne Institute, University of Leiden, who read a draft of the manuscript and offered many suggestions for improvement, as well as encouragement, support, and best of all, friendship. I have also enjoyed many hours of dispute with my friends and fellow-Spenserians, Drs Jan Karel Kouwenhoven and John Radcliffe. My greatest scholarly debt, however, is to Professor Alastair Fowler of the University of Edinburgh, who in supervising this work as a dissertation was always interested, patient, and rigorous in his criticism, to my incalculable benefit. All faults are, needless to say, my own responsibility. I should also like to thank my former colleagues in the Department of English, Bedford College, and my present colleagues in the Department of English Literature, University of Sheffield, for their tolerance and support; and the University of Sheffield Press Committee for the generous financial assistance which has rendered publication possible.

ABBREVIATIONS

References to parts of the Bible employ the standard abbreviations. In references to books, the place of publication, unless otherwise stated, is London.

BL British Library
BM British Museum
CSP *Calendar of State Papers*
EETS *Early English Text Society*
HLQ *Huntington Library Quarterly*
HMSO Her Majesty's Stationery Office
JEGP *Journal of English and Germanic Philology*
JWCI *Journal of the Warburg and Courtauld Institutes*
MLN *Modern Language Notes*
MLR *Modern Language Review*
MP *Modern Philology*
NY New York
N&Q *Notes and Queries*
OED *Oxford English Dictionary*
OUP Oxford University Press
PMLA *Publications of the Modern Language Association of America*
PQ *Philological Quarterly*
PUP Princeton University Press
RES *Review of English Studies*
SEL *Studies in English Literature, 1500-1900*
SP *Studies in Philology*
UTQ *University of Toronto Quarterly*
UP University Press

INTRODUCTION

This book considers a feature of *The Faerie Queene* hitherto largely unstudied: Spenser's use of the traditional symbolism of the actions and equipment of a knight. I argue that Spenser uses this 'martial and chivalric symbolism', as I have called it, throughout his epic poem.

My term implies that this kind of symbolism can be divided into two parts. The first is that composed of the symbolism of armour, weapons, and battles drawn on by Spenser to contribute generally to the expression of his allegory: for instance, in the first chapter I argue that the shields of Prince Arthur, Britomart, and Sir Arthegall develop our understanding of the virtues of which these figures are patron; and that they also convey the interrelation of the various figures and of their virtues.

These martial symbols — shields and their devices, weapons and the blows struck with them, the complete armour of the knight — constitute a group only because all of them are connected with combat, not because they are associated with any single theme or set of ideas. However the second group of symbols is that made up of those specifically identified with chivalry and used by Spenser to express what I take to be a chivalric theme and meaning in *The Faerie Queene*.[1] My discussion of this latter group will propose the existence of allusions to the institution of knighthood (and particularly to the Order of the Garter) by means of chivalric symbolism, especially in Books Three, Four, and Five of the poem.

In its use of martial and chivalric symbolism Spenser's poem employs a traditional mode of expression which existed both in antiquity and in Elizabethan England and which had its place in daily life as well as in literature. As we shall see, previous epic literature is prominent among Spenser's sources; and he draws extensively on Homer, Virgil, Ariosto, and Tasso. Equally prominent is the Bible. But Spenser also derives material from non-literary sources, particularly the political, social, legal, and heraldic symbolism of his own day.

Although this argument is not revolutionary it implies a reassessment of elements of *The Faerie Queene* which have, perhaps, for-

---

[1] The two groups are not, of course, exclusive. It will be seen that in certain contexts the general martial symbols take on specific chivalric meanings.

merly been passed over as insignificant. In the course of this book I hope to establish the need to attend to and interpret these martial and chivalric elements if we are to achieve a fuller understanding of the poem.

Despite the critical advances of the past twenty years, the martial and chivalric nature of *The Faerie Queene* has not been coherently studied.[2] Indeed critical commentary on the battles and warriors of the poem is comparatively rare: for every mention of Satyrane and Marinell's tournaments, the principal chivalric episodes of the poem, there are a host of articles on the Temple of Venus and the Garden of Adonis. And in particular any symbolic meaning contained in these martial passages has gone largely unremarked. This is not due to any lack of interest in the iconography of *The Faerie Queene*: the works of such scholars as Rosemond Tuve, Alastair Fowler, and Paul Alpers have alerted us to the far more pervasive and profound incidence of symbolic expression in the poem than had hitherto been suspected, even though some of their specific conclusions may be contested.[3] And of more recent contributions, James Nohrnberg's monumental commentary, *The Analogy of 'The Faerie Queene'* (Princeton: PUP, 1976), has proposed ever more labyrinthine complexities. Despite the lead of these scholars, however, little attention has been given to symbolism in the martial episodes of the poem.

One might have expected more of that school of criticism aiming to pay close attention to the surface of *The Faerie Queene*. These critics advocate, with A.C.Hamilton, the study of 'Spenser's art of language', the immediate, verbal expression of the poem.[4] As a result of their labours we now have a far wittier Spenser than that bequeathed to us by the Romantics and the Victorians. Between this group and the iconographers there is, of course, no necessary conflict (indeed they are by no means as discrete as this summary suggests): Jane Aptekar, an iconographical critic, describes Spenser as 'metaphysical'; but her Spenser manipulates his symbols as wittily as he does his words, a side to the poet also shown us by such scholars as René Graziani.[5]

---

2   The starting-point for the current Renaissance of Spenser studies would seem to be A.C.Hamilton's *The Structure of Allegory in 'The Faerie Queene'* (Oxford: Clarendon Press, 1961). Behind this, however, lie the seminal and stimulating works of C.S.Lewis.

3   Particularly in their respective books, *Allegorical Imagery: Some Mediaeval Books and their Posterity* (Princeton: PUP, 1966); *Spenser and the Numbers of Time* (Routledge, 1964); and *The Poetry of 'The Faerie Queene'* (Princeton: PUP, 1967). These three writers have each made significant contributions to the understanding of martial symbolism in the poem.

4   *The Faerie Queene*, ed. A.C.Hamilton (Longman, 1977), p.vii.

5   Jane Aptekar, *Icons of Justice: Iconography and Thematic Imagery in Book*

In outlining his approach, Professor Hamilton contends that 'interpretation may be controlled and refined by reading the words more carefully in context'.[6] But surprisingly, the context of Spenser's words has not included his poem's apparent genre.[7] Perhaps it has been thought too obvious to devote much attention to *The Faerie Queene*'s status as a work of chivalric literature. Certainly, in all the discussions of verbal and symbolic wit and of allegorical, theological, and philosophical subtleties, the knights and their battles have been left very much alone. Our growing awareness of *The Faerie Queene*'s debts to and connections with the classics and the European Renaissance has possibly rendered us less receptive to its apparently more medieval features: we are unwilling to turn from the clear vision of the Graces to the confusing, if not confused, 'Knights and Ladies gentle deeds' (I. Proem. 1.5) of which Spenser undertakes to sing.[8]

A common feature of both the critical schools I have mentioned is that they tend to avoid any discussion of passages portraying or describing martial action in *The Faerie Queene*. Modern scholarship has found its most fertile pastures to lie in the close analysis of near-static, tableau-like scenes; and this approach has yielded impressive results, revealing many qualities hitherto unnoticed. But it has also led us into the peril of seeing only the static in the poem; and that in acute isolation. Paul Alpers's *The Poetry of 'The Faerie Queene'* is the most challenging work to arise from this tendency. He divides the poem into stanzas and even lines of such independence as to deny any narrative, action, or drama. But however beneficial locally, this approach ignores aspects of *The Faerie Queene* which our responses as readers confirm to be present. Professor Alpers's partial view is betrayed by an analysis of the examples with which he supports his case. He discusses the Cave of Mammon in Book Two; but like many other critics completely ignores the context of this adventure: the presence, past and future, of the pagan brothers Pyrochles and

Five of 'The Faerie Queene' (New York: Columbia UP, 1969), p.3. Graziani demonstrates Spenser's witty adaptation of Philip II's Apollo *impresa* in 'Philip II's *impresa* and Spenser's Souldan', *JWCI* 27 (1964), pp.322-24.

6 'Our new poet: Spenser, "well of English undefyld" ' in *A Theatre for Spenserians*, eds Judith M. Kennedy and James A. Reither (Toronto: Toronto UP, 1973), p.103.

7 John Arthos's book, *On the Poetry of Spenser and the Form of the Romances* (Allen & Unwin, 1956), now seems a rather limited approach to this subject.

8 All quotations from *The Faerie Queene* are taken from *The Works of Edmund Spenser: A Variorum Edition*, ed. Edwin Greenlaw *et al.*, 9 vols (Baltimore: Johns Hopkins Press, 1932-49), hereafter cited as *Var*, unless otherwise stated.

Cymochles is not mentioned.[9] More revealing still is his account of Book Four, which omits any reference to the second, fourth, seventh, and ninth cantos, thus eliminating most of the action of the book. In particular the important narrative events of the two tournaments receive barely a mention.

The denial of narrative, action, and drama in *The Faerie Queene* is the exaggeration of a good point: the slower, more static scenes are frequently crucial. But this should not prevent our recognising the significance of other sections of the poem, sections likely, given the type of narrative, to be martial. T.K.Dunseath has also noted the scant attention given to such events as battles and his own studies lead him to oppose the consensus view:

> the neglected battles are every bit as important to the argument of the poem, and an understanding of them is essential. In these seemingly in-significant and endless Iliads, what seems occasional metaphor becomes ... an elaborate poetic order in which every image contributes to the progress of the argument.[10]

Although Professor Dunseath's claim is perhaps excessive in its absoluteness, his general point is correct: some of the martial scenes embody arguments integral to the poem; others, like the Red Cross Knight's combats with Errour and the Dragon and the tournaments of Books Four and Five, provide the essential encapsulation and resolution of some of the poem's principal themes.

In studying *The Faerie Queene* we should remember the counsel of E.H.Gombrich, who agrees with E.D.Hirsch in stressing 'that the intended meaning of a work can only be established once we have decided what category or genre of literature the work in question was intended to belong to'.[11] The genre of *The Faerie Queene* has perhaps been lost sight of in recent years. It comes into the same category as *Orlando furioso, Rinaldo,* and *Gerusalemme liberata*: a chivalric epic-romance. To be sure, each of these works is very different from the others in important ways. Nevertheless they are similar

---

9 *The Poetry of 'The Faerie Queene'*, pp.235-75. Frank Kermode, another of the seminal writers on this passage, also ignores the framing incidents involving Pyrochles and Cymochles, in 'The Cave of Mamon', *Stratford-upon-Avon Studies* 2 (1960), pp.151-73.

10 *Spenser's Allegory of Justice in Book Five of 'The Faerie Queene'* (Princeton: PUP, 1968), pp.32-33.

11 *Symbolic Images* (1972; 2nd edn., Oxford: Phaidon Press, 1978), p.5; citing E.D.Hirsch, *Validity in Interpretation* (1967). In general, of course, this comment begs the question of conscious genre theory in earlier periods. But in Spenser's case the *Letter to Raleigh* is sufficient evidence of Spenser's awareness of his poem's place within a genre.

in that they utilize a chivalric setting and martial activities. I have tried to go back to this first stage in interpretation in order to understand what use, if any, Spenser makes of the symbolic language that came to him with the genre.

The bias in some modern studies of *The Faerie Queene* against the poem's martial passages and characteristics is perhaps counterbalanced by a growing understanding of the intellectual and artistic climate of Elizabethan England. This understanding has been fostered by such scholars as Frances Yates, Roy Strong, and Stephen Orgel, who have taken us a considerable way towards comprehending the strange and eclectic world in which Spenser wrote.[12] Their works have concentrated on explicating the visual and poetic arts of the period and particularly on the courtly masques, pageants, and tournaments which combined literature and spectacle, and which are so important for *The Faerie Queene*. Of equal and largely unrecognised value to Spenser studies have been the pioneering examinations of the new knowledge available in the late sixteenth century. Stuart Piggott and, above all, T. D. Kendrick have revealed the significance of the development of antiquarianism and historiography in England.[13]

Spenser's epic is an element in the general upsurge of interest in chivalry in the England of the sixteenth century. Although its prominence among the arts of war had declined, chivalry never ceased to be a prized part of the aristocratic ethos in either of the principal kingdoms of northern Europe, England and France. Partly this was because of its kinship with the prevailing hierarchical structures of the state: earls, barons, and knights, though their position and power in renaissance England might stem from impersonal or financial sources, had originally been leaders of men in battle; and the spectacular and romantic arts of medieval combat continued to be prized as an expression of worth and honour. Spectacular they could certainly be: Henry VIII's extravagent display at the Field of Cloth of Gold in 1520 probably cost as much as any war it might have been designed to avoid; and the competitive glory of the French and

---

[12] Yates's most pertinent essays are collected in *Astraea: The Imperial Theme in the Sixteenth Century* (Routledge, 1975); Strong's in *The Cult of Elizabeth* (Thames and Hudson, 1977), which continues many of the themes of his earlier *Portraits of Queen Elizabeth I* (Oxford: Clarendon Press, 1963); and Stephen Orgel's works include *The Jonsonian Masque* (Cambridge, Massachusetts: Harvard UP, 1965), *The Illusion of Power: Political Theater in the English Renaissance* (Berkeley: California UP, 1975), and, with Strong, *Inigo Jones: The Theatre of the Jacobean Court* (Sotheby Parke Bernet, 1973).

[13] Stuart Piggott, *Ruins in a Landscape: Essays in Antiquarianism* (Edinburgh: Edinburgh UP, 1976); and T. D. Kendrick, *British Antiquity* (Methuen, 1950), especially his remarks on Spenser, pp. 126-32.

5

English monarchs on that occasion was shown in a series of opulent and magnificent tiltings and tournaments.[14]

England was well provided with appropriate forms for this enthusiasm: the pre-eminent European chivalric institution was the Order of the Garter, founded in 1344 by Edward III. But in the late fifteenth and sixteenth centuries English chivalry gained considerable new vigour as a result of events across the Channel, not so much in France itself, but in the now vanished independent territories of Burgundy. Its ducal courts seem, at this remove, almost incredible in their brilliance and colour; and the language and symbolism of chivalry was certainly their chosen element for the purposes of display. In imitation of the Garter, which by then was somewhat neglected and in eclipse, the Burgundian rulers launched their own version, the Order of the Golden Fleece, more magnificent and more directly geared to ostentation and propaganda than the Garter. The impact was immediate: the independent duchy may have been doomed to transience, but its princes flashed as bright as any comet across the fifteenth-century sky, dominating courtly fashion all over northern Europe. As Gordon Kipling has demonstrated, the Tudor dynasty in its early years enthusiastically took up many Burgundian forms and conventions, and made them its own.[15]

The mid sixteenth century, however, was not particularly sympathetic to chivalry. The death of Henri II in a tilt in 1559, scaring accidents to Henry VIII, and the latter's inactive and irascible old age were inhibiting factors;[16] but more actively hostile were the increasingly anti-chivalric attitudes of the English Reformation.[17] Edward VI's government, more radically Calvinist than his father's had been, had little time for what it perceived as Papistical relics of former, corrupt times, and the king himself was reported to have poured scorn on the principal badge of the Garter, idolatrously depicting its patron St George.

One might suppose that a sickly boy king followed by two female monarchs would have given this aggressively masculine ideal the *coup de grace*. But it was not so: although Queen Mary's reign made little use of chivalry in pageantry, that of her sister saw a resurgence. As the possibility of Elizabeth's marriage lessened, towards the middle of her reign, an idealized vision of her as the Virgin Queen took

---

[14] See Sydney Anglo, *Spectacle, Pageantry, and Early Tudor Policy* (Oxford: Clarendon Press, 1969), pp.150-156 especially.

[15] Gordon Kipling, *The Triumph of Honour: Burgundian Origins of the English Renaissance* (The Hague: Leiden UP, 1977).

[16] *Spectacle, Pageantry, and Early Tudor Policy*, p.261.

[17] *Spectacle, Pageantry, and Early Tudor Policy*, pp.298-301.

shape; and this was accompanied by a revival in the forms and festivals of chivalry, over which the queen presided as the ever-unattain-
able heroine of an infinite and infinitely beautiful romance. The
story was acted out in pageant and entertainment wherever Elizabeth
went; but the key episodes were the Accession Day Tilts, held each
year on 17 November to celebrate her reign. These, superbly revealed
for us by Frances Yates, were first recorded in 1581; and they
represent the apogee of the neo-medieval court culture of the
Elizabethan age, the equivalent in movement of the great 'fantasy
houses', such as Hardwick, Wollaton, or Burghley, with their crenell-
ations and other pseudo-Gothic features.[18] Unlike these, the tournaments were essentially ephemeral, which even at the time must have
been part of their charm. But we can glimpse their wonders in contemporary descriptions, in the occasional Gheerearts or Segar painting of a man in tournament costume, or above all in the exquisite
world of the Hilliard miniature: delicate, brilliantly coloured, and
delighting in recondite and involved meaning.

One cannot hope to explain the phenomenon of Elizabethan neo-
medievalism completely. But one reason for the growth in interest in
chivalry later in the sixteenth century must have been the cultural
nationalism of the age and a partial rejection, or at least modulation
and Anglicization, of the newer arts of display of continental Europe:
England had not thrown off one form of Roman domination merely
to take up another unthinkingly. The Elizabethans's embattled
political and religious situation led not, as is often stated, to enforced
isolation from the Renaissance in the rest of Europe, but to a
conscious espousal of England's indigenous culture. When Spenser
praises the illustrations of the *Shepheardes Calender* as equal to or
better than anything by Michaelangelo, we do not take his art criticism seriously; but as an expression of the cultural self-esteem of the
age his words speak powerfully. And the constituents of chivalry
were not excluded from this enthusiasm for the English and the
medieval: heraldry's supposed antiquity (even the ancients were
thought to have borne arms and the origins of chivalric symbolism
were occasionally traced to Troy) made it, perhaps, a native equivalent to the more European art of the emblem, counterbalancing the
latter's aura of Platonism and pseudo-Egyptian hieroglyphics with an
heroic, military, and above all English vocabulary of images. The
revival of interest in King Arthur also has this nationalistic motive, at

[18] See *Astraea*, pp. 88-111. The architectural neo-medievalism and the chivalric
entertainment come together most clearly after Spenser's death, in the entertainment for Charles I and Henrietta Maria at Bolsover Castle in 1634, *Love's
Welcome at Bolsover.*

least in part; for Arthur was fabled to have thrown off the Roman yoke and, indeed, to have gone beyond that and become emperor himself. The British history of King Arthur and the Round Table thus possessed considerable attractions for English historians and people alike.

Indeed, English history as a whole exercised considerable fascination for Spenser's contemporaries. The revival of scholarship associated with humanism led to new ways of looking at and documenting not just the classics and the ancient world, but also the national past of England (though ultimately this would spell doom for the legend of King Arthur). England's past included the ancient British period, the Anglo-Saxon invasions, the Norman conquest and the later middle ages. Again, this interest was inextricably bound up with the form taken by the English Reformation: when Matthew Parker (1504-75), Archbishop of Canterbury, set out and defended the *via media* of Anglicanism, he did so by direct appeal to the antiquity and purity of the national church, in a work fittingly entitled *De Antiquitate Britannicae ecclesiae et priveligiis ecclesiae Cantuariensis cum archiepiscopis eiusdem 70* (1572). And it was under his patronage that, again in 1572, the first Society of Antiquaries was established for the study of all aspects of English history. Among its members was Ben Jonson's schoolmaster and Spenser's friend, William Camden (1551-1623), whose historical labours resulted in the successive editions of the *Britannia* (first published in 1586) and the *Remaines ... concerning Britaine* (1605), among much else.

Camden, like many of the distinguished antiquarians of the sixteenth and seventeenth centuries, was fascinated by the subject of heraldry; he became Clarenceux King of Arms in 1597. Although the College of Arms was in some ways a public scandal in the Elizabethan period, it nevertheless possessed (as it still does) a unique body of manuscript material relating to chivalry and heraldry.[19] And to more than that: because the heralds were required to undertake 'visitations', journeys into each area under their jurisdiction in order to maintain heraldic legality and correctness, they had an unrivalled opportunity to survey the entire country and explore the history of each locality. As a result, some of the outstanding early historians were heralds: Camden himself, founder of the first university chair of history in Britain; Sir William Segar (d. 1633), Garter King of Arms and author of *Honor, Military and Civil* (1602); Sir William Dugdale

---

[19] See Sir Anthony Wagner's *Records and Collections of the College of Arms* (Burke's Peerage, 1952); and for the disrepute of the College in the sixteenth century, the same author's *Heralds of England: A History of the Office and College of Arms* (College of Arms, 1967).

(1605-86), Garter King of Arms and author of the influential *Antiquities of Warwickshire* (1656); Elias Ashmole (1617-92), Windsor Herald and author of the *Institution, Laws and Ceremonies of the most Noble Order of the Garter* (1672) and founder of the Ashmolean Museum; and John Anstis (1669-1744), Garter King of Arms, whose many works are among the basic texts for the modern study of heraldry and chivalry.

To this group, although not formally members of the College of Arms, should be added John Selden (1584-1654), who contributed the antiquarian notes to Drayton's *Polyolbion* (1612) and whose *Titles of Honour* (1614) is the most chivalric of his many historical treatises; John Speed (1552?-1629), the map-maker and historian; and Sir Robert Cotton (1571-1631), pupil, friend, and patron of Camden, the 'general Maecenas' of the antiquarian movement in the later Elizabethan and Jacobean periods.

Many of these authors' works deal with chivalry and heraldry; but in the process they necessarily touch on and explore much more. Camden's interests included archaeology, etymology, and numismatics, even the influence of Old Norse on the English language. The title-page alone of *Remaines ... concerning Britaine* specifies that the book will treat 'the inhabitants thereof, their Languages, Names, Surnames, Empreses, Wise Speeches, Poesies, and Epitaphs'. Far from being trapped into a narrow and recondite subject, the heraldic antiquarians found that their studies led them into an ever-growing multitude of disciplines.

This breadth of vision is obviously shared with Spenser's epic. *The Faerie Queene* uses all those kinds of knowledge which fascinated the antiquarians: etymologies, names, and the history of ancient peoples, their institutions, laws, and ceremonies (to adapt Ashmole's title). Above all, perhaps, it uses historical iconography: the standard chivalric images which were the heralds's principal concern as well as the 'Empreses' mentioned on Camden's title-page. Like the historians, Spenser refers far beyond chivalry and heraldry as narrowly defined; and, particularly, he uses martial and chivalric symbolism as an instrument for the introduction and discussion of some of the central themes of his poem.

In the following chapters I do not attempt a comprehensive survey of all the instances on which martial and chivalric symbolism is used in *The Faerie Queene*. Rather I have selected examples which seem to me to convey most successfully the scope and uses of this symbolism. In the first three chapters I discuss the meanings attached to the armour, weapons, and martial actions of knights throughout the poem. In Chapter Four I concentrate on the martial symbolism of Book One, isolating this book because of its widespread use of

9

material drawn exclusively from the Scriptures and other Christian sources. Chapters Five and Six turn specifically to chivalric symbolism; and each has as its focal point one of the poem's two tournaments. At these, I suggest, chivalric symbolism is pervasive; and comprehension of it is essential to an understanding of Spenser's meaning, both locally and throughout the poem.

I: THE SHIELD

1. Prince Arthur's Shield

I

'The shelde', writes Ramon Lull, 'is gyven to the knight to sygnefye the office of a knight'.[1] Lull succinctly places the shield at the heart of chivalric symbolism, as the emblem of knighthood itself. His emphasis was common; in the sixteenth century, the shield and its device were widely used on all those occasions when display was required. With an established tradition and a developed taste and understanding among his readers, the shield was entirely suitable for Spenser as a means of expression, and in this chapter I shall discuss the uses to which it is put in *The Faerie Queene*. Some shields, such as those of Sans foy and his brothers in Book One, can be read with comparative ease (although even in these cases exact interpretation is difficult given the deliberately cryptic quality of the devices); but I shall show Spenser using the subtle arts of reference and allusion in the shields of more prominent and complex figures, particularly Prince Arthur, Britomart, and Arthegall, to contribute to the unity of his poem, and to relate these figures to the themes, moral and political, of *The Faerie Queene*.

Spenser's period abounds in examples of shields used symbolically to convey complex meanings. As the principal form taken by the coat-of-arms the shield was central to the art of heraldry, and as such it appeared in symbolic contexts with extraordinary frequency, in particular with reference to the monarch. In 1588, for instance, Elizabeth I embellished the landing stage at Greenwich with four royal beasts, each holding a shield, which reminded the onlooker of the queen's political and dynastic claims: her royal ancestry; her Welsh forebears and the connection with King Arthur; her alliances with various noble houses; and above all the political unity and stability achieved by the Tudors, represented by the Tudor double-rose.[2] It is an eloquent testimony to the decay of this kind of sym-

---

[1] *The Book of the Ordre of Chyvalry*, ed. A.T.P.Byles [*EETS* OS. 168] (1926), p. 82.
[2] See H. Stanford London, *Royal Beasts* (East Knoyle: Heraldry Society, 1956), p. 7.

11

bolism that when these beasts reappeared, along with six others, at Westminster Abbey in 1953 to greet Elizabeth II for her coronation, they served purely decorative functions, to such an extent that they were not allowed to be painted in their correct colours (essential to any interpretation of their significance) because these would not harmonize with the blackened Abbey.[3] But in 1588 their symbolic function was very much alive. And we shall find Spenser alluding to Elizabeth I's personal, political, and dynastic associations through shields and emblems in the same way.

Coexisting with this traditional role for the shield was the newer use of tournament shields which did not employ standard heraldry. Witty, learned, and totally unsuitable for battle, these fabrications were purely symbolic. Their splendidly abstruse charges are well represented by those collected in Camden's *Remaines* (1605), many of which are thought to have been used in the Accession Day Tournaments held on November 17 each year to celebrate Elizabeth I's reign.[4] These tournaments were occasions for personal display, rather than dynastic identification, and the devices tended to be of the *impresa* type: the point is neatly made in one of Sir Philip Sidney's favourite *impresa* mottoes, *vix ea nostra voco*. The shields also reflect courtly compliment of Elizabeth; but now as an individual (albeit an individual monarch) rather than as the representative of English kingship in abstract, as can be seen from these examples:

> He referred Fate, Fortune and all to his Soveraign which drew for himselfe the twelve houses of heaven, in the forme which Astrologians use, setting downe neither Signe nor Planet therein, but onely placing over it this word, *DISPONE*.
> The like reference had he which onely used a white shield, and therein written, *FATUM INSCRIBAT ELIZA*.
> It may bee doubtfull whether hee affected his Soveraigne, or justice more zealously, which made a man hovering in the aire, with *FEROR AD ASTRAEAM*. (p.169)

None of these examples has any connection with traditional heraldry. Camden makes it clear that these emblems are to be read by means of the references they contain. And the reader of *The Faerie Queene* recognizes some of the same mythological and astrological references thought to underpin the imagery and iconography of Book Five.[5] It is also noticeable that these *imprese* draw on a wider range of sources,

---

3 London, p.2.
4 See Frances Yates, *Astraea*, p.107.
5 See, for instance, Yates, *Astraea*, pp.69-72; Alastair Fowler, *Spenser and the Numbers of Time*, Chapter 12; and Jane Aptekar, *Icons of Justice*, Chapter 2.

including classical mythology and astrology, than the heraldic shields, which mainly employ medieval chivalric symbolism.

Both kinds of shield-symbolism influence sixteenth-century literature. Perhaps the most famous example is the *New Arcadia* in which, Frances Yates and others have suggested, some of the details of the Elizabethan tournaments in which Sidney took part may be reflected.[6] Be that as it may, learned significance and outrageous unrealism combine in both literature and life to produce the energetic *jeux d'esprit* characteristic of the age, culminating in the hilarious anarchy of symbolic ornament paraded in the tournament of *The Unfortunate Traveller*.[7] However, in both art and reality tournament shield symbolism has its serious side: the deeper meanings and allusions of the devices carried in the *Four Foster Children of Desire* have yet to be plumbed; and Marlowe relies on popular knowledge of such matters when, in an anachronistic tournament, Edward II demands to see the witty *imprese* devised by his barons, only to be confronted by emblems representing his disgrace and their threatened revolt.[8]

Both Edward's eagerness to see the shields and their striking quality are reflections of contemporary tournaments. We may surmise that Spenser's audience was capable of understanding and was even expecting the complex uses to which shield and device are put in *The Faerie Queene*. His early readers would have enjoyed, as we barely can, the references to the arts of *impresa* and *blazon* central to their own pageantry and display. Drawing on contemporary usage, interest, and knowledge, Spenser can achieve highly concentrated expression. And through the shields of *The Faerie Queene* he develops and expounds his moral and political themes.

II

Having emphasized the significance of the device, it may seem perverse to begin by considering Prince Arthur's shield, which is

---

6 *Astraea*, pp.88-94; James Holly Hanford and Sara Ruth Watson, 'Personal Allegory in the *Arcadia*: Philisides and Lelius', *MP* 32 (1934), pp.1-10; D. Coulman, ' "Spotted to be known" ', *JWCI* 20 (1957), pp.179-80; and Katherine Duncan-Jones's two articles, 'Nashe and Sidney: The Tournament in *The Unfortunate Traveller*', *MLR* 63 (1968), pp.3-6 and 'Sidney's Personal *Imprese*', *JWCI* 33 (1970), pp.321-24.
7 Thomas Nashe, *The Unfortunate Traveller* in *The Works of Thomas Nashe*, ed. R.B.McKerrow, 5 vols (1904; revised reprint, Oxford: Blackwell, 1958). Vol.2, pp.271-79.
8 *Edward II* II.ii.11-28; see also *Pericles* II.ii.14-58.

blank and normally covered by a veil. Yet Camden's selection includes a contemporary instance in which blankness does not mean emptiness of meaning, but instead is used expressively. Reasons why Spenser chooses a blank shield for Arthur involve not only his presentation as an individual character, but also the organization and structure of the poem.

Both Spenser and the bearer of the blank shield in Camden's list draw on the medieval tradition in which a young knight, before he proved himself, bore a shield without device. Thus Sir Gawain is given arms of a single colour when he exchanges clothing with a young knight:

> Then were brought the arms of Helain ... and the shield was completely blank as it was new, as it was the custom at that time that new knights bore a shield of one tincture alone for the first year they were knights.[9]

The time limit of a year is more specific than is usual in the Romances, these arms being retained until the performance of some notable deed. And in the *New Arcadia* also, Sidney uses this tradition when he describes 'a great nobleman of Corinth, whose device was to come without any device, all in white like a new knight (as indeed he was)'.[10]

Spenser's hero is also at the outset of his career, as the poet tells us in the *Letter to Raleigh*:

> after his long education by Timon ... [having] seene in a dream or vision the Faery Queen, with whose excellent beauty ravished, he awaking resolved to seeke her out, and so being by Merlin armed, and by Timon throughly instructed, he went to seeke her forth in Faerye land.[11]

The newness of both knight and armour is stressed. Arthur himself tells Una and the Red Cross Knight that he embarked on his adventures 'in freshest flowre of youthly yeares, / When courage first does creepe in manly chest' (I.ix.9.1-2). Conventionally, the love of a mistress has taken the young man from his 'looser life' (I.ix.12.6) and set him on the pursuit of honour and love.

The newness of Arthur, perhaps insufficiently recognised by the critics, links him with the Red Cross Knight in the initiating trials of

---

9 *Vulgate Version of the Arthurian Romances*, ed. H.Oskar Sommer, 8 vols (1909-1916). Vol.3, *Le Livre de Lancelot del Lac, Part 1*, p.299:
   Lors furent aportees les armes helain ... et li escus tous blans comme nois. si comme a chel tans estoit coustume. que chevaliers nouiax portoit escu dun seul taint le premier an que il lestoit.
10 *The Countess of Pembroke's Arcadia*, ed. Maurice Evans (Harmondsworth: Penguin, 1977), pp.354-55. Hereafter referred to as the *New Arcadia*.
11 *Var*, Vol.1, p.168.

the first book. As well as distinguishing the poem's Prince from the King Arthur of legend, this newness suggests that the young 'gentleman or noble person' is to identify in part with the Prince in his education in 'vertuous and gentle discipline' (*Var*, Vol.1, p.167). The Prince's inexperience and immaturity are conveyed by the blank shield, a clean slate in a sense. In the course of the poem, the reader will be instructed in the meaning of the virtues; and gradually, the meaning of Arthur's all-inclusive magnificence will become apparent.

The bearing of a blank shield implied no lack of dignity: writers of romance did not demand quarterings with the rigour of Madame la Baronne de Thunder-ten-tronckh.[12] On the contrary, the simplicity of a shield was taken, in retrospect, to be a sign of honour and antiquity. In times when heraldry was becoming ever more complex, the imagined simplicity of former ages was associated with unblemished chivalry and national success. Geoffrey of Monmouth tells us,

> For at that time was Britain exalted unto so high a pitch of dignity as that it did surpass all other kingdoms in plenty of riches, in luxury of adornment, and in the courteous wit of them that dwelt therein. Whatsoever knight in the land was of renown for his prowess did wear his clothes and his arms all of one same colour.[13]

The late sixteenth century was an age of highly developed heraldry with which Arthur's blank shield would have contrasted sharply. The difference would have imparted a sense of other-wordly antiquity and simple honour to its bearer.

But as well as drawing on common heraldic knowledge, Spenser relies on our recognition of his literary sources in the description of Arthur's shield. Chief among these is the shield of Atlante in the *Orlando furioso*, and the connections between these two shields have been studied at length by Paul Alpers.[14] However it is the shield's difference from this and other analogues that interests us here. It was early recognised that whereas Atlante's shield is made of carbuncle, Spenser informs us that Arthur's is composed of 'Diamond perfect pure and cleene' (I.vii.33.5). This alteration was noted by D.C. Allen; but his rigorous interpretation of the shield as symbolising repentance (following an occasional allegorisation of the diamond in renaissance

---

12 Voltaire, *Candide* in *Romans et Contes*, ed. René Groos (Paris: Gallimard, 1954). Candide's supposed father was *infra dig*, 'parce qu'il n'avait pu prouver que soixante et onze quartiers', p.149.
13 Geoffrey of Monmouth, *History of the Kings of Britain*, tr. Sebastian Evans (1912; revised, Dent, 1963), pp.201-202. See also Gerard J. Brault, *Early Blazon: Heraldic Terminology in the Twelfth and Thirteenth Centuries with Special Reference to Arthurian Literature* (Oxford: Clarendon Press, 1972), pp.29-30.
14 *The Poetry of 'The Faerie Queene'*, pp.168-79.

lapidary works) seems too limited in the context of this poem.[15] Some earlier critics, perhaps as a result of drawing on the cruder manifestations of the renaissance love of allegory, were excessively concerned to discover detailed, precise moral allegories, a tendency perhaps comparable with the problems of historical allegory, which suffers from over-rigorous equations with Spenser's contemporaries. In both fields, Spenser's allegory operates by temporary and suggestive associations, rather than rigid and permanent identifications.

Allen's error lies in assuming that, because the Red Cross Knight's shield is connected in the *Letter to Raleigh* with the 'shield of faith' of the Epistle to the Ephesians, so Arthur's must be equally specific and yet different. However, everything we know concerning Arthur suggests that he is less different from the other knights than superior to them. So much is conveyed in the inevitable comparison between the Prince's shield and that of the Red Cross Knight; a deliberate comparison, one feels, because they are the only two described at any length in Book One and appear in similar positions at the beginning of each half of the book.[16]

The Red Cross Knight bears a

> silver shielde,
> Wherein old dints of deepe wounds did remaine,
> The cruell markes of many' a bloudy fielde   (I.i.1.2-4)

Perhaps to point the comparison, the neologism 'dint' (as the result of the blow rather than the blow itself) recurs in the description of Prince Arthur's shield, although there in its normal sense after an initial ambiguity. Spenser contrasts the obviously embattled shield of the Christian soldier with that of his rescuer, whose shield was

> Hewen out of Adamant rocke with engines keene,
> That point of speare it never percen could,
> Ne dint of direfull sword divide the substance would.

                                                        (I.vii.33.7-9)

Arthur's impregnable shield transcends the heroic vulnerability of the Red Cross Knight's. The comparison between the two shields reveals not only the relationship between these knights but also their profound difference.

The distance between them is nowhere clearer than in the rescue of the Red Cross Knight. Whereas the Knight falls to Duessa and Orgoglio, Arthur is able to defeat them in circumstances strongly

---

15 'Arthur's Diamond Shield in the *Faerie Queene*', *JEGP* 36 (1937), pp. 234-43.

16 The Red Cross Knight enters the poem with Una and the Dwarf at I.i; Prince Arthur enters exactly six cantos later at I.vii, when he meets Una and the Dwarf.

reminiscent of the Harrowing of Hell. The Prince's Christ-like role should not surprise us after the description of his arms, for his diamond shield has, as its primary symbolic significance, Christ. Valeriano, for instance, writes of *adamas*:

> this is set down concerning Christ: 'Truly, from the Father to the earth was sent the unique, divine, heavenly, and incorruptible Diamond, only begotten God, of whom God the Father says: "Behold I place a Diamond in the midst of my people, whom neither the fire of temptation in the wilderness will weaken, nor the blows, scourging, and wounds of the wicked on the cross will weaken or make less, whom neither burial nor descent into the underworld will be able to harm in the slightest, but he will certainly overcome all and prove a divine and incorruptible Diamond"'.[17]

Arthur's diamond shield is superior to that of the Red Cross Knight as Christ is superior to the Christian soldier. Spenser may well intend us to recognise as much as a result of the reference to 'Adamant rock': the Latin *adamas* is obviously suitable for puns on the relationship between St George, as the 'old Adam', and his saviour or redeemer Prince Arthur as the new. Indeed Spenser may be suggesting that Arthur is associated with Christ in his initial lines on the shield, where the insistent negative applied to 'earthly mettals' places diamond in the heavenly sphere:

> Not made of steele, nor of enduring bras,
> Such earthly mettals soone consumed bene:
> But all of Diamond perfect pure and cleene
> It framed was   (I.vii.33.3-6)

The perfection and purity of the diamond, and its superiority, apply equally to the shield's bearer and his virtue.

Other aspects of the symbolism of the diamond, such as fortitude, have been suggested in the discussion of Arthur's shield. Although no doubt apt for the poem's preeminent hero, these suggestions add little to our understanding of the Prince's role. However, referring again to the shield of Atlante in the *Orlando furioso* may be more enlightening: Fornari, Ariosto's commentator, occasionally interprets this shield as divine grace.[18] Spenser's alteration of the substance

[17] Valeriano Bolzoni, *Hieroglyphica* (Basle, 1575), f.306ʳ:
   Mox illa de christo subjecit: 'Sic namque et singularis et divinus, coelestis atque incorruptibilis Adamas unigenitus Deus a patre ad terras missus, de quo dicit Deus Pater: Ecce ego pona Adamantem in medio populi mei, quem neque ignis tentationum in deserto comminuet, quem ictus, verbera plagaeque impiorum in cruce non atterent comminuentue, quem neque sepultura, neque descensus ad inferos vel minimum violare poterunt, sed enim omnia superabit, seque divinum et incorrupatabilem probabit Adamantem'.
[18] *The Poetry of 'The Faerie Queene'*, p.166 ff.

from carbuncle to diamond makes this connection more definite, because the diamond was frequently associated with grace in the Renaissance, as in Picinelli's account of *adamas*:

> Thus although great men shine by natural gifts, by no means however do they shed around great light as much as when they receive at the same time the rays of divine grace, which make greater their splendor.[19]

The association of diamond and divine grace is particularly apt in view of the shield's being veiled; because St Augustine also says that divine grace,

> lay hidden in the Old Testament under a veil. It is revealed in the gospel of Christ.[20]

Augustine's words provide an especially illuminating context for the sudden revelation of Arthur's shield, in the battles with Orgoglio and the Souldan for instance. Significantly, Orgoglio 'read[s] his end' in the shield, rather than merely seeing it (I.viii.21.4). And subsequent to this, the gospel of Christ and the diamond box are gifts exchanged by the Red Cross Knight and Prince Arthur after the former's rescue. The stanza describing them carefully relates the two gifts, not least in the final line's description of the Bible as a 'worke of wondrous grace' (I.ix.19.9). The symbolism of the diamond thus joins other features of his first appearance to suggest Arthur's role as an agent of Christ.

III

Spenser's description of the powers possessed by Arthur's shield suggests references both literary and mythological:

> Men into stones therewith he could transmew,
> And stones to dust, and dust to nought at all;
> And when him list the prouder lookes subdew,
> He would them gazing blind, or turne to other hew.
>
> (I.vii.35.6-9)

The immediate renaissance prototype, Atlante's shield, was capable of blinding the onlooker, but not of petrifying. Spenser has overgone

---

[19] D. Philippo Picinelli, *Mundus Symbolicus* (1681), p.682:
Ita viri magni etsi naturalibus splendeant donis, numquam tamen majorem sibi circumponunt splendorem, quam ubi gratiae Divinae radios simul excipiunt, iisque claritatem suam adaugent.
[20] *Augustine: Later Works*, tr. John Burnaby (S.C.M. Press, 1955), p.216.

Ariosto here by returning to the latter's source, the shield of Minerva, for this further power. And in doing so he suggests the superiority of both hero and armour to those of one of the most popular of renaissance epics. This superiority is also to be found in the pervasive religious and moral concentration of *The Faerie Queene*, in comparison with the shifting perspectives and intermittent allegory of the *Orlando furioso*.

The moral intensity of *The Faerie Queene* is further emphasised by Arthur's shield's proving even more powerful than the mythological original. Minerva's shield could petrify; Arthur's can annihilate. The difference is significant: it indicates the altogether more absolute power of the Christian's weapons, not only to kill but to destroy opponents entirely. In the overthrow of the Souldan following the uncovering of Prince Arthur's shield, this sense of infinite, menacing power is revealed, in the terror of the horses and the final dispersal of the Souldan's body. All that is left of him is his empty armour and his usefulness as 'an eternall token' (V.viii.44.4) of the operation of divine justice. Arthur takes,

> Onely his shield and armour, which there lay,
> Though nothing whole, but all to brusd and broken, ...

> So on a tree, before the Tyrants dore,
> He caused them be hung in all mens sight,
> To be a moniment for evermore.   (V.viii.44.1-2; 45.1-3)

Although Arthur's shield achieves the absolute disintegration of the Souldan by means besides those of petrification and annihilation, the effect is that specified in the original description. And the manner and tone of his death confirm the rigour implied in the comparison with the shields of Atlante and Minerva.

The relationship between Minerva's shield and Arthur's resides not only in their powers but also in their physical characteristics. Hers was diamond or crystal, and, before the addition of the Gorgon's head, blank. Enid Welsford describes a tournament of 1509 'in which certain knights, scholars of Pallas ... were headed by a Goddess bearing a crystal shield'.[21] Minerva and her shield are shown in Mantegna's 'Wisdom leading the Virtues against the Vices' and here she performs a role similar to that of Prince Arthur in *The Faerie Queene*, as the leader of the warriors of virtue.

Allegorisations of Minerva's shield lend weight to the interpretation of Arthur's as symbolising the grace of God and divine intervention

---

[21] *The Court Masque* (Cambridge: Cambridge UP, 1927), p.123. I am indebted to Professor Alastair Fowler for this reference.

in human affairs. Natalis Comes, for instance, comments on the lending of Minerva's shield to Perseus:

> This, the escaping of the Gorgons' attack and the beheading of Medusa whom no-one might even look upon freely, conceals how all human prudence through itself is feeble without God's aid; without which it is not sufficient to shun the inducements of pleasure: and in fact, to be a good man is the gift of God.[22]

And elsewhere Comes comments,

> for unless we are provided with precepts from heaven and God's aid to us, scarcely any reason can govern the inducements of pleasure.[23]

The frailty of man in the battle with the forces of evil characterises the episodes in which Prince Arthur appears in the first two books. This is obvious in the first, the rescue of the Red Cross Knight; in the second, Arthur protects the body of Guyon from Pyrochles and Cymochles. When the Prince's spear, his only weapon, is rendered useless, the shield emerges as his only protection until the Palmer gives him Guyon's sword. In this episode, which will be discussed more fully in Chapter Three, Arthur's shield functions in the same way as Minerva's does in Comes's allegorisation: it is the defence against the forces of passion and pleasure, symbolised by the two brothers. At the beginning of this episode, the protection which man receives from evil is asserted to be a manifestation of God's compassion and aid; and this applies to Arthur's defeat of the Pagan brothers as well as to the Cupid-like angel who stands guard over Guyon's body. The Palmer's prayer to Arthur, asking for his protection for Guyon, repeats two significant words from the introductory stanzas on the compassion of God: 'succour' (II.viii.2.2; 25.7) and 'grace' (1.5; 25.6). We have already seen the association of both these ideas with Prince Arthur's shield.

---

[22] *Natalis Comitis Mythologiae, sive explicationum fabularum, Libri decem* (Paris, 1583), p. 811:
Hic fingitur Deorum ope Gorgonum impetum evasisse, Medusamque obtruncasse, quam neque intueri quidem ulli licebat: quia omnis humana prudentia per se debilis est sine Dei auxilio sine quo voluptatem illecebras effugere non satis possumus: est enim et hoc ipsum, esse virum bonum, Dei munus.

[23] Comes, p. 746:
nam nisi divinitus praeceptis instruamur, nobisque Deus auxilio sit, vix ulla ratione a voluptatum illecebris temperare possumus.

IV

Discussion of the traditional associations of the Minervan shield must include the Perseus legend. Arthur's encounter with Orgoglio in the first book of *The Faerie Queene* has several parallels with the defeat of the Gorgon by Perseus, the use of the shield and the decapitation of the loser being but two. Almost inevitably, Perseus was allegorised in Christian terms; and, as the son of Zeus miraculously conceived by Danae, he was equally inevitably seen as a figure of Christ. For our purposes the most interesting reading of the legend is found in the *Ovide Moralisé*, which comments,

> when the Son of God, at his own volition, descended from heaven to the earth ... it was he who despoiled the three daughters of Phorces [the Gorgons] of their rule by force; these were the daughters of the devil. ... The first was pride, the other avarice, and the third carnal delight.[24]

The allegorisation of the three Gorgon sisters follows the standard division of the totality of sin into three categories, the world (avarice), the flesh (carnal delight), and the devil (pride). Patrick Cullen has attempted to demonstrate the uses of this division in the first two books of *The Faerie Queene*, notably in the Red Cross Knight's battle with the Dragon and Guyon's journey through the Cave of Mammon, and one might suggest a number of other episodes which could be interpreted using this triadic structure.[25] But Cullen fails to note a larger-scale application in the very ordering of the first three books of the poem. In Book One, Prince Arthur confronts pride (Orgoglio / *orgeulz*), using the Minervan shield and decapitating the defeated giant, and this is strikingly similar to the *Ovide Moralisé*'s version of the Perseus legend. In Book Two Guyon's principal enemy is Mammon, whose realm is pervaded by the considerations of the world and whose initial description vividly suggests

---

[24] *Ovide Moralisé*, ed. C. de Boer, 5 vols (Amsterdam, 1915-38). Vol. 2 (1920), pp. 132-33:   Quant li filz Dieu, par son plesir,
    Fu descendus dou ciel en terre ...

    C'est cil qui de lor regne a force
    Despoulla les trois filles Phorce,
    Ce sont les filles au diable,
    Le roi cruel, le roi doutable ...

              La premeraine
    Fu orguelz, et l'autre avarice,
    Et la tierce charnel delice.   (IV. 5825-45).

[25] See *Infernal Triad: The Flesh, the World, and the Devil in Spenser and Milton* (Princeton: PUP, 1974), Chapter One; and 'Guyon *microchristus*: The Cave of Mammon reexamined', *ELH* 37 (1970), pp. 153-74.

avarice.[26] Finally, throughout the third book, Britomart encounters lust in its myriad forms. Although other evils are certainly present in each book (indeed, all seven Deadly Sins *in propria persona* in Book One), underlying the structure of the first instalment of *The Faerie Queene* is this three-fold division of sin. As Cullen suggests, Spenser uses this division because it 'comprised all temptations faced by the First Adam, by the Second Adam, and by all men'.[27] Its use as a larger structure for the first three books is initiated by Prince Arthur's use of his shield to defeat Orgoglio, which alludes to Perseus's use of Minerva's shield to defeat the Gorgon, 'Orgeulz'.

V

His role in initiating the structure suggested above corresponds with the overall function Arthur is assigned in the *Letter to Raleigh*: 'So in the person of Prince Arthure I sette forth magnificence in particular, which vertue for that (according to Aristotle and the rest) it is the perfection of all the rest, and conteineth in it them all' (*Var*, Vol. 1, p.168). The inclusiveness and supremacy of the Prince is reflected in the relationship between his shield and those of the first three knights-patron.

Two figures in *The Faerie Queene* are related to Minerva.[28] The first is Prince Arthur, who is associated with the goddess through his shield and baldric. The latter has at its centre,

> one pretious stone
> Of wondrous worth, and eke of wondrous mights,
> Shapt like a Ladies head, exceeding shone,
> Like *Hesperus* emongst the lesser lights,
> And strove for to amaze the weaker sights; (I.vii.30.1-5)

The position of the stone, in the centre of Arthur's chest, and its power to 'amaze the weaker sights', recall the traditional use of Medusa's head, as the centrepiece of Minerva's *aegis*. We recognize Arthur's 'Ladies head' not as Medusa but as Gloriana. The implied comparison between the two would seem unflattering until we remember the legend in which Medusa was famous for her beauty, and was envied by the goddess.[29] The allusion then becomes compli-

---

[26] Although I identify Book Two and Mammon with the temptations of the World, I do not mean to rule out Cullen's suggestion that there is a three-fold structure within this episode as well.

[27] 'Guyon *microchristus*', p.156.

[28] I do not include, for the moment, the shadowy figure Sir Paladine.

[29] This is, of course, the version found in Ovid's *Metamorphoses* IV.790ff.

mentary to Gloriana or Elizabeth and thus resembles the frequent comparisons of the queen with mythological beauties, such as in the painting at Windsor Castle in which she is compared, through a variation on the Judgement of Paris, with Juno, Venus, and Minerva. Not surprisingly the comparison is favourable to her.[30] Like Medusa, it is Gloriana's beauty that has the power to amaze.

The other traditional position of the Gorgon's head, on the shield, is that which is used for the poem's other Minervan figure. As Alastair Fowler has shown, both the events of Book Three and the descriptions of Britomart herself have a definite Minervan flavour.[31] On one occasion she is explicitly likened to the goddess:

> Like as *Minerva*, being late returnd
>   From slaughter of the Giaunts conquered; ...
>   Hath loosd her helmet from her lofty hed,
>   And her *Gorgonian* shield gins to untye
> From her left arme, to rest in glorious victorye.

(III.ix.22.1-2; 7-9)

The simile works in many ways. But one point at which these figures do not correspond is in their magical weaponry. Although Britomart has the spear associated with Minerva, her shield possesses none of the qualities or powers of the '*Gorgonian* shield'; as will be seen later in this chapter, the symbolism of Britomart's shield operates in different ways. But Arthur's shield does possess these physical qualities, and both possesses and exceeds the powers. The various links between Arthur and Britomart have been noted by several critics. To these we may now add a common use of Minervan iconography, in ways which qualify and elucidate the relationship between them. As Arthur's shield exceeds the power of the goddess's, so Arthur the supreme hero exceeds the virtue of the patroness of Chastity.

To appreciate the connections between Arthur's shield and those of the other two knights-patron of the first instalment of *The Faerie Queene*, it is necessary to move from the realms of myth to those of legend. One of the remarkable features of the description of Spenser's Prince is the minimal use made of material taken from descriptions of the legendary King Arthur. The only detail resembling King Arthur's arms is the Prince's dragon-crest; and, as I shall argue in the following chapter, that probably derives from elsewhere as well. Nowhere is the abandonment of the traditional heraldry of King Arthur more evident than in the Prince's shield, for nowhere is King Arthur

---

[30] See Strong, *Portraits of Queen Elizabeth I*, p.79.
[31] *Spenser and the Numbers of Time*, pp.122-32.

said to possess a blank or diamond shield. And, vice versa, King Arthur's various devices are never used by Spenser's Prince. But although the Prince seems to have few traditionally Arthurian connections, two of the emblems closely associated with the legends of King Arthur and the Round Table do appear on the shields of other figures.

Firstly, the Red Cross Knight's shield can be seen to have a possible Arthurian origin. In the sixteenth century, Gerard Legh reports that King Arthur was thought to have borne the red cross shield of St George, just as Spenser's Knight does.[32] A further Arthurian link is that Sir Galahad, in the *Tale of the Sank Greal*, bears a similar red cross shield. It is perhaps this emblem that has prevented the recognition that the powers and features of Galahad's shield are strikingly reminiscent of Prince Arthur's. In the *Tale*, Galahad is told that this shield once belonged to King Evelake; and when the king

> was in the batayle there was a clothe sette afore the shylde, and whan he was in the grettist perell he lett put awey the cloth, and than hys enemyes saw a vigoure of a man on the crosse, wherethorow they all were discomfite.[33]

The device on the shield is similar to the Red Cross Knight's. But the power of the shield to dismay opponents, and particularly the unveiling of the shield only *in extremis* resemble Prince Arthur's:

> His warlike shield all closely cover'd was ...

> The same to wight he never wont disclose,
>   But when as monsters huge he would dismay,
>   Or daunt unequall armies of his foes,
>   Or when the flying heavens he would affray;

(I.vii.33.1; 34.1-4)

Prince Arthur only reveals his terrifying shield at moments of the greatest danger, and this action is always the turning point of the battle. Its effect is exactly that of King Evelake's. Orgoglio sees it first in the poem and is immediately drained of his capacity to fight:

> for he has read his end
> In that bright shield, and all their forces spend
> Themselves in vaine: for since that glauncing sight,
> He hath no powre to hurt, nor to defend;   (I.viii.21.4-7)

As in the case of the Minervan shield, Spenser has divided the allusion. Here, although the Red Cross Knight's shield has the same device as

[32] *Accedens of Armory* (1562), fol. 47ᵛ.
[33] *The Works of Sir Thomas Malory*, ed. Eugène Vinaver, 3 vols (1947; revised edition, Oxford: Clarendon Press, 1967). Vol. 2, p. 880.

Galahad's, Prince Arthur's has the covering and the divine powers. Through this division, paradoxically, Spenser connects the overall hero of *The Faerie Queene*, Prince Arthur, with the local hero of Book One, the Red Cross Knight.

Secondly, the shield of the following hero, Sir Guyon, also has Arthurian connections. The Red Cross Knight describes Guyon's device, which is,

> that faire image of that heavenly Mayd,
> That decks and armes your shield with faire defence:

(II.i.28.7-8)

Later in the second book we are told that the 'heavenly Mayd' is none other than the Faery Queen herself; in other words, a similar image to that borne by Prince Arthur on his baldric: the two are already being linked through their emblems. But at this stage in the opening canto of the second book Spenser does not explain the identity of the figure; he allows us instead to believe that Guyon's shield bears an image of the greatest 'heavenly Mayd', the Virgin Mary. Such a shield is again thought to have been used by King Arthur. Camden writes that,

> the victorious *Arthur* bare our Ladie in his shield, which I do the rather remember, for that *Nennius*, who lived not long after recordeth the same.[34]

Elias Ashmole, virtually quoting Nennius, confirms this:

> King *Arthur* himself is reported to bear a *Shild* called *Pridwen*, whereon was painted the Image of the *blessed Virgin.*[35]

Given that Gloriana is closely associated with Queen Elizabeth, and that the English reformation had rejected the cult of the Blessed Virgin, Spenser's ambiguity may seem tactless. But the connection between the Virgin Mary and Queen Elizabeth was one that trembled on the edge of Elizabethan iconography, to be admitted fully only after her death.[36] We see in Spenser's subtly ambiguous reference all the delicacy required for successful panegyric. The glancing allusion to the Virgin Mary recalls King Arthur's shield Pridwen.

In each of the three opening books, then, the relationship between the local hero, the knight-patron of that particular book, and the universal hero, Prince Arthur, is expressed in terms of the relationship between the patron's shield and that of the Prince. A further

---

[34] *Remaines* (1614), p.178.
[35] *Institution, Laws and Ceremonies of the most Noble Order of the Garter* (1672), p. 96.
[36] See Strong, *Portraits of Queen Elizabeth I*, pp.42-43; p.154.

comment should be made. The emblems of the first two knights-patron, the Red Cross Knight and Sir Guyon, are both associated with King Arthur and the institutions that seek to recall him and his glory. Chief among these institutions is the Order of the Garter, the rituals of which consciously sought (and still seek) to recreate those of the Round Table. After four centuries of Protestantism, we have forgotten the intense devotion to the Virgin Mary manifested in many facets of English national life. And this devotion to Mary was present in the Order of the Garter. Its patrons were St George, who was symbolised in the Order's regalia by the red cross; and the Virgin Mary, who was represented in the regalia by her image. It is interesting to note that Spenser's poem opens with two books whose knights-patron bear the most common emblems of the Order of the Garter (apart from the garter itself), a subject returned to in the fifth and sixth chapters.

2. Arthegall's Shield

I

Discussions of Arthegall's shield are beset by one immediate problem: which shield are we to discuss? We never receive a definitive description of Arthegall's arms and armour. Instead we are left with a choice of three shields. In Book Five he fights using Braggadocchio's sun-like shield; and a strong case has been made for regarding this as Arthegall's principal emblem in that book.[37] In Book Four he fights using the emblem of a Salvage Knight, but only as a disguise as far as the narrative goes. And in Book Three he appears bearing a totally different, carefully described shield. But *appears* is the word implicitly questioning this shield, because we only see Arthegall in Book Three in Britomart's vision of her future husband in King Ryence's magical mirror. It is with this shield that we are concerned here; but it is necessary to bear in mind the uncertainty of Arthegall's *blazon* to comprehend its meaning fully.

The vision of Arthegall shows him in full armour:

> His crest was covered with a couchant Hound,
> And all his armour seem'd of antique mould,
> But wondrous massie and assured sound,
> And round about yfretted all with gold,

37 See Jane Aptekar, *Icons of Justice*, pp.77-78.

26

In which there written was with cyphers old,
Achilles armes, which Arthegall did win.
And on his shield enveloped sevenfold
He bore a crowned litle Ermilin,
That deckt the azure field with her faire pouldred skin.

(III.ii.25)

The description is detailed, especially with regard to the shield. Its sevenfold nature may be explained by the epic convention that heroes often have sevenfold or foursquare shields: the well-armed protagonist should never be without one. It is the *blazon* that is particularly interesting and initially baffling. T.K.Dunseath has made an interesting attempt to explain its significance by relating the shield to justice and to Hercules.[38] According to Dunseath, blue as an heraldic colour is 'particularly appropriate to the virtue of justice' (p.58). And he adds that the shield of Hercules, according to Hesiod, had plates of blue enamel. However, he is only able to cite Gerard Legh in favour of this interpretation of blue; and Legh is going against the mass of evidence suggesting that this colour is most closely associated with the symbolism of the sky and the heavens. We need only cite Sir Philip Sidney's comment on blue as an heraldic colour in the *New Arcadia*, where Phalantus wears armour 'blue like the heaven'.[39]

Dunseath's comments on the ermine are also questionable. He states that 'it is consistent with Spenser's poetic design that his hero display such an emblem on his shield, as the ermine (any weasel which turns white in winter) is the animal held sacred to [Hercules]' (p.56). Dunseath then gives ample evidence of the weasel's association with Hercules. But this evidence is irrelevant to the central interpretation of the shield. Spenser's animal is heraldic, not zoological, and in heraldry the distinction between an ermine and a weasel is absolute. This is all the more so because the ermine's fur has a distinct place in heraldry whereas the weasel's does not. Although Dunseath may find the leap from *mustela erminea* to *mustela* worthy only of a short parenthesis, one doubts whether Spenser's symbolically nicer contemporaries would have agreed.

Dunseath's identification of the 'weasel/ermine' (p.58) with Hercules alone is explained partially by his failure to see the shield in

---

[38] T.K.Dunseath, *Spenser's Allegory of Justice*, pp.55-58.
[39] *New Arcadia*, p.497. At a deeper level, this conflict in interpretation perhaps disappears. In Samuel Daniel's masque *The Vision of the Twelve Goddesses* (1604), Astraea the goddess of justice is said to be 'clad in celestial hue (which best she likes)' (l. 330). See *A Book of Masques: In Honour of Allardyce Nicoll*, eds T.J.B.Spencer and S.W.Wells (Cambridge: Cambridge UP, 1967), p.34.

context. His interpretation suits Book Five, the subject of his study, but is worse than redundant in Book Three because it obscures the shield's true meaning. The ermine itself, rather than the transformed weasel, has a long and established tradition as a symbol of purity and chastity, stemming from the legend that the ermine would rather die than soil its coat. Again we may seek corroboration of the currency of this legend from a similar heraldic use in the *New Arcadia*, in which Clitophon bears 'the Ermion [Ermine] with a speech that signified, "Rather dead than spotted" ' (p.165).

The ermine's presence in the Renaissance as a symbol on banners and shields derives largely from its use in the immensely popular *Trionfi* of Petrarch:

> Hyr vyctoriouse standerde was this:
> In a greene felde a whyte armyne is
> With a chayne of golde about his necke;[40]

Although these lines occur in the *Triumph of Death*, the banner in question is that of Chastity (although we should not lose sight of the wider meaning of purity, to which I shall return). In addition to the ermine, the azure of Arthegall's shield is, as we have remarked, a colour closely associated with heaven and the Virgin Mary. Upton tells us that, in heraldry, azure is symbolic of loyalty, fidelity, and chastity.[41] Taken together, the ermine device and the azure field seem to point towards an interpretation of the shield highly appropriate to Book Three: as symbolic of chastity.

In all this I do not wish to deny the ermine shield any application to Sir Arthegall himself; indeed it may be appropriate to him in ways hitherto unrecognised. As in Leonardo da Vinci's 'Lady with an Ermine' in Cracow, now thought to be a portrait of Cecilia Gallerani, Spenser may be punning on the Greek word for ermine, *galee*.[42] The ermine on the shield would then be an example of canting heraldry, where the device puns upon the name of the bearer: in this case, Arthe*gall*. But an allusion to his name should not blind us to the shield's more consistent reference to Britomart; and we should also

---

40 *Lord Morley's 'Tryumphes of Fraunces Petrarcke'* ed. D.D.Carnicelli (Cambridge, Massachusetts: Harvard UP, 1971), 'Triumph of Death', ll. 25-27 (p.117). Petrarch, *Rime e Trionfi*, ed. Ferdinando Neri (Turin: Unione Tipografico, 1966), p.556:
>   era la lor vittoriosa insegna
>   in campo verde un candido ermellino,
>   ch'oro fino e topazi al collo tegna   (ll. 19-21)
41 *The Faerie Queene*, ed. John Upton (1758), Vol. 2, p.527.
42 See Martin Kemp, *Leonardo da Vinci: The Marvellous Works of Nature and Man* (Dent, 1981), p.200.

be aware of the possibility that the device cants or puns on her role through the name of one of her literary prototypes. In Tasso's *Gerusalemme liberata* Tancred finds himself in a situation closely paralled in Arthegall's predicament in Book Five of *The Faerie Queene*: both are captured by female warriors; and in both cases women in love with them assume armour belonging to another female knight in order to rescue them. In Spenser's poem the heroine is of course Britomart; in *Gerusalemme liberata* her name is, almost inevitably, Erminea.

II

But this does not explain why Arthegall should be bearing a shield so symbolic of chastity. It would seem more fitting for Britomart to do so. To understand the reasons why this shield is Arthegall's will take us to the heart of some of Spenser's themes in the story of Arthegall and Britomart.

Britomart first sees Arthegall in a vision of the future. That vision is seen in a magical 'glassie globe' (III.ii.21.1); but the globe is also referred to frequently as a mirror (for example III.ii.Arg.3; 17.4; 22.5) or as a 'looking glasse' (III.ii.18.8). Spenser clearly expects us to add to the iconographical associations of the glass globe (primarily, the fragility of marriage) those of the mirror. However, the normal function of a mirror, to reflect the viewer's image, appears to be unfulfilled. But we may suggest that, in two different ways, Britomart is reflected and that the image in the mirror embodies aspects of her self.

Firstly, her gazing in the mirror and thinking of those things 'that mote to her selfe pertaine' (III.ii.22.9) carry the implication that the process of falling in love involves the recognition of something of one's self in the beloved. This is a very old idea; and in the *Romance of the Rose* is expressed in terms similar to Spenser's. There, the Lover gazes into a fountain at the bottom of which are two crystal stones. The crystal is described as,

> the mirrour perilous,
> In which the proude Narcisus
> Saw all his face fair and bright,
> That made hym sithe to ligge upright.
> For whoso loketh in that mirrour,
> Ther may nothyng ben his socour

That he ne shall there sen somthyng
That shal hym lede into lovyng.[43]   (ll. 1601-1608)

In the *Romance*, the Lover gazes and sees two reflecting crystals, one suspects his own eyes. In them is reflected the 'roser' containing the fateful Rose. In *The Faerie Queene*, Britomart gazes similarly and sees a knight bearing, in the azure and ermine of his shield, emblems of her own, characteristic virtue. She has indeed seen things 'that mote to her selfe pertaine' and fallen in love with the bearer of them.

Secondly, Britomart's quest, as the heroine of Book Three, is for Arthegall. But it is also a quest for chastity. Britomart is seeking the ideal form of the virtue of which she is patron with which to become united. What she sees in the mirror is that ideal in the person of her future husband bearing the attributes of heavenly chastity. In retrospect we perceive that these emblems may contain meanings taken up in Arthegall's own book, as suggested by Dunseath, but, for the time being, the mirror's image may be read in terms of the quest for chastity and the quest for Britomart's 'selfe' in the person of her future husband. In Britomart's search for her reflected but separated self in Arthegall we may see the influence of the *Symposium*, and Aristophanes's theory of the androgyne (189c-193e). Having seen her other half in the mirror, it is no wonder that she envies (or 'halfe' envies) Amoret and Scudamour in the cancelled ending to Book Three, who find each other and form 'that faire *Hermaphrodite*', 'growne together quite' (III.xii.46.2; 5 [1590]). They have achieved the union of selves that she is seeking.[44]

In the significance of Arthegall's shield we find the first instance of the complementariness of these two figures. In Britomart's second vision, at Isis Church, we see in effect a mirror image of the vision in King Ryence's 'glassie globe' (III.ii.21.1). In the mirror, emblems borne by Arthegall display Britomart's virtue of chastity. At Isis Church, the vision includes two symbols associated with Britomart: the lion of her shield and the Minervan dragon. But in this latter vision her symbols are used to explore Arthegall's virtue, that of Justice.

43 *The Works of Geoffrey Chaucer*, ed. F.N.Robinson (1933; second edition, OUP, 1957), p. 580.
44 Britomart's 'halfe' envy and initial uncertainty as to the cause of her 'melancholy' (III.ii.27.9) are also consistent with Aristophanes's theory. The separated lovers are unaware of the cause or nature of their longings; they desire,
>   something else which the soul of either evidently desires and cannot tell,
>   and of which she has only a dark and doubtful presentiment,   (192c-d)
(*The Dialogues of Plato*, tr. Benjamin Jowett, 4 vols (1868-71; 4th edition, corrected reissue, OUP, 1964). Vol.1, p. 523).

30

III

In the story of Britomart and Arthegall, the fictional ancestors of the Tudors, Elizabeth I is praised. Although occasionally critical of the reality, Spenser never wavers in his glorification of the queen's ideal self, her Platonic idea. In the Proem to Book Three, Spenser calls the queen's attention (and with it the reader's) to his method of portraying her; he instructs her how to read his work and her image within it:

> Ne let his fairest *Cynthia* refuse,
> In mirrours more then one her selfe to see,
> But either *Gloriana* let her chuse,
> Or in *Belphoebe* fashioned to bee:
> In th'one her rule, in th'other her rare chastitee.
>
> (III.Proem.5.5-9)

The reference to 'mirrours more then one' may be no more than a transient metaphor. But the presence in Book Three of such a prominent and significant mirror as that in which Britomart sees Arthegall should make us wary of disregarding Spenser's instruction.

Britomart sees a reflection of her ideal self unfolded in the person of her future husband and his armour. It is possible that this vision refers not only to Britomart, but also to Elizabeth. Bearing in mind that this is a vision of the Arthegall of the future and not the present, it shows an armed knight (we are later to know him to be the patron of justice) bearing the shield of heavenly chastity; the combination expresses just those qualities singled out in the Proem: chastity and rule. Arthegall never achieves the perfection implied here (at least in the poem as we have it); the synthesis of his and Britomart's virtue to which the vision looks forward is left to their progeny. And perhaps we are meant to feel that this synthesis is only achieved in their ultimate offspring, the queen herself.

Support for this interpretation of Arthegall's shield can be found in the iconography of Elizabeth I, particularly in the so-called Ermine Portrait at Hatfield House. This depicts the queen, plainly dressed, holding in her right hand an olive branch, with her left hand touching a table beside a sword. Olive branch and sword probably symbolise peace and justice respectively. Resting on her left arm is an ermine with a small crown round its neck. This last detail distinguishes the portrait from the general tradition descended from Petrarch, in which the ermine wore a gold collar studded with topaz. Spenser's description of the ermine on Arthegall's shield agrees with the portrait in this detail: his has no collar but is a 'crowned litle Ermilin'. Both Elizabethan ermines may be an adaptation of Petrarch's image to suit the royal object of praise. The ermine in the portrait joins the other attributes to form an emblematic representation of the qualities of Elizabeth I's reign: justice and peace, political and personal purity. Close attention to the portrait reveals that the colours of the ermine, black and white, predominate, colours which became the queen's personal emblem of her purity in her later days.[45]

The Ermine Portrait is a subtle work. The ermine as a symbol, although derived from the *Trionfi* in large measure, also had its political significance, as purity in public, as well as private, affairs. Two other queens, Anne, wife of Francis I, and her daughter Claude, wife of Louis XII, used this emblem. So too did John of Gaunt's descendants, the Dukes of Lancaster, who were connected with the Duchy of Brittany. Ashmole explains the use of the ermine emblem as deriving from the creation of the Order of the Ermine by Duke John of Brittany, 'by which he made known the greatness of his courage, and rather than fail of his word, that he would undergo any misfortune'.[46] The ermine's refusal to stain its fur may obviously be interpreted as implying steadfastness and purity, not only in personal morality, but also in religious and political affairs. As such its presence on Arthegall's shield may contain not only a reference to the Belphoebean chastity of Elizabeth, but also to her Mercillan justice and integrity.

3. Britomart's Shield

I

Britomart enters the poem as an unknown knight, distinguished only by her spear and her shield. The latter 'bore a Lion passant in a golden field' (III.i.4.9). Perhaps distinguished is the wrong word: the lion is one of the commonest heraldic beasts in literature. Britomart received the shield as part of the armour hanging in King Ryence's church and which formerly

> long'd to *Angela*, the Saxon Queene,
> All fretted round with gold, and goodly well beseene.
> (III.iii.58.8-9)

Arthegall's armour was also 'round about yfretted all with gold' (III. ii.25.4) and these are the only armours thus decorated in *The Faerie*

---

45 See Strong, *Portraits of Queen Elizabeth I*, p.21.
46 Ashmole, p.118.

Queene. Britomart, one might say, has already begun to model herself on the image in the mirror and Spenser has begun to link these figures and their attributes.

However, the charge on Britomart's shield remains unexplained. Given its origin, we may speculate that Spenser is using this charge to indicate Britomart's symbolic and actual progenitors. The lion of course is the regal animal *par excellence*, and is the basis of the English royal coat-of-arms.[47]

It was suggested by Church that Britomart's arms, although spoil in terms of the narrative, are hers by virtue of her ancestor Brutus (*Var*, Vol.3, p.203). His arms (*or, a lion gules*) are found frequently in sixteenth and seventeenth-century works dedicated to the praise of the monarch and to the support of his right to the throne. Thus in Sir William Segar's fine illuminated pedigree of James VI and I, the arms of Brutus begin the series of James's ancestors (illus. 1).[48]

Interesting though this suggestion is, Church has only traced half the history of these arms, for Brutus inherited them from the pre-eminent medieval hero, Hector of Troy. His arms are thus described by Benoit de Sainte-Maure:

> On his shield was just a lion, but it was gules, surrounded by gold; so were his emblems, and the ensigns of his lances.[49]

These arms are also found in visual representations of Hector as in the tapestry representing his funeral from Tournai, now in the Burrell Collection.[50] In the course of Britomart's adventures the Trojan war and its causes receive farcical retelling in the liaison between Paridell and Hellenore. But the comedy should not blind us to the more serious themes involved in the Trojan legend, nor to the significant ways in which the Trojan legend underlies *The Faerie Queene*. During the episode in Malbecco's castle, Britomart reveals her own

[47] The animal is a lion and not a leopard as sometimes stated.
[48] BL Harley MS 6085, f.3r.
[49] *Roman de Troie*, ed. Léopold Constans, 6 vols (1904-12). Vol.1 (1904), p.437:   En son escu n'ot qu'un lion,
        Mais vermeuz fu, d'or environ;
        Autreteus sont ses conoissances
        E les enseignes de ses lances.   (ll. 8065-68)
The heraldry of Hector has been the subject of some discussion, with articles by R.S.Loomis ('The Heraldry of Hector or Confusion Worse Confounded', *Speculum* 42 (1967), pp.32-35) and R.A.Dwyer ('The Heraldry of Hector and its Antiquity', *JWCI* 34 (1971), pp.325-26). However both these articles are concerned only with Hector's arms as part of the tradition of the Nine Worthies, in which special, confusing features are found.
[50] See Margaret R.Scherer, *The Legends of Troy in Art and Literature* (New York: Phaidon Press, 1963), pp.93-94 and plate 76.

33

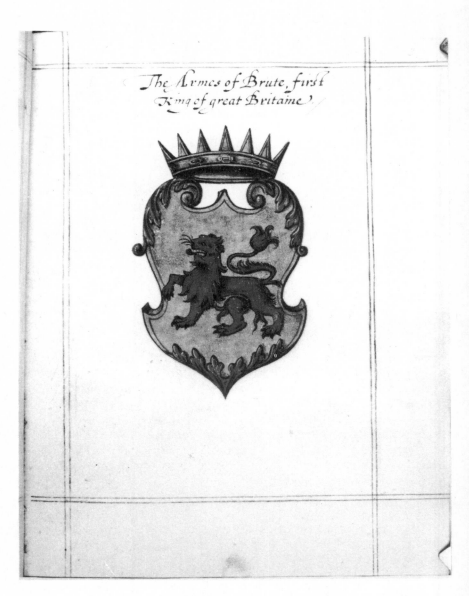

The Armes of Brute, first
King of great Britaine

1. The Arms of Brute. From BL Harley MS 6085, f.3: *Sir William Segar's Book of Royal Arms and Badges 1604*. (British Library)

Trojan ancestry; and as Paridell's debased and falsified version of the legend makes her sincerity more obvious, so his description of his ancestor as the 'most famous Worthy of the world' (III.ix.34.1) serves to heighten the true nobility (and true membership of the Nine Worthies) of Hector, whose arms she bears.

Once again, as the reader will have noticed, the discussion has returned to a point of contact between Britomart's arms and those of Arthegall. As her shield derives from Hector's, so he wears,

> *Achilles armes, which Arthegall did win.* (III.ii.25.6)

Critical comment on this line has been confused. Kathleen Williams sees this as the 'near identification' of Arthegall and Achilles, where-as Jane Aptekar concludes that 'Spenser seems to have had it in mind to associate Artegall with Achilles as well as with Hercules; but the Achilles relationship is not worked through'.[51] T.K.Dunseath, also concerned to establish a connection with Hercules, suggests the rather laboured contortion, 'Achilles' armor here is Spenser's sly reference to the fact that Hercules fought at Troy, and Arthegall is to unite with Britomart, thereby continuing the Trojan line in Britain' (p.59). Sly indeed. Dunseath is right in bringing in the Trojan destiny, but we must surely reject the reference to Hercules: '*Achilles armes*' is a reference to Achilles.

II

In associating these two figures with the adversaries in the most famous of all wars, Spenser is setting up once more the greatest opposition in all epic literature: Hector against Achilles, Troy against Greece. In this, Spenser follows the example of Virgil, who rematched the two heroes in Aeneas and Turnus, initiating a tradition of re-working the legend. Spenser imitates Virgil in allowing the Trojan side to triumph (at least initially), because Arthegall is overcome by Britomart in the tournament for Florimell's girdle. But he ultimately revolutionises the legend's ending: by embodying in a woman the Trojan stock, he makes possible the conclusion of the feud through a marriage alliance, combining the virtues of both sides. There was an element of this in the genealogy of Brutus himself, as Nennius tells us: 'According to the annals of the Roman history, the Britons

---

[51] Kathleen Williams, *Spenser's 'Faerie Queene': The World of Glass* (Routledge, 1966), p.133; and Aptekar, p.236, n.12.

deduce their origin both from the Greeks and Romans'.[52] Spenser, we notice, has the resolution of the feud in Book Four of *The Faerie Queene*, the book of *discordia concors*.

The union achieved works not only in terms of the epic tradition, but also in terms of the Tudor dynasty's own history. The offspring of Britomart and Arthegall are to be English sovereigns down to Elizabeth herself. The Tudor dynasty had been safely established as a result of just such a marriage alliance between two warring groups, thus ending the Wars of the Roses. The association was by no means new to Spenser: there is a wealth of evidence in the pageant tradition to support its commonness; as Frances Yates puts it, 'Closely related to the imperial theme of the Trojan descent of the Tudors is the theme of the united monarchy which they established through joining the houses of York and Lancaster'.[53] There is also a suggestion of this in the combination of weapons and armour borne by Britomart. She bears the armour of Angela, the Saxon queen; but she also carries the spear of Bladud, the Briton king. Spenser's innovation lies in the juxtaposition of Britomart and Arthegall, Elizabeth of York and Henry VII, the warring protagonists of Homer's epic, and the feuding monarchs of the tribes of Britain.

III

Two of the principal attributes mentioned in this chapter have several features in common. Prince Arthur's shield and Britomart's magical mirror are both crystal; both mirror-like; both magical; and both made by Merlin. It may be that they are in some way related.[54]

As we have seen, Britomart's vision presents an emblematic representation of herself and also, perhaps, of Queen Elizabeth's ideal self. The queen is counselled to see herself in mirrors and is also described as the 'Mirrour of grace and Majestie divine' (I.Proem.4.2). This latter description suggests the powers of Arthur's shield. The diamond shield, we have seen, is symbolic of grace and divine intercession. A complex of fleeting associations is built up in the poem, from which we may deduce that the queen's ideal virtues are in some way connected with the Prince's shield. This connection is certainly present in the description of the baldric, which has a portrait of

52 Nennius, *The History of the Britons* in *The Works of Gildas and Nennius* (1841), p.7.
53 Yates, *Astraea*, p.50.
54 I am indebted to Mr J.G.Radcliffe for bringing to my attention the resemblance between these objects.

Gloriana in its central stone. If we are correct in seeing an association between the Prince's armour and the Virgin Queen, then we may be able to solve the riddle of the armour and its present whereabouts:

> But when he [Arthur] dyde, the Faerie Queene it brought
> To Faerie lond, where yet it may be seene, if sought.
>
> (I.vii.36.8-9)

If one knows where to seek this armour of grace and divine intercession, then one will find it: in the queen herself.

II: ARMOUR

1. Body Armour

I

The charges of shields have always been intended to carry some significance, whether simply as a means of identification or more sophisticatedly for the expression of subtler matters. It is normal, then, for shields to fulfil symbolic functions. But this is by no means true of the rest of a knight's equipment; and the question must therefore arise of whether we have any justification for regarding body-armour in *The Faerie Queene* as an active constituent of the poem's symbolic language. This question would be all the more pressing if Spenser could be shown to have another end in view in his description of armour, perhaps the accurate representation of contemporary or carefully archaized armour; the implication of which would be that the requirements of verisimilitude governed the details of armour in *The Faerie Queene*.

Spenser's forerunners in the depiction of armour in poems often display just this interest and pride in historical accuracy. Irving Linn has shown how Chaucer in the *Tale of Sir Thopas* employs considerable knowledge of the arming of a knight; and he points to several equally detailed passages in other works of medieval literature.[1] That Spenser recognized the authenticity of such detail is demonstrated by his invocation, in *A View of the Present State of Ireland*, of the arming of Sir Thopas to clinch a point concerning the origins of the 'Checklaton'.[2]

Fortunately, the accuracy of the various suits-of-armour in *The Faerie Queene* has been studied by Allan H.Gilbert, and we may repeat his conclusions:

> It would seem that in the equipment of his knights [Spenser] was satisfied with a general suggestion of 'antique history' and did not make an attempt to find a norm to which the outward appearance of a cavalier must conform. In other words, there is no indication that he carefully visualized the

[1] Irving Linn, 'The Arming of Sir Thopas', *MLN* 51 (1936), pp.300-11.
[2] *Var*, vol.9, p.121.

details in the armor of his heroes; indeed he has less feeling for the niceties of armor than his Italian predecessors in romantic poetry.[3]

Gilbert demonstrates that such terms as 'plate' and 'mail' cannot be read in their technical, literal senses in this poem, but are frequently used as poetic alternatives for 'armour' (p.987).

Although somewhat harshly expressed, Gilbert's main conclusion is essentially correct. Judged for its accuracy, Spenser's armour would have suffered at the hands of Tristram Shandy's Uncle Toby as did Parson Yorick's ill-imagined seige metaphor:

> Aye, ... aye, *Trim*! quoth my uncle *Toby*, shaking his head, ... these are but sorry fortifications, *Trim*.[4]

But Spenser, like the unfortunate Parson, is concerned more with literary than martial effectiveness. On the one hand, his use of technical vocabulary creates, when required, the illusion of a physical reality; on the other, as the following pages will suggest, his selection of chivalric detail is frequently motivated by a desire to employ the symbolism of armour. And in such cases, *pace* Gilbert, there is every 'indication that he carefully visualized the details in the armor of his heroes'; but for purposes other than the realistic or the decorative.

Further examination of *The Faerie Queene* reveals that the same is true of many of the details of combat. On several occasions the poet praises the size and weight of the equipment used by his characters: Arthegall's 'wondrous massie' armour (III.ii.25.3), for instance, or Satyrane's 'huge great speare' (IV.iv.17.2). But contemporary writers on the art of warfare ridiculed the very qualities Spenser stresses. Matthew Sutcliffe tells a cautionary tale:

> The Frenchmen in time past had some ... that were armed, as they saie, *de cap en pied* at which the Romane souldiers laughed. For that they were unable by reason of the weight of their armes, eyther to strike the enemie, or to defend themselves. Therefore did they hew them downe with billes, and pollaxes.[5]

Armour such as that used by some of Spenser's knights would have made them prey to every wild man in the woods. Sutcliffe would no doubt have congratulated Guyon on the loss of his 'loftie steed with golden sell, / And goodly gorgeous barbes' (II.ii.11.6-7), for,

---

[3] Allan H. Gilbert, 'Spenserian Armor', *PMLA* 57 (1942), p.987.

[4] Laurence Sterne, *The Life and Opinions of Tristram Shandy, Gentleman*, ed. G. Petrie (Harmondsworth: Penguin, 1967), p.146.

[5] Matthew Sutcliffe, *The Practice, Proceedings, and Lawes of Armes* (1593), p.187.

The barded horsemen both for their heavines, and great charge, I thinke not very needefull. When Lucullus his men were much afraide of Tygranes his barded horses, he willed them to be of good cheere, for that there was more labour in spoyling them being so armed, then in foyling them: they were so unweldy.[6]

The fact that his impressive weaponry and armour might be cumbersome and immobilizing is irrelevant in Spenser: Guyon's 'golden sell', no doubt impossible and unliftable, has symbolic functions that override the demands of realism and verisimilitude.

II

Before considering some of the individual suits-of-armour in the poem, we should refer to the general properties of the symbolism of armour in *The Faerie Queene*. This symbolism becomes most evident when Spenser explicitly draws our attention to characteristic actions involving armour: its assumption, retention, and removal.

There are times when this symbolism remains dormant and unevoked. When Prince Arthur and Sir Guyon, having toured Alma's castle, come to pay court to her damsels, we are never informed that they have disarmed in the meantime. Nonetheless, we do not imagine them clanking in habergeon and cuirass as they traverse the floor: in Alma's castle, awareness of the continued presence of the suit-of-armour is allowed to fade, because its symbolism is irrelevant.

But at other times and in other places this is not so. Throughout Britomart's adventures, armour is brought to the forefront of our attention; and I shall therefore use her armour as my principal example. First Spenser informs us that at Malecasta's house,

> The *Redcrosse* Knight was soone disarmed there,
> But the brave Mayd would not disarmed bee,   (III.i.42.6-7)

Spenser's lines make us aware that we are now to focus on seemingly mundane actions involving armour.

The six knights who earlier opposed the Red Cross Knight also disarm. But Britomart resists all Malecasta's entreaties to remove her inhibiting martial equipment. Only when she retires alone to bed does Britomart,

> her selfe despoile,
> And safe commit to her soft fethered nest   (III.i.58.6-7)

6 P.183. Spenser's form 'barbes' is a corruption of that used by Sutcliffe (*OED* Barb sb1). The bards made up the 'protective covering for the breast and flanks of a war-horse' (*OED* Bard sb1).

In view of later events, the second line's implication of security is ironic. The seed of disquiet, however, is already sowed in the term 'despoile': although on the surface this merely means to remove an outer garment, in a martial context 'despoile' carries the sense of forcible deprivation, usually associated with the plundering of the dead and defeated in battle.[7] We realise, perhaps only in retrospect, that Spenser has revitalized this near-dead martial sense in order to undermine for the reader the character's impression of safety and security and to convey the hazard of Britomart's action in disarming.

Interpretation of these lines and the action they describe can be taken further. As a result of her voluntary disarming Britomart renders herself vulnerable; and she is indeed wounded by Gardante, a wound associated with sexual or amorous attraction. This sequence of events suggests more than that Britomart has been smitten by love. It also implies that her wound is in part self-inflicted: 'she gan *her selfe* despoile' (my italics). In her partial defeat by love she is both victor and victim. The play on pronouns in this line is recalled when we are later told the circumstances of her vision of Arthegall in King Ryence's mirror, a passage discussed in the previous chapter. This vision is preceded by her self-contemplation:

> she gan againe
> *Her* to bethinke of, that mote to *her selfe* pertaine.
>
> (III.ii.22.8-9; my italics)

Significantly, her assailant in Malecasta's house is Gardante, the personification of the phase of 'looking' in the Ladder of Lechery.[8] Britomart's exposure to the dangers of love is thus implied to be partially voluntary and her response to it appears ambivalent.

Britomart certainly learns from this experience in Malecasta's dangerous house. In the lust-laden atmosphere of Busyrane's castle she prudently remains fully armed:

> Yet nould she d'off her weary armes, for feare
> Of secret daunger, ne let sleepe oppresse
> Her heavy eyes with natures burdein deare,
> But drew her selfe aside in sickernesse,
> And her welpointed weapons did about her dresse. (III.xi.55.5-9)

---

[7] *OED*, Despoil v3c; v2a. See also Spenser's other uses of the term: I.x.17.7; V.iv.31.3; VI.vi.34.6; and VI.vii.26.9.

[8] See Allan H. Gilbert, 'The Ladder of Lechery, *The Faerie Queene*, III, i, 45', *MLN* 56 (1941), pp. 594-97; James Hutton, 'Spenser and the "Cinq Points en Amours"', *MLN* 57 (1942), pp. 657-61; and Alastair Fowler, 'Six Knights at Castle Joyous', *SP* 56 (1959), pp. 583-99. More recently and more generally, see Lionel J. Friedman, 'Gradus Amoris', *Romance Philology* 19 (1966), pp. 167-77. For the translation as 'looking', see especially Fowler, pp. 584 and 598.

Resisting the temptation to disarm and sleep, presented in a highly seductive manner, she has good reason to feel that she is 'in sickernesse' or 'a state or condition of being secure'.[9] Spenser's elided form 'welpointed' allows a pun, implying that Britomart's weapons have been prudently sharpened as well as retaining the normal sense of her being properly equipped. The passage as a whole conveys her greatly increased safety and knightly competence. But it does so, significantly, through stressing two connected aspects of Britomart: she is well armed against external attack; but this goes alongside her psychological alertness, her self-awareness and self-protection.

Finally, Spenser seems to invite us to study the role of her armour in the adventure at Dolon's castle: both incidents occur at the beginning of a quest for Sir Arthegall and in both cases the host mistakes her sex. Dolon imitates Malecasta in entreating Britomart to disarm:

> But she ne would undressed be for ought,
> Ne doffe her armes, though he her much besought. (V.vi.23.4-5)

This time Britomart also refuses to lie in a perilous bed, but maintains her vigil and thus avoids the trap. Lying in such a bed would undoubtedly have carried sexual overtones.[10] But her prudence, constancy, and love for Arthegall have now developed sufficiently to prevent her falling into dangers similar to those faced at the beginning of her quest.

While this summary of Britomart's adventures makes clear the importance in them of actions involving armour, it does not establish the meaning of the suit-of-arms in the allegory. But any reader of renaissance literature knows that it is almost axiomatic that full armour is an attribute of personified virtue; and this is the principal iconographical tradition on which Spenser draws.[11] In other contexts than that of moral allegory armour may have different significations: it may, for instance, be an attribute of Mars, and thus denote war.[12] But although other associations are occasionally intended in *The*

---

9 *OED* Sickerness 3a.

10 Compare, for instance, Sir Gareth's temptations and symbolic wounding in his left thigh in *The Works of Sir Thomas Malory*, vol.1, pp.332-36. That Spenser was fully aware of this passage and had it in mind while composing the story of Britomart is supported by the resemblances between Dame Lyoness's nocturnal visit to Sir Gareth and that made by Malecasta to Britomart. Both seductresses, for example, are dressed in ermine mantles: 'dame Lyonesse [came] wrapped in a mantell furred with ermyne' (p.333); Malecasta 'with a scarlot mantle covered, / That was with gold and Ermines faire enveloped' (III.i.59.8-9).

11 I omit, until the fourth chapter, the specifically Christian symbolism of armour.

12 See Guy de Tervarent, *Attributs et Symboles dans l'Art Profane 1450-1600: Dictionnaire d'un Langage Perdu*, 3 vols (Geneva: Droz, 1958-64), cols 33-34.

Faerie Queene, symbolic armour in this poem is principally connected with the inclusive abstraction, virtue. Armour is frequently used with this meaning in the visual arts of Spenser's period. The opposition between armed Virtue and 'loose' Vice is perhaps most clearly seen in the various versions of the 'Choice of Hercules'. Hadrianus Junius (1575) and Geoffrey Whitney (1586) in their popular emblem books both differentiate Virtue and Vice by having the former personification armed.[13] The meaning of the contrast is mentioned by neither author, testimony to the commonness of the allusion. A more polished and consciously artistic version of the same subject is that by Gaspar de Crayer (1584), who also uses an armed Virtue, again without annotation. And an explicit acknowledgement of this meaning of armour is found in Alciati's *Emblemata* (1621), where he states that 'the armed girl signifies a wise man arming himself against all perturbations of mind, and resisting vices with a strong hand'.[14] Finally, to anticipate the discussion of the Christian warrior's arms in Chapter Four, Marcus Gheeraerts the Elder's etching of William I cf Orange (William the Silent) as St George shows the knight fully dressed in the armour of virtue; what is more, the armour is identified as representing the various specific virtues in the margin (illus. 2).

It is equally clear that the representation of virtue as an armed female must have been related, or thought to have been related to representations and interpretations of the goddess Minerva. The latter is often found in the role of leader of the Virtues, engaging in combat with the Vices.[15] Tracing the development of Minerva's interpretation over the period of the Renaissance, Rudolf Wittkower sums up the 'literary and pictorial tradition of the Middle Ages' as showing 'Minerva in full armour as the warlike defender of wisdom and virtue'.[16]

But this quotation introduces a second point, as did that from Alciati. As well as representing virtue in general, Minerva was held to

---

[13] Hadrianus Junius, *Emblemata* (1565; facsimile edition, Scolar Press, 1972), Emblem 44; Geoffrey Whitney, *A Choice of Emblemes*, (1586; facsimile edition, ed. Henry Green, 1866), p.40. The engraving after Gaspar de Crayer is illustrated in Erwin Panofsky, *Hercules am Scheideweg und andere Bildstoffe in der Neueren Kunst* (Leipzig: Teubner, 1930), plate 34.

[14] *Emblemata cum commentariis* (1621; facsimile edition, ed. Stephen Orgel [*The Renaissance and the Gods*, vol.25], New York: Garland, 1976), p.123: 'Puella igitur armata virum sapientem adversus omnes animi perturbationes se armantem, et vitiis animo forti resistentem significat'. The translation is quoted from Fowler, *Spenser and the Numbers of Time*, p.126.

[15] See Mantegna's *Wisdom Overcoming the Vices* and Perugino's *Combat of Love and Chastity* for example.

[16] Rudolf Wittkower, 'Transformations of Minerva in Renaissance Imagery', *JWCI* 2 (1938-39), p.199.

2. William of Orange (William the Silent) as St George. Marcus Gheeraerts the Elder. (British Museum).

be patroness of more specific qualities; and these are transferred to armour, her characteristic attribute. They are also transferred to those figures associated with Minerva in *The Faerie Queene*. Britomart, as Alastair Fowler has shown, possesses many of the goddess's attributes, not least her armour.[17] Of the moral qualities associated with Minerva, Britomart partakes not only of her chastity, but also of her prudence, her wisdom. At least, Britomart does so by the end of her quest; and it is in this context that we can best understand her education in virtue. Her devotion to chastity is rarely, if ever, in question. But what she does learn throughout her adventures is the self-awareness and self-possession required to retain intact her chastity and her integrity.[18] And it is this lesson that is represented in her changing responses to the promptings and temptations, from within and without, to remove her armour.

The true test lies in her conduct in Busyrane's castle. One cannot feel here that Britomart is greatly perturbed by the lurid scenes depicted in the tapestries, nor by the pageant she witnesses.[19] Rather, in the gathering of her armoury about her and her drawing 'her selfe aside in sickernesse', we are aware of the prudent watchfulness, the wise self-possession she now displays, in contrast to her too-ready sense of security in Malecasta's house.

III

The lessons learnt in the course of Britomart's adventures may help in the difficult task of comprehending the meanings of armour in Book Six.

As A.C.Hamilton has commented, 'for no other book does the usual kind of allegorical interpretation seem so entirely inadequate, irrelevant and disposable'.[20] As if deliberately to confirm this, Spenser presents the disarming of characters such as Aladine without

---

17 *Spenser and the Numbers of Time*, pp.124-26.
18 The value Spenser places on such qualities is eloquently expressed in *Amoretti* LVIII and LIX: 'Most happy she that most assured doth rest, / but he most happy who such one loves best' (LIX.8-9).
19 Discussion of the House of Busyrane in the foregoing pages has covered some of the same ground as James Nohrnberg's account in *The Analogy of 'The Faerie Queene'* (pp.471-490). However, Professor Nohrnberg makes little of the Minervan theme of wisdom in this episode; and his conclusions vary from the unexciting (Britomart as *Custodiendas Virgines*, love defeating love [p. 486]) to the irresponsible (her possible 'skeptophilia' or voyeurism [p.473]).
20 *The Faerie Queene*, ed. A.C.Hamilton, p.621.

the moral condemnation found elsewhere on similar occasions. Aladine is discovered, attacked, and wounded while he and Priscilla are

> Joying together in unblam'd delight,
> And him unarm'd, as now he lay on ground.   (VI.ii.43.3-4)

Unlike the implied openness to lust in the unarmed encounter at Malecasta's house, or the obvious lustfulness of the disarmed Red Cross Knight (I.vii), of Cymochles (II.v), and of Verdant (II.xii), the activities of Aladine and Priscilla are explicitly 'unblam'd'.

A solution to our difficulties in interpreting disarmings and re-armings in Book Six may be found through study of Calidore's actions at the beginning and end of his sojourn in the pastoral world. Calidore disarms in order to melt into the shepherds' life and particularly to render himself acceptable to Pastorella. Finding the shepherdess unimpressed by his courtly accomplishments, 'his layes, his loves, his lookes' (VI.ix.35.9), he

> thought it best
> To chaunge the manner of his loftie looke;
> And doffing his bright armes, himselfe addrest
> In shepheards weed   (VI.ix.36.1-4)

Calidore is successful in his limited aim and Pastorella looks kindly on him. But this success is precarious: as soon as the pastoral world is challenged from the outside, his new equipment, 'in stead of steele-head speare, a shepheards hooke' (VI.ix.36.5), proves utterly inadequate. The limitations of the attributes of his new role are powerfully and ironically pointed by the kidnapping of Pastorella herself.

Calidore's response to the invasion of the pastoral world takes the form of his rearming. But it is a rearming which constitutes the most subtle and resonant image of courtesy in the poem. He resolves, with the cowardly Coridon, to rescue Pastorella:

> So forth they goe together (God before)
> Both clad in shepheards weeds agreeably,
> And both with shepheards hookes: but *Calidore*
> Had underneath, him armed privily.   (VI.xi.36.1-4)

Calidore's dress now combines the emblems of arcadian peace and harmony with the armour of the warrior.

This armour too must be interpreted. Spenser never describes Calidore's equipment, not even his shield. Yet this lack of definition gives his arms, like Prince Arthur's blank shield described in the first chapter, a fertile inclusiveness and enables them to partake freely of the developing meanings attached to armour in the course of *The Faerie Queene*. Among these, the dominant theme has been that of armour representing virtue and wisdom. And we may interpret Calidore's wearing of armour concealed by 'shepheards weed', not as the renunciation of the pastoral ideal, but as indicating the essential grounding in virtue and prudence required for the survival of the precious qualities represented by the attributes of the arcadian.

The image of Calidore as an armed shepherd, but a shepherd nonetheless, perfectly expresses courtesy as Spenser preceives it. Courtesy implies a society; but society since the Fall (or the end of the Golden Age, in another pastoral tradition) is corrupt. Aladine and Priscilla's error is not lust: their love is innocent, 'unblam'd'. But they may, perhaps, be censured for imprudence. They have behaved, in the naive gratification of their love and their failure to guard against attack, as though the world had returned to its ancient, uncorrupt state (as indeed both their names imply), when it 'without a law, of its own will, kept faith and did the right'.[21] In a sense they have misjudged the extent and scope of Arthegall's success in Book Five, taking it as absolute and implying the return to earth of Astraea. But Arthegall's achievement is severely limited and entails the enforcement of law rather than its supercession.

In studying Britomart's career it was noted that her armed virtue included wisdom: it is her prudent wariness that saves her in Dolon's house and Busyrane's castle. Britomart is, latterly, well aware of the pitfalls and perils of the world, even for those disposed to goodness; and in Book Six Calidore also requires an education in this aspect of virtue. He retreats, as Meliboee had before him, from the corrupt outside world, experimenting with the unrestrained freedom and contentment of a separate, pastoral existence. The destruction of the village forces a reassessment of his response to the imperfections of humanity and human society. Calidore's solution is not to reject all that he has discovered during his 'truancy'. Instead, he combines, emblematically, the inner virtue, prudence, and integrity (symbolized by his armour) necessary for the protection of the self with the social qualities of courtesy symbolized by the 'shepheards weed'.

Even as one makes them, such cut-and-dried distinctions seem an inadequate formulation of our response to this book: the subtlety and delicacy of Spenser's achievement in Book Six make the critic a clod-hopping Calidore blundering through Colin's vision. Perhaps it is more satisfactory, then, to imitate Calidore and resolve the problem by stressing the essential unity of the theme of this book and that of the whole of *The Faerie Queene*. Courtesy, in a sense, is not *a* virtue;

---

21 Ovid, *Metamorphoses*, ed. and tr. Frank Justus Miller, 2 vols (Loeb Classics, 1916; 3rd edn., revised by G.P.Goold, Heineman, 1977), I. 90:
sponte sua, sine lege findem rectumque colebat.

it is Virtue in its social manifestation. As with Holiness at the beginning of the poem, it is difficult to restrict this virtue to a narrow compass. As Holiness encompasses all the virtues in a religious context, so courtesy does in the context of human society. The emblematic dress of Calidore, the paradoxical armed arcadian able to achieve the equal paradox of bringing Pastorella to the non-pastoral world, would seem to confirm this.

I stress deliberately the 'paradox' of Calidore here. Spenser has placed his knight in an impossible position, requiring him to be a 'gentle' man and yet also to indulge in the beastliness of combat with brigands and thieves. That conflict of roles is suggested by and rendered tangible in the armings and disarmings of his hero; and Spenser uses armour, the adopted outer protection of the warrior, in combination with an internal or external difference to express this kind of conflict and paradox. Britomart suppresses her feminity, literally enclosing it within an outer case, in adopting masculine armour; yet this is to achieve her true fulfilment, sexual and dynastic, through discovery of and union with Sir Arthegall. The image of armour, the case or outer skin, either covering the real self or itself covered, becomes one of Spenser's most powerful and most human metaphors, a vehicle for profound and mysterious comment on the moral and psychological dilemmas and tensions confronted by his characters.

Our interpretation of armour in *The Faerie Queene* must then include a Minervan refinement on the simpler symbolism of virtue. However, the inclusion of wisdom is to some extent true of the poem as a whole. Set within the archaized and romantic landscapes of Faeryland are explorations of all-too-timeless human dilemmas. Spenser rarely presents the opposition between good and evil in terms of a clear-cut *psychomachia*. Rather, despite the poem's limitations when judged by novelistic standards, the nature and the difficulties of the virtuous life are presented through recognizable and common human situations. Although his readers will never come face to face with an Acrasia or a Despair, the moral problems presented in such figures, and presented through Spenser's art so vividly and compellingly that we are involved in the moral drama, are accessible to us all. Perhaps one of Spenser's most significant divergences from the simple allegory of abstract virtues is the realization in his poem of the indispensability of self-awareness and self-possession; in fact the additional quality of prudence necessary to the preservation of every other virtue when the abstract is put to the concrete test. And this extra, ever-present virtue is expressed symbolically in the armour his heroes learn always to wear. The knight is the basic building block of *The Faerie Queene*; and his characteristic garb, armour, is not left as mere decoration, but is central to the presentation of Spenser's intensely human moral allegory.

2. Arthur's Armour

I

It is perhaps surprising that Prince Arthur's armour has received so little attention from the critics of *The Faerie Queene* and that no sustained attempt has been made to account for its prominence. A few authors have dealt with elements of this suit-of-armour in passing; Kathleen Williams briefly discusses the helmet and her conclusions are largely reiterated by Maurice Evans.[22] More recently, James Nohrnberg has commented on the baldric.[23] But although these scholars have made some valuable individual points, there has been a general failure to see the armour as a whole. Williams and Evans, to take an extreme example, do not even consider the helmet as a single entity, but discuss its various details in isolation from each other. The result of such piecemeal discussion is that the concentrated effect achieved by Spenser in his single, narrative-arresting description is dissipated and the armour's power as a symbol is greatly reduced.

Our first impression of the Prince comes as Una sees him marching towards her:

> His glitterand armour shined farre away,
> Like glauncing light of *Phoebus* brightest ray;
> From top to toe no place appeared bare,
> That deadly dint of steele endanger may: (I.vii.29.4-7)

We are made immediately aware in this description of two of the themes which will recur in virtually all Prince Arthur's appearances in the poem: his symbolic relationship with the sun and his ultimate invulnerability. The significance of the first can best be seen in his battle with the Souldan, whose catastrophic inferiority is conveyed by his being likened to Phaeton (V.viii.40).[24] The significance of the latter is pervasive in all of the Prince's adventures.

---

22 Williams, p. 22; and Maurice Evans, *Spenser's Anatomy of Heroism: A Commentary on 'The Faerie Queene'*, (Cambridge: Cambridge UP, 1970). p.104.
23 James Nohrnberg, *The Analogy of 'The Faerie Queene'*, p.40.
24 Prince Arthur's battle with the Souldan shows a direct engagement with a Phaeton-figure. It should however be noted that Book One has already contained its antitype to the Prince who is also defined in this way. The description of Lucifera's throne contains elements similar to the later description of

This much has been noted by many critics. However, there is more to these lines than is normally allowed. As well as introducing such general themes, Spenser may also be making statements about the standing of his central hero in comparison with the heroes of other epics, and in particular with Achilles.

The description of Arthur's perfect, glittering armour recalls details of the combat between Achilles and Hector in the *Iliad*. When Achilles seeks a vulnerable spot in which to wound his opponent, Homer comments on the integrity of the latter's suit-of-armour. These arms had, of course, previously belonged to Achilles, until Hector had plundered them from Patroclus's body. Achilles looked,

> upon his fair flesh to find where it was most open to a blow. Now all the rest of his flesh was covered by the armour of bronze, the goodly armour that he had stripped from mighty Patroclus when he slew him.[25]

Hector's *cap-a-pie* armour seems flawless and impenetrable as does Prince Arthur's. But Achilles's own armour is even more extraordinary, as its shining demonstrates:

> all around about the bronze flashed like the gleam of blazing fire or of the sun as he riseth.[26]

Spenser's Arthurian armour is, if anything, more amazing still, glittering like '*Phoebus* brightest ray'.

Neither of these resemblances is sufficient to make an allusion definite: they may be no more than the stock images and comparisons of epic. But Spenser describes the baldric Arthur wears in terms which seem more certainly derived from Homer. As he does on several other occasions, Spenser alters the weapon or garment to which an image or simile applies in his source while transferring it to his own poem. In this case the simile travels from Achilles's spear to Arthur's baldric, which bears a central jewel in the shape of a lady's head; and this,

---

Arthur: she shines 'as *Titans* ray' (I.iv.8.5); has a dragon as a symbolic attribute (10.5); and is compared with '*Phoebus* fairest childe' (9.1). As a false version of royalty and magnificence, she should perhaps be contrasted with Prince Arthur, as well as more obviously with Mercilla in Book Five.

[25] Homer, *The Iliad*, ed. and tr. A.T.Murray (Loeb Classics, 1925), pp.478-79:
χρόα καλόν, ὅπη εἴξειε μάλιστα.
τοῦ δὲ καὶ ἄλλο τόσον μὲν ἔχε χρόα χάλκεα τεύχεα,
καλά, τὰ Πατρόκλοιο βίην ἐνάριξε κατακτάς.

[26] 22. 134-35:
ἀμφὶ δὲ χαλκὸς ἐλάμπετο εἴκελος αὐγῇ
ἢ πυρὸς αἰθομένου ἢ ἠελίου ἀνιόντος.

exceeding shone,
Like *Hesperus* emongst the lesser lights. (I.vii.30.3-4)

Homer describes Achilles's spear in these terms:

> As a star goeth forth amid stars in the darkness of night, the star of evening,
> that is set in heaven as the fairest of all; even so went forth a gleam from
> the keen spear that Achilles poised in his right hand.[27]

Like Arthur's baldric, the spear is compared to Hesperus, and then its
singularity conveyed in Hesperus's beauty and superiority when compared to other stars in the heavens. In this connection it is also
interesting to note that Hesperus was used in the pageantry of
Catherine of Aragon's entry into London in 1501 as a symbol of her
intended husband, Henry VII's eldest son Prince Arthur; and so there
may well have been in Spenser's mind a pre-existing connection
between his overall hero and the star. In Catherine of Aragon's entry,
the association of Prince Arthur and Hesperus formed part of a
greater compliment to the Prince of Wales through an allusion to
Christ.[28]

Returning to the specifically Achillean context of Prince Arthur's
armour, in addition to the suggested verbal allusions we may note
more general resemblances between the martial equipment of the
two heroes. Both sets of armament are made by divine or magical
figures, Hephaestus and Merlin respectively. Both include an extraordinary shield. And Hephaestus also provided Achilles with a shining
baldric to support his shield (*Iliad* 18.480). These general resemblances, together with the similarities of phrasing and imagery already
noted, suggest that Spenser intends us to see a comparison between
Prince Arthur and Achilles conveyed through their arms.

Such a juxtaposition should come as no surprise to us. In the
Letter to Raleigh Spenser had indicated his intention to compare
Arthur with the heroes of classical and contemporary epic.[29] But although unsurprised we should not dismiss the advantages and prestige
to the poet of a comparison with the paramount epic hero of earlier
literature: Spenser exalts both hero and poem by this means. Furthermore, Achilles ultimately performs a role in the *Iliad* not unlike that

[27] 22. 317-20:

οιος δ ἀστὴρ εισι μετ' ἀστράσι νυκτὸς ἀμολγῶ
ἕσπερος, ὃς κάλλιστος ἐν οὐρανῶ ἵσταται ἀστηρ,
ὡς αἰχμῆς ἀπελαμπ' εὐήκεος, ἣν ἄρ' Ἀχιλλεὺς
πάλλεν δεξιτερῆ

[28] See Sydney Anglo, 'The London Pageants for the Reception of Katherine of
Aragon: November 1501', *JWCI* 26 (1963), pp.74-76. Anglo calls the allusion
to Christ 'a refulgent, and shameless' compliment!

[29] *Var*, Vol.1, p.167.

of Spenser's Prince Arthur. Homer's hero intervenes decisively to save the nearly-defeated Greeks, rescuing them from Hector and finally killing him, the chief threat to a Grecian victory. Spenser takes this interventionist role for Prince Arthur, a role which dominates his appearances in *The Faerie Queene* almost to the exclusion of all others. On this level, then, the comparison of Prince Arthur and Achilles is both general and pervasive.

A second function of the comparison is to provide another point of contact between Prince Arthur and Sir Arthegall, a connection at the heart of much of the political and moral allegory of Books Three to Five. Arthegall, as well as performing frequently in an Achillean role, wears a suit-of-armour which is explicitly said to have belonged to Achilles: '*Achilles armes, which Arthegall did win*' (III.ii.25.6). In fact, there is nothing particularly Achillean about these arms, since they derive neither from Homer's descriptions nor from any of the other suits-of-arms given to Achilles by later writers. But part of Spenser's intention may lie in this discrepancy: the inconsistency here parallels that in the comparison of Britomart's shield with Minerva's. In the first chapter it was noted that although the 'martiall Britoness's' shield was explicitly compared with that of the goddess, it was Arthur's shield which was, in fact, Minervan both in physical resemblance and in its petrifying powers. And it was suggested that through this split reference to Minerva Britomart and her arms were linked to Prince Arthur. We may now suggest that the same process links Sir Arthegall to the Prince: the former's arms are said to be Achillean in the poem; but the latter's are the arms really derived from the *Iliad*.

II

In addition to its relevance to the poem as a whole, Arthur's arms play an integral part in the symbolism of the first book. Kathleen Williams perceptively notes this when she comments that 'Arthur's dragon [on his crest] is now part of his strength, Red Crosse's is still to fight' (p. 22). This dragon-crest is described in great detail:

> For all the crest a Dragon did enfold
> With greedie pawes, and over all did spred
> His golden wings: his dreadfull hideous hed
> Close couched on the bever, seem'd to throw
> From flaming mouth bright sparkles fierie red,
> That suddeine horror to faint harts did show;
> And scaly tayle was stretcht adowne his backe full low.
>
> (I.vii.31.3-9)

In discussing Prince Arthur's dragon crest we should be aware of two traditions. Firstly, there is the tradition that the legendary King Arthur wore 'a helm of gold graven with the semblance of a dragon'.[30] However, we should be cautious in assuming that Spenser's source is Geoffrey of Monmouth or one of his followers. We possess, as did Spenser's own time, a considerable wealth of detail concerning King Arthur's arms, from Geoffrey, Nennius, and the iconography of King Arthur as one of the Nine Worthies. But Spenser, excepting this dragon crest, appears to refer to none of this. There is no trace among the attributes of *The Faerie Queene*'s Prince of Excalibur, the spear Ron, the shield with the three crowns motif, or, indeed, any of King Arthur's weaponry.

Furthermore, Spenser's description of the helmet seems to derive more from a second, non-Arthurian tradition, that of Virgil and Tasso and the European epic. And Spenser seems specifically to allude to the Sultan's helmet in the *Gerusalemme liberata*. But in considering these allusions, we should be at least as aware of the differences as we are of the similarities. The Sultan's dragon takes up an aggressive stand on his helmet: it 'raises itself up on its legs, and spreads its wings, and curves up in an arc its forked tail'.[31] This is indeed a ferocious beast. But although Prince Arthur's dragon is also awesome, and its wings are likewise outspread, its position on the helmet is strikingly different. This is most noticeable in the line, 'his dreadfull hideous hed / Close couched on the bever'. The position of the dragon's head is surprising: the beaver, technically the area below the vizor but frequently used for the vizor itself, is well below the crest of the helmet. This dragon's head, far from being raised in attack, is bent right down, if anything in a defensive position. Similarly Prince Arthur's dragon has its 'scaly tayle ... stretcht adowne his backe full low', contrasting radically with the Sultan's dragon, the tail of which is vitally curled up and forked. Arthur's dragon's tail is ennervated, stretching limply down.

These contrasting details allow us to perceive crucial differences between these two helmets. The dragon on the Sultan's crest conveys his evil vigour and power. Prince Arthur's dragon, on the other hand, carries with it auguries of the defeat of the real Dragon at the end of Book One. Kathleen Williams's comment, that these two dragons of the first book are meant to be compared, is surely correct. The

[30] Geoffrey of Monmouth, p.188.
[31] Torquato Tasso, *Opere*, ed. Bortolo Tommaso Sozzi, 2 vols (1956; 3rd edition, Turin: Unione Tipografico-Editrice Torinese, 1974). Vol.1 *Gerusalemme liberata* 9.25.3-4:
        su le sampe s'inalza, e l'ali spande,
        e piega in arco la forcuta coda

defeated and defensive stance of Arthur's 'tamed dragon' conveys, as Williams says, its subordination to the Prince, especially when compared with its fellow in *Gerusalemme liberata*.

The impression of the dragon's submission is strengthened by Spenser's use of the word 'couched'. The poet avoids the normal heraldic term for this type of pose, 'couchant', although he uses it on other occasions (notably in the description of Sir Arthegall's greyhound crest). Instead Spenser uses a form associated with the behaviour of real, rather than symbolic animals. 'Couched' describes an animal crouching or cowering 'in obedience, fear etc.' (*OED* 'couch' v1 16b and 17a). The *OED* cites a cutting simile, in which 'couch' is applied to false ministers of the Gospel: 'yf they [these dombe dogges] be but ones byde cowche ... they draw the tayle betwine the legges' (*A Supplication of the Poore Commons* [1546]). Prince Arthur's dragon, its tail stretched down well out of the way, has also been mastered; and the use of 'couched' vividly conveys as much, by transforming momentarily a symbolic representation into a life-like beast, susceptible of fear.

The simile applied to the plume of the helmet also contributes to the overall impression of Prince Arthur's victoriousness:

> Upon the top of all his loftie crest,
>   A bunch of haires discolourd diversely,
>   With sprincled pearle, and gold full richly drest,
>   Did shake, and seem'd to daunce for jollity,
>   Like to an Almond tree ymounted hye
>   On top of greene *Selinis* all alone,
>   With blossomes brave bedecked daintily;   (I.vii.32.1-7)

The reference to 'greene *Selinis*' appears to be an allusion to Virgil's phrase 'palmosa Selinus' (*Aeneid* III.705). R.D.Williams, following Servius, has suggested that the epithet 'palmosa' may refer to the plant *apium*. This plant was used on the coins of Selinus, and the crown given to the victor of the games was formed of it.[32] It is possible that the plume or 'bunch of haires' on Arthur's helmet should be read in part as the Prince's victory wreath suspended over the defeated dragon.

As several critics have remarked, the reference to 'an Almond tree' is probably an allusion to 'Aaron's budding rod which yielded almonds and so marked him as the chosen priest of the Lord'.[33] The

---

[32] *The Aeneid of Virgil*, ed. R.D.Williams, 2 vols (Macmillan, 1972-73). Vol.1, p.330. A.C.Hamilton has arrived at similar conclusions independently (*The Faerie Queene*, ed. A.C.Hamilton, p.103).

[33] *The Faerie Queene*, ed. A.C.Hamilton, p.103; see also Kathleen Williams, p.22; and Evans, p.104.

allusion would obviously be suitable to Arthur's frequently Christ-like role. But we may now go further by considering the helmet as a whole, instead of as a collection of unrelated parts. Prince Arthur's crest is formed of a dragon, seemingly cowed and defeated; it lies beneath a plume associated both with the tree of victory and with the tree of divine election. The combination recalls those images of the Crucifixion which show the Cross or Tree of Victory with the defeated serpent or dragon at its foot. As a single entity, then, the helmet expresses Prince Arthur's function in *The Faerie Queene* as a saviour who is at times closely associated with Christ.

In her illuminating and perceptive comments on this helmet, Kathleen Williams divided the symbolism from the joyful tone of this description:

> far more important than the traditional symbolism is the effect inherent in the image, the lightness and life and untroubled joy. (p.22)

We should now reintegrate these two sides of the description. The sense of vitality and gaiety she perceives and conveys so vividly derives from and is generated by the optimistic and prophetic symbolism of man's salvation which the helmet, as a whole, contains.

Until now I have made no attempt to integrate the helmet with the rest of Prince Arthur's armour. One of the most significant functions of this armour is to connect Arthur with Achilles. The dragon-crest is not to be found in the *Iliad*, nor in any other literary source I have found. But it is the crest given to Achilles in some visual representations of the Trojan legend, as can be seen in Giulio Romano's version of the hero in the Palazzo Ducale in Mantua. The currency in contemporary England of the association of Achilles with a dragon-crest is supported by the alterations to the frontispiece to Chapman's *Homer*, first published in 1610. For the second edition of 1611 William Hole revised his engraving, correcting a number of mistakes and anachronisms; and prominent among his alterations is the substitution of a dragon-crested helmet for the rather plain casque-type originally worn by the figure of Achilles on one side of the architectural surround.[34] Hole's correction implies that either he or someone else associated with the publication was sufficiently aware of the iconography of Achilles to point out the omission of his characteristic helmet. In addition to these connections through the visual arts, there is a further link through the dragon's presence on the Sultan's helmet in *Gerusalemme liberata*: for the Sultan is modelled on

---

[34] See Hind, *Engraving in England in the Sixteenth and Seventeenth Centuries. Part II: The Reign of James I*, p.332; and Margery Corbett and Ronald Lightbrown, *The Comely Frontispiece: The Emblematic Title-Page in England 1550-1660* (Routledge and Kegan Paul, 1979), pp.112-18.

Turnus, the 'apud Achilles' of the *Aeneid*. As well as its Arthurian, Christian, and triumphal connotations, then, the dragon-crest may continue the association with Achilles that was found in other elements of Spenser's description. The helmet thus combines allusions which relate Prince Arthur specifically to both Achilles and Christ, paramount heroes of the classical and Christian ages.

This analysis of Prince Arthur's armour confirms and expands points made concerning his shield in the previous chapter. There it was noted that the shield revealed through its symbolism above all a Christ-like role for the Prince: through it he appeared as the consummate hero, the ultimate and triumphant opponent of the forces of evil, and the bearer of grace to the aid of fallen humanity. Now it can be seen that this role is further emphasized in the description of the rest of his armour: his helmet relates him to the epic hero Achilles; it alludes to the Red Cross Knight's victory at the end of Book One; but also, taken as a whole, it betrays him as the elect of God, the saviour of the poem, whose battles are necessarily triumphant.

It is this note of triumph that marks the description as a whole. With St George's defeat at the hands of Orgoglio, the very first book of *The Faerie Queene* seems to have wandered, like the Knight himself, into error and defeat. The progress of the individual towards salvation has been arrested and reversed; and the total frustration of the plan is conveyed by the return of the Knight's 'forlorne weed', the armour he was given at the outset of his quest, to Una:

> His mightie armour, missing most at need;
> His silver shield, now idle maisterlesse;
> His poynant speare, that many made to bleed,
> The ruefull moniments of heavinesse   (I.vii.19.4-8)

Una recognises the symbolic quality of these arms and of their return, seeing them as 'the signes, that deadly tydings spake' (20.6). But the desperate mood her understanding of the symbolism breeds is not allowed to persist. At this nadir, for both Knight and poem, Spenser introduces Prince Arthur; but he does so without naming or otherwise identifying him, concentrating the eight, uninterrupted stanzas of his description on the Prince's external appearance. The depression fostered by the return of the 'ruefull moniments' of the Red Cross Knight is eliminated by the magnificence of Prince Arthur's arms; as Kathleen Williams implies, the poem seems suddenly spacious and optimistic once more. The Prince's arms in general speak his triumph; but also each element in his equipment participates in the detailed expression of both his magnificence and his role in the poem.[35]

---

[35] These details have been discussed with the exception of the sword and baldric, which will be considered in the third and sixth chapters respectively.

3. Arthegall and Britomart

I

Discussion of Prince Arthur's crest leads to the only other helmet described in detail in the poem: when Arthegall appeared to Britomart in the magical mirror,

> His crest was covered with a couchant Hound   (III.ii.25.1)

The hound has puzzled those critics who have written about it. John Upton attempts to explain its presence by suggesting that it is a reference to Spenser's superior in Ireland, Lord Grey de Wilton:

> I formerly said that Arthur Lord Grey de Wilton was imaged in *Arthegall*, which name corresponds to his Christian name *Arthur*, and means *Arthur's peer* — The arms here likewise seem devised in allusion to his name *Gray*:
> ... For *Griseum* in the barbrous Latin age signified fine furr or *ermine* ... The crest likewise of the knight's helmet is a GRAY hound, couchant.[36]

The possible reference to a greyhound and the ingenious pun on 'gris' would perhaps be more acceptable today were they not connected with so-called 'historical allegory'. Upton's comment has been largely discounted and is not recorded in recent annotated editions of the poem.[37]

However, the further etymological pun on Arthegall's name mentioned in the preceding chapter, through the Greek for ermine, 'galee', may provide at least circumstantial support for Upton's case. And the possibility of a reference to Lord Grey may also be defended by comparison with a similar possible allusion in the work of one of Spenser's predecessors. At the beginning of the *Divine Comedy*, when Dante finds himself in the 'selva oscura', he is terrified by three beasts: a Leopard, a Lion, and finally a Wolf. Virgil, comforting him, provides an enigmatic interpretation of the encounter and predicts the defeat of the Wolf, which has emerged as the most prominent adversary:

> Many are the creatures with which she mates and there will yet be more, until the hound comes that shall bring her to miserable death.[38]

---

[36] *The Faerie Queene*, ed. John Upton, vol. 2, p. 527.

[37] See the notes on this passage in the recent editions by A. C. Hamilton (1977) and T. P. Roche (1978).

[38] Dante Aligheri, *Divine Comedy*, ed. and tr. John D. Sinclair, 3 vols. Vol. 1 (1939; revised edition, OUP, 1975), p. 27:
> Molti son li animali a cui s'ammoglia,
> e piu saranno ancora, infin ch'l Veltro
> verrà, che la farà morir con doglia.   (*Inferno* I.100-102)

The identity of this messianic Hound has been discussed for centuries; but a persistent early suggestion was that Dante alludes to the noble-man who was his patron and protector, Cangrande I della Scala. Cangrande was seen as a potential saviour of Italy, the possible embodiment of the imperial order for which Dante longed. Vellutello, one of the early commentators on the *Divine Comedy*, subscribes to this interpretation of the Hound:

> Feigning in this to prophesy concerning Can Grande I della Scala, Lord of Verona, through this [Dante] speaks of that which was present [by the time he was writing]: because Dante, in his exile, was greatly aided in his needs by this lord.[39]

As in Upton's suggestion concerning Lord Grey de Wilton, the basis of Vellutello's identification of the Hound is a pun on the name: Cangrande, 'cane grande', or 'great dog'.

Cangrande's family were great users of canting heraldry, 'della Scala' being represented in their arms by a ladder; and it is therefore not surprising that the pun on 'cane' was used frequently by Cangrande himself. On his magnificent funerary monument in Verona, his coat-of-arms is held by a greyhound. More interesting still is the equestrian statue of Cangrande surmounting the monument (now a copy: the original is in the Castelvecchio museum, also in Verona). Ruskin describes it thus:

> Above ... [a recumbent effigy of Cangrande], a bold arched canopy is sustained by two projecting shafts, and on the pinnacle of its roof is the statue of the knight on his war-horse; his helmet, dragon-winged and crested with the dog's head, tossed back behind his shoulders.[40]

Cangrande's crest (illus. 3) is a hound, as is Arthegall's in the magical mirror. If Upton is right in his identification of Arthegall with Lord Grey, then Spenser may have evolved his hero's crest through a pun similar to that which lies behind Cangrande's, and which was thought to be the basis of Dante's allusion to his patron.

[39] *Dante con l'espositione di Christoforo Landino, et di Alessandro Vellutello* (Venice, 1564), f 8r:
> Fingendo per quello pronosticar di Cane grande primo della Scala Signor di Verona, e perdire ciò che allhora era presente; Perche Dante, nel suo esilio, fu molto souvenuto ne' suoi bisogni da questo Signore.

[40] John Ruskin, *Stones of Venice*, 3 vols (1851-53). Vol.3, p.71. For this quotation, and for his aid in tracing illustrations of this monument, I am indebted to Professor John Dixon Hunt.

3. Effigy of Can Grande I della Scala, Verona (detail)
Photography: Julian Gardner

59

There are further analogies between Sir Arthegall and the enigmatic Hound of the *Divine Comedy*. Another interpretation of Dante's cryptic prediction places the Hound in precisely the mythological context Spenser gives the patron of his fifth book:

> some say that Dante, a great lover of the doctrine of Virgil, wishing to be ambiguous and obscure in this place, imitated this passage of the Bucolics, where he says: 'Iam redit et virgo redeunt saturnia regna: Iam nova progenies coelo dimittitur alto'.[41]

This commentator, Christopher Landino, discussed the suggestion that the Hound represents Christ in his second coming, allegorically the successor to Astraea:

> these verses have so much obscurity and are so ambiguous that some have interpreted them as concerning the coming of Christ.[42]

At the beginning of Book Five of *The Faerie Queene*, the book of Justice, Spenser makes Arthegall the chosen and nurtured representative of Astraea:

> For *Artegall* in justice was upbrought
> Even from the cradle of his infancie,
> And all the depth of rightfull doome was taught
> By faire *Astraea* (V.i.5.1-4)

The coming of Arthegall is set in the context of Virgil's prophecy, the same context discussed by Landino and thought by others to lie behind Dante's prophecy of the Hound. As a result, both Arthegall and the mysterious Hound have something of the status of saviours, as representatives of divine justice.

For both the Hound of the *Divine Comedy* and Sir Arthegall the ultimate foe is a wolf-like beast. James Nohrnberg in *The Analogy of 'The Faerie Queene'* (p.693) has briefly mentioned the existence of Dante's animal. We may go further and note distinct similarities between the Wolf of the *Inferno* and the Blatant Beast.

---

41 *Dante con l'espositione*, f 8r:
　　i quali dicono, che Dante molto amatore della dottrina di Virgilio, vuole in questo luogo esser ambiguo, e oscuro, a imitatione di quello passo della bucolica, ove egli dice. 'Iam redit et virgo redeunt saturnia regna: Iam nova progenies coelo dimittitur alto'.
42 *Dante con l'espositione*, f 8r:
　　i quali versi hanno tanta oscurità, e sono sì ambigui ch'altri gl'interpreta per l'avenimento di Christo.

The Hound will finally kill the Wolf after a long chase:

he shall hunt her through every city till he has sent her back to Hell whence envy first let her loose.[43]

The pursuit 'through every city', 'per ogni villa', resembles that which Calidore undertakes to capture the Blatant Beast:

> who seeking all this while
> That monstrous Beast by finall force to quell,
> *Through every place*, with restless paine and toile
> Him follow'd, by the tract of his outragious spoile.
>
> (VI.xii.22.6-9; my italics)

In the description of the pursuit and, particularly, in the italicized phrase, Spenser may be alluding to Dante's prophesy.

Furthermore, just as the Wolf was set loose by Envy in the *Divine Comedy*, so in *The Faerie Queene* the Blatant Beast is set on Sir Arthegall by Detraction and another personification, whose

> name was *Envie*, knowen well thereby   (V.xii.31.1)

The Wolf and the Blatant Beast have similar origins and are pursued in similar ways. Together with the Astraean and Virgilian contexts, and the common symbolism of the hound on the crest, these resemblances suggest that Spenser's descriptions of Sir Arthegall and the Blatant Beast may in part derive from Dante.

The principal result of these similarities, however, is to bring into sharp focus crucial differences. In the prophecy at the beginning of the *Divine Comedy*, the Wolf is to be killed and Italy, in the allegory, is to be saved. In *The Faerie Queene* the converse turns out to be true: Sir Arthegall is impotent against the Blatant Beast; and even Calidore only manages to capture it temporarily,

> Untill that, whether wicked fate so framed,
> Or fault of men, he broke his yron chaine,
> And got into the world at liberty againe.   (VI.xii.38.7-9)

Despite the suggestions of a Messiah in Arthegall's role (suggestions present even if the allusion to Dante is not allowed), the Blatant Beast remains at liberty and grows even more powerful.

It is perhaps in these differences that Spenser's intention lies. The resemblances noted to the *Divine Comedy* and Sir Arthegall's Astraean pedigree raise expectations of a return of Justice to the

---

[43] *Divine Comedy*, vol.1, p.29:
> Questi la caccera per ogni villa,
> fin che l'aura rimessa nello 'nferno,
> la onde invidia prima dipartilla.   (*Inferno* I.109-11)

world, of a new Golden Age. In the course of Book Five, these expectations are mercilessly dashed. Through Virgil's prophecy of the Hound, Dante allows his desire for the end of disorder and evil to be fulfilled in the emergence of a saviour. But Spenser's subject is as much the limitations of human virtue as it is its power for good. Throughout *The Faerie Queene*, knights-patron reach the climax of their quests only to find that there is yet more to be done: the Red Cross Knight in the joy of his betrothal

> nought forgot, how he whilome had sworne,
> In case he could that monstrous beast destroy,
> Unto his Fary Queene backe to returne:
> The which he shortly did, and *Una* left to mourne.

(I.xii.41.6-9)

However much the combat with the Dragon seems to represent the final defeat of evil, Spenser deliberately warns us that there is still work to be done. As in his impassioned prayer at the end of the *Mutabilitie Cantos* (VII.viii.2), Spenser is desperately hoping for the return of Christ and the defeat of evil; but he seems intent on showing us that in the meantime human virtue is a poor substitute at best.

In his references to Astraea and, possibly, to the Hound, Spenser suggests that the Patron of Justice is to be an omnipotent, messianic figure. Within a few stanzas, the mere possibility of the fulfillment of these hopes has been dashed. This is particularly true if Spenser is alluding to Lord Grey de Wilton in his portrayal of Sir Arthegall. However much Spenser respected and admired him, Lord Grey had manifestly failed. Of course, so did Cangrande della Scala; of his failure, and of the barenness of Dante's prophecy, Spenser may have been aware.[44]

---

[44] In suggesting some relationship between *The Faerie Queene* and the *Divine Comedy* I am going against the prevailing opinion that Dante's greatest work was little regarded in Elizabethan England. However, because Spenser's contemporaries were more impressed by the recent triumphs of Ariosto and Tasso this does not mean that they ignored Dante. Matthew Tosello, I.M.C., ('Spenser's Silence about Dante', *SEL* 17 [1977], pp.59-66) states the case for revising this assessment of Dante's reputation; and in particular he lists probable debts in Spenser's works. More generally we may note that Sidney in the *Apology* mentions both Dante and Beatrice; and in addition that William Drummond of Hawthornden, one of the few poets of the age whose libraries are known to us in detail, possessed the *Divine Comedy* and noted in his copy of *The Faerie Queene* some of Spenser's other unacknowledged Italian borrowings. See *The Library of William Drummond of Hawthornden*, ed. Robert H. MacDonald (Edinburgh: Edinburgh UP, 1971), catalogue entry 1219; and Alastair Fowler and Michael Leslie, 'Drummond's Copy of *The Faerie Queene*', *TLS* 17 July 1981, pp.821-22.

III

In the first chapter it was suggested that the device on Arthegall's shield, the ermine, formed part of an emblematic reference to the dynastic and imperial claims of Elizabeth I through her heraldry. There are grounds for suggesting that the hound on Sir Arthegall's helmet contributes further to this reference and to the historical or political allegory in the poem.

Although the royal arms of Britain and their heraldic supporters have remained largely unchanged for several hundred years, they were hardly constant in the sixteenth century and before. As each dynasty, and each monarch, gained the throne, so their possession was signalled by the incorporation of elements of their personal or familial heraldry into the royal bearings. When the Tudors assumed the crown, they brought with them as supporters to their arms the dragon of Cadwallader (to symbolize their connection with Wales and the ancient British monarchs) and their family's own badge, the Tudor or Beaufort greyhound. These two beasts were used extensively by Henry VII: for instance, they are the dominant motif on the wrought-iron screen surrounding his tomb in Westminster Abbey. Henry also used them as supporters of his emblem (the Tudor rose) at the head of the sarcophagus (illus. 4).

After his death, other members of the Tudor dynasty continued to use the greyhound, although less frequently. In Elizabeth's reign, two sets of supporters are recorded: the lion and the dragon, and less commonly the dragon and the greyhound.[45] In other contexts besides the coat-of-arms, the greyhound appears extensively in Elizabeth's reign; it was, for instance, one of the four royal beasts set up at the landing-stage at Greenwich in 1588.[46]

In the greyhound Sir Arthegall bears as his crest one of the distinguishing emblems of the Tudor dynasty. As an emblem of Queen Elizabeth the greyhound joins those other details of Arthegall and Britomart's armour which were noted as relating to Elizabeth in the previous chapter. Taken together, the lion, ermine, and greyhound depict the queen's ideal self through the medium of her imperial, personal, and dynastic emblems. As Britomart's lion suggests the lion of England; and the ermine the queen's political and personal purity; so the greyhound introduces the Tudor and Beaufort houses of which Elizabeth was the descendent.

Only the crests of Prince Arthur and Sir Arthegall are described in any detail in *The Faerie Queene*. As well as being related by their

[45] See *Boutell's Heraldry*, revised by J.P.Brooke-Little (Warne, 1978), p.212.
[46] See H.Stanford London, *Royal Beasts*, p.2.

4. Tomb of Henry VII, Westminster Abbey (detail)

names, as Upton and latterly Dunseath have noted, this concentration on their crests forms another link between them. And on one particular occasion, the crests appear to be used in conjunction by Spenser to allude to an aspect of Elizabeth's role as monarch.

When Arthur and Arthegall arrive at the court of Mercilla, they find her sitting amid a plethora of royal symbols. She sits on a throne 'all embost with Lyons and with Flourdelice' (V.ix.27.9); in other words, her throne is decorated with the dominant heraldic motives of the kingdoms to which English monarchs laid claim: the lions of England and the lilies of France. In addition, Mercilla bears her sceptre, has by her the sword of state, and the royal lion lies beneath her feet. And immediately they arrive in her court she resumes the kingly role of judge, in order to preside over the arraignment of Duessa.

Recognizing the partial allegory of the trial of Mary Queen of Scots, various critics have suggested that Mercilla's court is intended to allude to some specific branch of the Elizabethan judiciary. Identification of the particular court Spenser had in mind is difficult because of peculiarities in his description. The monarch had not, of course, actually taken the role of judge for centuries (although James I characteristically made a point of so doing as soon as he ascended to the English throne). We may surmise that Spenser is, in a sense, reversing the normal symbolism of the courts, in which the monarch's presence, giving authority to the judge, is implied iconographically by the royal coat-of-arms. At Duessa's trial, on the other hand, the monarch's real presence symbolizes justice and the court.

But which court? Spenser's version cannot directly represent the reality: Mary Queen of Scots was tried by an *ad hoc* body of dubious legal status and Elizabeth adamantly refused any meeting with her cousin. Nevertheless several candidates have been put forward, including the supreme court of Parliament.[47] This is indeed possible; but the evidence is not so overwhelming as to produce conviction and it tends to be circumstantial: there is little in Spenser's lines to support this identification. However, another judicial body does seem to be alluded to in Spenser's description of Mercilla's court and its functions:

> She was about affaires of *common wele*,
> Dealing of Justice with indifferent grace,
> And hearing *pleas* of people *meane* and *base*
>
> (V.ix.36.3-5; my italics)

[47] Douglas A. Northrop, 'Spenser's Defence of Elizabeth', *UTQ* 38 (1969), pp. 277-294); and the same author's 'Mercilla's Court as Parliament', *HLQ* 36 (1972-73), pp. 153-58.

Spenser's description and phrasing suggest the Court of Common Pleas. This court, which developed from the Court of King's, or Queen's Bench after Magna Carta, differed from the latter in that it dealt specifically with čases in which the Crown was neither prosecutor nor defendant.[48] Its purpose was to adjudicate between citizen and citizen; to hear the 'pleas of people meane and base'.

Corroboration of the connection between the Court of Common Pleas and Mercilla's court may be found in the iconography of the former and Spenser's description of the latter. Mercilla invites Arthur and Arthegall to observe the case and takes them to her throne, where she

> placed th'one on th'one,
> The other on the other side, and neare them none.

(V.ix.37.8-9)

Spenser is precise about the position of the knights, which he stresses by separating them from anyone else present. They are to either side of Mercilla's throne which, we have already been told, is decorated with elements of Elizabeth's coat-of-arms. If we visualize the armour of the knights, and particularly their helmets, we can see that Spenser is further alluding to judicial and royal iconography. Prince Arthur's crest is a dragon; and the only crest of Arthegall's of which we ever hear is a greyhound. The seal of the Court of Common Pleas is the only judicial seal to incorporate all these elements, and particularly the relatively unusual combination of supporters, the dragon and the greyhound (illus. 5). The seal shows on one side an image of Elizabeth enthroned, with the sceptre and other symbols of royalty; and on the reverse the royal coat-of-arms of lions and fleur-de-lys in the shape of a shield, supported by the dragon and the greyhound. Spenser appears to have conflated the two sides of this seal in order to produce his image of Mercilla sitting to hear the people's indictment of a traitor.

Mary Queen of Scots was not tried by the Court of Common Pleas. But by setting Duessa's trial in this context Spenser can develop points concerning the nature of royal justice in such serious cases.

---

[48] See the entries for the Court of Common Pleas in *The Oxford Companion to Law* by David M.Walker (Oxford: Clarendon Press, 1980); also G.R.Elton, *England under the Tudors* (1955; 2nd edition, Methuen, 1974), pp.62-63. For the increasing prominence and business of the Common Pleas in the sixteenth century, see *A History of English Law* by W.S.Holdsworth, 17 vols (Methuen, 1903-72), vol.4 (2nd edition, 1937), pp.255-56. For a contemporary view of the function of the Common Pleas, see Camden's *Britannia*: 'the common Pleas hath that name because in it are debated the common Pleas between Subject and Subject, according to our law, which they call common' (p.179).

5. Seal of the Court of Common Pleas. BL Seal XXXIX
(British Library)

And, both as a subsidiary interest and as the specific example through which the general, philosophical statement is made, he can comment on the trial of Mary.

The Court of Common Pleas existed for the trial of cases between citizens, in which the Crown was not directly involved. We must ask why it is to this court that the 'tryall of a great and weightie case' (V.ix.36.7) is brought. Duessa is being accused of treason, as Mary was, but she is accused not by the impersonal state, nor by the possibly biased central administration, but by the ordinary people of Mercilla's realm. The trial is not presented as a case of '*Regina* versus Duessa' but as the people versus Duessa. Treason is not solely a crime against the individual monarch; rather it is a crime against the whole commonwealth, the 'common wele', which benefits from the rule of a just and merciful ruler. And it is the commonwealth, made up of the ordinary people of the land, which demands justice (just as the prosecution of Mary Queen of Scots was demanded by Parliament, not Elizabeth). Hence the trial, perhaps, takes place in the Court of Common Pleas, the court given over to such cases.

As one critic believes, the trial of Duessa is part of Spenser's 'justification for Elizabeth's rule'.[49] But it is more than that. Spenser uses the particular case of Mary Queen of Scots as a means of discussing Elizabethan justice. But he also uses a defence of Elizabethan justice as a means of discussing justice itself. In the case of Duessa's trial Spenser makes the point that crimes against the monarch are not crimes against an individual, but against state and people. In such cases the monarch must put aside personal feelings, and judge without either excessive rancour or excessive mercy. Rather he must display, as Mercilla does, an altruistic regard both for justice and mercy, and for the well-being of the commonwealth.

IV

As well as using the decoration on helmets for symbolic effect, Spenser draws on the traditional associations of this part of the knight's armour with love. The story of Britomart and Arthegall is punctuated by occasions on which helmets are removed, willingly or unwillingly, or the vizor lifted. On these occasions, the effect of the action involving the helmet is intense: when Britomart 'vented up her umbriere' (III.i.42.8) at Castle Joyous, she inadvertently stimulated Malecasta's perverted lust. She is herself struck by love for Sir

49 Northrop, 'Spenser's Defence of Elizabeth', p. 288.

Arthegall when he appears in King Ryence's mirror with his 'bright ventayle lifted up on hye' (III.ii.24.3). Sir Arthegall succumbs to her charms when he demolishes her helmet in battle (IV.vi.19-22); and her wrath is cooled when he and Scudamour 'their bevers up did reare' (IV.vi.25.8). Later Arthegall is equally vulnerable to Radigund's beauty as it is displayed when he removes her helmet; and Britomart finally concludes this play on helmets by refusing to remove Radigund's in their duel, but 'with one stroke both head and helmet cleft' (V.vii.34.6).

The prominence of helmets seen in these examples is peculiar to the story of Britomart and Sir Arthegall in *The Faerie Queene*, and it may be explained by reference to medieval and renaissance symbolism. In part of the prose *Lancelot*, such actions as the removal and replacement of the knight's helmet assume a similar significance to that noted above. Twice within a few pages Lancelot removes his helmet (because of the heat, a rare concession to practicality and comfort in these romances); and on both occasions, he enters immediately afterwards 'la forest perdue', in which compulsive dancing and merrymaking are taking place.[50] On the first occasion he is warned against proceeding further and turns back; but on the second he perseveres, and immediately loses his memory. Joining the revellers, he too begins to sing and dance, and his squire 'takes him for mad. And he sang a song concerning Queen Guinevere'.[51] The forest and the compulsive revellers seem to represent the darker side of the effects of love, of love madness. It is significant that in these surroundings Lancelot sings of Queen Guinevere, because elsewhere he is careful never to mention his particular devotion to her.

To enter the forest he removes his helmet. And the connection between the helmet and love is acknowledged when Morgan la fee, attempting to discover Lancelot's identity, commands him 'by the thing that you most love to remove your helmet'.[52] Later, at a tournament in which Lancelot and Bohort fight in disguise, Guinevere supplies them with armour. The queen helps them both to arm; but her lover is distinguished when it is stated that she laced on Lancelot's helmet herself.[53]

In the Renaissance, Valeriano explicitly connects love or sex and the helmet: 'the helmet ... signifies the hidden beginnings of gener-

---

[50] *The Vulgate Version of the Arthurian Romances*, vol. 5, *Le Livre de Lancelot del Lac, Part 3*, pp.120 and 122.
[51] *Lancelot*, p.123: 'la tient pour fol. Et it cantoient une cancon de la royne Genieure'.
[52] *Lancelot*, p.167: 'par la riens que vous plus ames que vous ostes vostre heume'.
[53] *Lancelot*, p.185.

ation'.[54] What this cryptic statement means is never fully revealed; Valeriano appears to leave it deliberately obscure. But we may note that his comment conveys the sense of something hidden, sexual, waiting to be revealed; and that it is with the removal of helmets in *The Faerie Queene*, as in the prose *Lancelot*, that sexual attraction is acknowledged.

It is, for instance, only when Britomart doffs her helmet that her sexual role is brought out into the open. Once her head is uncovered, or her vizor raised, she both reacts and is reacted to sexually. For example, the moving lament she utters during her first quest for Sir Arthegall occurs only when her helmet has been taken off:

> There she alighted from her light-foot beast,
>> And sitting downe upon the rocky shore,
>> Bad her old Squire unlace her lofty creast; ...
> Thereat she sighed deepe, and after thus complaynd.
>
>> (III.iv.7.1-3; 9)

At other times, she can only bemoan her lot when dressed as a woman, as when she suspects Sir Arthegall of having betrayed her (V.vi.3-6). The removal of her helmet allows her sexual feelings expression.

The same sequence, the removal of her helmet and the expression of her feelings, occurs during her vigil at Isis Church. Again, Spenser emphasizes the uncovering of her head:

> By this the day with dampe was overcast,
>> And joyous light the house of *Jove* forsooke:
>> Which when she saw, her helmet she unlaste,
> And by the altars side her selfe to slumber plaste.   (V.vii.8.6-9)

Spenser refers to none of the other elements of her armour, only the helmet. And this is the only time on her second quest for Sir Arthegall that she removes it. Immediately upon doing so, she has a dream which, although having a rich and varied meaning, is primarily expressed in sexual imagery. The crocodile she (or Isis) subdued,

> gan for grace and love of her to seeke:
>> Which she accepting, he so neare her drew,
>> That of his game she soone enwombed grew,
> And forth did bring a Lion of great might;   (V.vii.16.3-6)

This vision takes place only after she has removed the helmet. And the point that the helmet conceals her sexual identity, from men at

---

54 Valeriano, f. 316v: 'Galea ... significat occulta esse principia generationis'.

least, is made again with different emphasis when the priests explain her dream:

> Magnificke Virgin, that in queint disguise
>   Of British armes doest maske thy royall blood,
>   So to pursue a perillous emprize,
>   How couldst thou weene, through that disguized hood,
>   To hide thy state from being understood?
>   Can from th' immortall Gods ought hidden bee?
>   They doe thy linage, and thy Lordly brood;
>   They doe thy sire, lamenting sore for thee;
>   They doe thy love, forlorne in womens thraldome see.   (V.vii.21)

The priests say that the gods can see through the helmet, as men cannot, to Britomart's real self. And we should notice that what the gods see are her sexual roles as a woman: daughter to King Ryence; lover and wife to Sir Arthegall; and mother to a great dynasty.

The disguise of 'British armes' allows Britomart to appear in the full complexity of her role, a role intensely feminine yet expressed through the attributes and actions of a man. The rendering of such a paradox through martial costume and equipment is not unique to this passage: we have already seen Spenser achieving similar effects through Sir Calidore's wearing of both armour and pastoral clothing; and in the succeeding chapter Britomart's spear will be shown to indicate a similar paradox. The use of armour in this manner to convey tensions and paradoxes was not confined to literature in Spenser's day: disguising formed a significant part of both Henrician and Elizabethan entertainments and tournaments; and it was often used for the expression of contradictions within the individual, of psychological tensions frequently the result of a clash between the private self and the public role.[55] In precisely the same way Spenser reveals the complexities of such a figure as Britomart and the situations in which she finds herself: her essential feminity, crucial to Books Three to Five, to the praise of the queen, and indeed to the whole universe of *The Faerie Queene*, is forced by circumstances (both narrative and allegorical) to fulfil itself through an unnatural masculinity. That tense paradox at the heart of this section of the poem is embodied in Britomart's concealment within her armour, and in her own (and other's) attitudes to it.

The play on Britomart's armour throughout her career in the poem, then, is central to our understanding of Spenser's allegory.

---

[55] On this subject, see (for instance) Marie Axton, 'The Tudor Mask and Elizabethan Court Drama' in *English Drama: Forms and Development. Essays in Honour of Muriel Clara Bradbrook*, eds Marie Axton and Raymond Williams (Cambridge: Cambridge UP, 1977), pp. 24-47.

And in this context it may be permissible to suggest that the first line of the priests' reply to her account of her dream may contain a sexual pun: the helmet Britomart wears is indeed a 'queint disguise', in that it conceals, in Valeriano's phrase, the hidden beginnings of generation, her 'queint' or pudendum, the symbol of her essential femininity.

V

To comprehend fully Spenser's use of the helmet in the history of Britomart and Sir Arthegall we should also consider the helmet's part in the solar and lunar imagery connected with these figures. In her initial vision of her husband, Britomart sees that

> Through ... [his] bright ventayle lifted up on hye
> His manly face ...
> Lookt foorth, as *Phoebus* face out of the east,
> Betwixt two shadie mountaines doth arize;   (III.ii.24.3-7)

This simile, likening his face radiating from the helmet to the rising sun perceived between mountains, begins a series of images connecting Arthegall with the sun (and thus of course with Prince Arthur). The simile follows the traditional symbolism of the helmet: Valeriano explains that the helmet 'is interpreted ... as the sun, during the time when it circles remote from our part of the world throughout the winter'; and he relates this interpretation to the myth of Proserpina.[56] The association of the hidden sun and the hidden face within the helmet parallels Sir Arthegall's constant use of disguise until he claims the sun shield from Braggadocchio at Marinell's tournament. Having adopted the sun-shield, which as Jane Aptekar has explained is ambiguously presented as Arthegall's own, he emerges for the first time as the near-equal of Prince Arthur and the second most important hero in the poem.[57] And his emergence is presented as an uncovering: he watches Braggadocchio's infamous conduct while 'in the preasse close covered'; until he 'unto all himselfe there open shewed' (V.iii.20.2; 5). By his uncovering he reveals himself as the true solar hero.

That Arthegall and Britomart are made for each other is established by a similar use of cosmological imagery. When they fight after Satyrane's tournament, Arthegall hews away Britomart's ventail, leaving her face uncovered:

---

56 Valeriano, f.316v: 'Solem interpretantur, eo tempore quo hyemem remotas a nobis mundi partes circuit'.
57 Aptekar, p.77.

> With that her angels face, unseene afore,
> Like to the ruddie morne appeard in sight,   (IV.vi.19.5-6)

Her face, like Arthegall's in the magical mirror, is compared to the rising sun. The effect on Arthegall is immediate: he falls to his knees and drops his sword involuntarily. This is similar to the effect of Radigund's face upon him in the following book: having stunned her, he goes to remove her helmet and behead her. But although this helmet is 'sunshynie' (V.v.11.8), her face is significantly different from those of Britomart and Arthegall: it is,

> Like as the Moone in foggie winters night   (V.v.12.8)

Radigund's face, like her arms, is associated with the moon; and it is thus in opposition to those of Britomart and Arthegall.

The removal of helmets to reveal sun-like features may be interpreted with Valeriano as signifying the re-emergence of the life-giving sun after the winter. The symbolism of the helmet joins that noted in the Isis Church episode by Alastair Fowler as indicating renewal and fertility.[58] The uncovering of Britomart's head in Isis Church leads to a dream of sexual fulfilment and fruition, prophetic of her future progeny. In conclusion, this dream may be read allegorically as predicting a time when there will be peace and fertility in the land, the result of a marriage between equity and justice, to be brought about by the descendent in the poem of Britomart and Arthegall, the new Astraea.

---

[58] Fowler, *Spenser and the Numbers of Time*, pp. 211-15.

III: WEAPONS AND BATTLES

The previous two chapters have discussed various arms and suits-of-armour as they occur in descriptions that stand apart from the general narrative of the poem; such as the arms of Prince Arthur and of Sir Arthegall as he appears in the magical mirror. But although these descriptions have been related to some of the battles and events of *The Faerie Queene*, martial symbolism as it operates and develops in meaning within narrative passages has yet to be considered. In this chapter I shall suggest that Spenser does use the symbolism of weapons in the combats of his poem; and that, through the interaction of various weapons and the interplay of narrative and allegory, the individual arms are made capable of complex and subtle expression although themselves relatively simple in signification.

It is particularly valuable to consider weapons in the context of the narrative. Because of the physical nature of most weapons Spenser cannot invest them with meaning in the ways analysed in previous chapters. The poet develops and particularizes the meaning of Sir Arthegall's helmet and shield, for example, by having them curiously and uniquely decorated. For a sword or spear this method of individuation is inappropriate: there is simply not room on a spear for much in the way of symbolic decoration.[1] Spenser does individuate weapons occasionally, as will be seen; but mainly he relies on the telling evocation of the general signification of the group. However, his use of these traditional associations is far from simple, and an understanding of his intentions requires close study of the details of combats and battles.

This chapter takes two weapons as its principal examples: Britomart's spear and Prince Arthur's sword Morddure. The former is characterized by Spenser through its magical powers; but a wider discussion of spears and related weapons in *The Faerie Queene* will reveal that Britomart's spear cannot simply be discussed as symbolic

---

1 It is interesting to note that, despite the otherworldly and magical qualities of *The Faerie Queene*, Spenser can sustain the illusion of realism when it suits him and does not describe impossibly decorated armaments. The plausible emblems on his shields contrast with those belonging to the heroes of Virgil and Homer, although Jasper Griffin makes the point that Homer manipulates the reader's awareness of illusion in similar ways (*Homer* [OUP, 1980], p.33).

of chastity. Rather, the discussion of her 'weapon keene' (III.i.10.5) will suggest the complexity of her virtue and the psychological state it implies.

Unlike Britomart's spear, Prince Arthur's Morddure is particularized through its name and the detailed description of its fabrication. Exploration of this description will again show Spenser using Arthur's attributes to relate him to the heroes of earlier literature; and through them to disclose his role within the poem.

Finally, an interpretation of one of the principal battles of the poem, that over Guyon's body (II.viii), will be offered; and in this the meanings of Morddure and the spear, as well as other martial attributes, are crucial. Although the events preceding Guyon's faint have frequently been discussed, especially his journey through Mammon's realm, the combat between Arthur and the Pagan brothers Pyrochles and Cymochles has recieved little attention; and, as a result, much of it remains obscure in signification. Yet detailed and 'blow by blow' consideration of the battle's incidents can lead us to the heart of Spenser's meaning, not just in this canto, but in Book Two as a whole. And necessarily this meaning is expressed primarily through the symbolism of the weapons used.

1. Britomart's Spear

I

Spears in general and Britomart's in particular have been too easily interpreted as representing chastity in *The Faerie Queene*: on close analysis there are many occasions on which such a reading is implausible. Does Satyrane's 'huge great speare' (IV.iv.17.2) represent chastity when he opens a tournament effectively for the possession of the false Florimell's body? Or Scudamour's when he gains forcible entry to the Temple of Venus? Or Britomart's own when she so grievously wounds the celibate Marinell? Yet on each of these occasions it is the character's spear which Spenser stresses. Equally interesting are those occasions on which the spear is missing: why does Britomart use only her sword and shield to defeat Radigund or in the rescue of Amoret?

For some critics these questions are too hair-splitting. A.C. Hamilton in his edition of *The Faerie Queene* deals with the latter by explaining that 'since Britomart is on foot, her sword substitutes for her "enchaunted speare" ... whose virtue manifests the magical power of chastity' (p.406). Hamilton contends that the difference between these weapons is insignificant and his explanation neutralizes it.

To counter the attractive simplicity of this explanation we may note that specific weapons are prominent in the story of Amoret and Scudamour, and that Spenser seems to associate the latter with the spear in particular. His doing so makes it unlikely that the substitution of one weapon for another should be lightly discounted. Furthermore, as many critics have noted, there are strong resemblances between Britomart's invasion of the House of Busyrane and Scudamour's of the Temple of Venus: but there are also crucial differences which centre on the weapons used. At the Temple, Scudamour does not dismount until he has gained entry, and his principal weapon for doing so is his spear. Conversely, at Busyrane's house Britomart dismounts for her second and successful attempt at entry, and abandons her characteristic weapon, the spear. Rather than ignore these differences we should explore them to see whether they help us to understand why Britomart is successful and Scudamour is not in their attempts to free Amoret. Far from being insignificant, both the resemblances and the differences are of great importance to our comprehension of the story of Amoret and Scudamour; and as such have a direct bearing on our understanding of Britomart herself.

Various critics, especially Alastair Fowler, have drawn attention to the Minervan connotations of Britomart's weapon, and have noted that the spear is thus a fitting attribute for the knight-patron of chastity.[2] But a brief study of the connotations of spears and spear-like weapons in Books Three and Four of *The Faerie Queene* muddies these clear waters by suggesting associations which go beyond this simple equation. In particular, one group of weapons specifically challenges and contradicts that standard meaning.

In the third book, Britomart and Sir Palladine, a shadowy knight associated with her, each chase a hideous giant.[3] Sir Palladine is briefly glimpsed pursuing a female monster, Argante; and Spenser's description leaves little doubt concerning the nature of her vice:

> over all the countrey she did raunge,
> To seeke young men, to quench her flaming thrust,
> And feed her fancy with delightfull chaunge: (III.vii.50.1-3)

---

2   *Spenser and the Numbers of Time*, pp. 124-25.
3   Also a female knight, Palladine's name connects her with Minerva. For a discussion of the connections between Palladine and Britomart, see Josephine Waters Bennett, *The Evolution of 'The Faerie Queene'* (Chicago: Chicago UP, 1942), p.20; Fowler, *Spenser and the Numbers of Time*, p.127n; and Nohrnberg, *The Analogy of 'The Faerie Queene'*, p.456.

In view of her aggressive, predatory sexual excess, it is not surprising that Argante's weapon turns out to be a phallic 'huge great yron mace' (III.vii.40.1).

Similar weapons are used by Orgoglio and Corflambo, both again with obvious sexual connotations. Orgoglio's 'mortall mace' (I.vii. 10.9) is also referred to as a club on several occasions; and with the word 'club' we reach the heart of this group of weapons.[4] When Timias attempts to rescue Amoret from the personification of Lust in Book Four, that giant 'with his craggy club in his right hand, / Defends him selfe' (IV.vii.25.6-7). In *The Faerie Queene* clubs and maces are primarily the attributes of figures either representative of or strongly associated with lust.[5]

The phallic and more specifically lustful connotations of the club or mace are transfered to Satyrane's spear. Before Sir Palladine frightens Argante away, the giantess has dealt successfully with Satyrane, hitting him so hard with her 'huge great yron mace' that he is stunned and she is able to capture him. Satyrane replaces the discarded Squire of Dames in the compromizing position 'before her lap' (37.6). His defeat by such a figure, as well as the manner of it, makes it no surprise that when he returns to where he left the defeated Hyena, that animal has broken Florimell's girdle and escaped. Satyrane's attempt to control his concupiscence, the struggle represented by his wrestling with the Hyena, has been unsuccessful; and his capture by Argante signifies as much. This awakened lustfulness is fully evident when we next see him, as he opens his tournament: to begin the jousting, he takes

<blockquote>
in hand
An huge great speare, such as he wont to wield   (IV.iv.17.1-2)
</blockquote>

The transference to Satyrane's spear of the adjectives and, by implication, the priapic connotations of Argante's mace signals that the tournament for the cestus, an emblem of chastity, will degenerate into a squalid dispute over the rights to the body of the false Florimell. Satyrane's spear has come to represent the opposite of chastity, aggressive and violent incontinence.

Such spears as this undermine the simple identification of this weapon and chastity. And only if we are aware of these lustful connotations of the spear in *The Faerie Queene* can we understand the power of Sir Paridell in Book Three. When he fights against Britomart outside Malbecco's castle, unpredictably he achieves more than any other knight in the poem against her:

---

4 E.g. I.viii.7.3; 10.1; 10.4; 18.4.
5 Clubs are, of course, used by some other figures, notably both Disdains, and Hercules, who is said to bear 'the club of Justice dread' (V.i.2.9). But these are isolated instances.

> Their steel-hed speares they strongly coucht, and met
> Together with impetuous rage and forse,
> That with the terrour of their fierce affret,
> They rudely drove to ground both man and horse,
> That each awhile lay like a sencelesse corse.   (III.ix.16.1-5)

Spenser's unusually placed caesura in the first line emphasizes the ferocity of the combat; and for the first and only time in the entire poem Britomart is fairly and squarely matched in a tilt. Though she still manages to unhorse Paridell, he does the same to her. Sir Guyon could not achieve such a feat; that is the point of his encounter with Britomart in the first canto of this book, when the Palmer has to warn him against trying again. And even Arthegall is unable to force her from the saddle, except by the accidental maiming of her horse: in their bitter combat after Satyrane's tournament, neither he nor Scudamour can withstand 'that enchaunted lance' (IV.vi.14.7).

But this last quotation highlights a curiosity in the encounter with Paridell. Spenser describes Britomart's weapon as 'enchaunted' both in the fight with Arthegall in Book Four and when she defeats Guyon (III.i.9.9); but he in no way differentiates her weapon from that of Paridell when they clash. And the resulting impression of equality-in-opposition is confirmed when their shared Trojan ancestry is revealed in Malbecco's castle, establishing a close relationship between them. Yet in the same episode Paridell is shown to be the very embodiment of callous and dishonourable sexual excess (as his name suggests); and his powerful spear is hardly that of chastity. It is, rather, the symbol of his aggressive lust. The fact that he alone can unhorse Britomart using the weapon primarily associated with her, and the fact that he does so in the episode in which she is explicitly compared to Minerva (III.ix.22.1), should cause us to question any simple interpretation of her spear.

II

The phallic associations of the spear are directly relevant to the story of Scudamour's success and failure to win Amoret. As he later relates, Scudamour had begun the process of gaining Amoret through the power of his spear:

> Before that Castle was an open plaine,
> And in the midst thereof a piller placed;
> On which this shield, of many sought in vaine,
> The shield of Love, whose guerdon me hath graced,

> Was hangd on high with golden ribbands laced;
> And in the marble stone was written this,
> With golden letters goodly well enchaced,
> *Blessed the man that well can use his blis:*
> *Whose ever be the shield, faire Amoret be his.*
>
> Which when I red, my heart did inly earne,
> And pant with hope of that adventures hap:
> Ne stayed further newes thereof to learne,
> But with my speare upon the shield did rap,
> That all the castle ringed with the clap.
> Streight forth issewd a Knight all arm'd to proofe,
> And bravely mounted to his most mishap:
> Who staying nought to question from aloofe,
> Ran fierce at me, that fire glaunst from his horses hoofe.
>
> (IV.x.8-9)

The vigour with which Scudamour beats his spear against the shield of love testifies to the aggressive nature of his passion. And in this context there may be sexual puns intended in 'ringed' and 'clap'.[6] Scudamour defeats the knight who rides against him, and nineteen more, using the same spear so well that he gains entry to the Temple.

The spear is again prominent when Britomart discoveres him lying in despair before Busyrane's castle, in which Amoret is imprisoned:

> she at last came to a fountaine sheare,
> By which there lay a knight all wallowed
> Upon the grassy ground, and by him neare
> His haberieon, his helmet, and his speare;   (III.xi.7.2-5)

Scudamour's very posture indicates that his sexuality is in some way reprehensible: he has taken up a position common to those characters in *The Faerie Queene* overcome by lust, a position for which the word 'wallow' is frequently used, as here. But the clearest impression of the meaning of 'wallow' for Spenser comes not from *The Faerie Queene* but from the *Hymne of Heavenly Love* where this word seems to sum up all the distinctions between the earthly and the heavenly:

> Then rouze thy selfe, O earth, out of thy soyle,
> In which thou wallowest like to filthy swyne,
> And doest thy mynd in durty pleasures moyle,
> Unmindfull of that dearest Lord of thyne;   (ll.218-221)

---

6   See Eric Partridge's discussions of 'ring' and 'clap' in *A Dictionary of Slang and Unconventional English*, 2 vols (1937-38; 5th edition, Routledge, 1961); and *OED* Clap sb2.

Of the characters discovered wallowing in *The Faerie Queene* we may best compare Scudamour with the Red Cross Knight in Book One.[7] He is also found stretched out, his arms cast aside, lying by a fountain; and the looseness and fluidity of the Knight's physical state, similar to that of Cymochles, Verdant, and more tragically Mortdant in Book Two, indicates a morally culpable sexuality, a mental propensity for 'durty pleasures'. Scudamour's posture implies that Amoret's captivity and his failure to release her do not solely represent her fear of marriage and sex in the abstract, but derive in part from the manner of his wooing.

Scudamour's excessive sexuality is initially implied by the position in the poem of the description quoted above. Britomart discovers him while unsuccessfully pursuing Ollyphant. In a book using *entrelacement* so thoroughly we do not expect any great narrative connection between the stories of Ollyphant and Scudamour. But there is a thematic connection: Ollyphant, the brother of Argante, has been seen chasing a 'fearefull boy' (III.xi.4.6), and we are told that he 'surpassed his sex masculine, / In beastly use' (4.3-4).

The fact that he is chasing a boy has caused some critics to imply that he is a representative of sodomy, or at least to exaggerate the scope of his 'beastly use'. But as is the nature of a *psychomachia*, the external threat in the narrative signifies an internal characteristic, in this case the 'fearfull boy's' own lust. A similar case, and one in which we see Spenser unfolding and explaining the relationship between the two figures in the narrative, is the struggle witnessed by Guyon in Book Two, where he sees how

> A mad man, or that feigned mad to bee,
> Drew by the haire along upon the ground,
> A handsome stripling with gret crueltee   (II.iv.3.5-7)

Here the aggressor is Furor. But the murderous fury thus personified is that within the 'handsome stripling', occasioned (and the Occasion is also personified) by his believing slander of his bride-to-be. The passionate excess is externalized and personified, but it remains that of the individual we see attacked in the narrative.

Using the Furor episode as a model for the interpretation of Ollyphant's pursuit of the boy, the identification of the giant as the personification of the young man's lust seems more satisfying than seeing him as an isolated instance of homosexuality. If the former interpretation is correct, then the thematic connection between

---

7   Hamilton's comparison of Scudamour with Adonis in III.vi surely mistakes the tone of one or other of these passages; unless he silently intends us to see the contrast as well as the similarity. See *The Faerie Queene*, ed. A.C. Hamilton, p.402.

Ollyphant's pursuit of the boy and Britomart's discovery of Scudamour is clear: chasing a personification of aggressive and excessive masculine sexuality Britomart comes upon Amoret's husband, whose wooing displayed just this characteristic. And it is clear that Scudamour has been trying to rescue her from Busyrane using his spear, the very weapon calculated to increase her terror.

The symbol of that terror is the fire at the castle gate which has prevented Scudamour's entry. Britomart's response to the flames that rise up as they approach confirms the nature of Amoret's fear and Scudamour's thematic connection with Argante and Ollyphant. As she and Scudamour retreat from the fiery gate, she compares their efforts with those of the Titans who rebelled against Jove:

> What monstrous enmity provoke we heare,
> Foolhardy as th'Earthes children, the which made
> Battell against the Gods? so we a God invade.   (III.xi.22.7-9)

In effect Britomart is comparing them with Argante and Ollyphant, who are said to be the children of 'the *Titans* which did make / Warre against heaven' (III.vii.47.3-4). As Alastair Fowler has noted, the war of the Titans has a particular meaning in *The Faerie Queene*:

> Spenser ... gives it a sexual application. Argante's and Ollyphant's wilfulness rebels specifically against the natural law of normal sexuality.[8]

When Britomart compares their joint attempt to enter the castle to the war of the Titans, Spenser is implying that the flames at the gate are in part a just, defensive response to Scudamour's aggressive and over-forceful sexual advances.

Before leaving the subject of Scudamour's spear it is worth noting that this weapon has another range of meanings associated with marriage, and which may be relevant. T.P. Roche has reminded us that the Masque of Cupid is, on one level, a wedding-masque presented by Busyrane at the nuptials of Amoret and Scudamour.[9] Valeriano's interpretation of the spear contains the following grim role for it in the Roman marriage ceremonies:

> Hence also the custom among the Romans that the heads of brides were adorned with [a pin called] a *coelibaris* or spear, because the newly married must subject themselves to the rule of the husband. They call that

8 *Spenser and the Numbers of Time*, p.128.
9 *The Kindly Flame: A Study of the Third and Fourth Books of Spenser's 'Faerie Queene'* (Princeton: PUP, 1964), pp.73-81.

spear *coelibaris* which remains fixed in the body of a gladiator, overthrown and killed.[10]

Ovid also refers to this ornament in the *Fasti*:

> And O, thou damsel, who to thine eager mother shalt appear all ripe for marriage, let not the bent-back spear comb down thy maiden hair![11]

The grotesque practice revealed in these quotations puts a terrible face, at least for the wife, on the institution of marriage into which Amoret is literally forced.

Both the phallic connotations of the spear and the context supplied by Valeriano of masculine rule and domination within marriage suggest reasons for Britomart's unusual actions when gaining entry to Busyrane's castle: she dismounts and discards her spear. A mounted rider is traditionally a symbol of authority and power, and so it is in *The Faerie Queene*.[12] When Scudamour approaches the first gate of the Temple of Venus he does so on horseback; and he does not ask for entry but demands it:

> to the Bridges utter gate I came:
> The which I found sure lockt and chained fast.
> I knockt, but no man aunswred me by name;
> I cald, but no man answerd to my clame.
> Yet I persever'd still to knocke and call,
> Till at the last I spide within the same,
> Where one stood peeping through a crevis small,
> To whom I cald aloud, halfe angry therewithall.   (IV.x.11.2-9)

Whatever the traditional attitude of the lover, Scudamour is no courtly suppliant: he commands instead. Britomart's action in dismounting before trying to enter Busyrane's house dissociates her from the husband's power and authority; equally, her abandonment of the spear removes the threat of violent and excessive sexuality this weapon has come to represent for Amoret. It is because she does not threaten Amoret in the ways that Scudamour does that she can gain entry; and the fact that she does not threaten her so is conveyed through her dismounting and the relinquishing of her characteristic weapon.

---

[10] Valeriano, f.311r: 'Hinc etiam mos apud Romanos fuit, ut nuptarum capita coelibari hasta comeruntur, propterea quod quae nuberet, imperio viri subjecerent. Coelibarem autem hastam vocabant, quae in corpore gladiatoris abjecti occisique stetisset'. The Latin 'subjecerent' and 'abjecti' make the point even more forcefully than the English translation, of course.

[11] *Ovid's Fasti*, ed. and tr. Sir James George Frazer (Heineman, 1931), pp.96-7: 'nec tibi, quae cupidae matura videbere matri, / comat virgineas hasta recurva comas' (II.559-60).

[12] See for example Valeriano, f.33v.

82

The principal conclusion to be drawn from this study of Scudamour's spear is that the significance of this weapon is far from unambiguous. It is the traditional attribute of Minerva and thus of chastity. But at the same time it is associated in the poem with lust and forceful sexuality: in fact with chastity's inverse, incontinence. In the past the two sides of the spear's meaning have, when recognized, been kept distinct; and Britomart's spear in particular has been cordoned off as entirely virtuous.

This distinction and separation are surely unjustified. The paradoxical double meaning of the spear in *The Faerie Queene*, that it represents chastity *and* aggressive sexuality, is precisely appropriate to the character with whom this weapon is most closely associated: it is the tension between Britomart's role in seeking sexual fulfilment while remaining the patroness of chastity which lies at the heart of her fascination for us. Any attempt to explain that tension away diminishes the poem: Britomart is the fitting heroine for a book containing Argante, Ollyphant, and Paridell, not because she is their polar opposite, but because she is so like them. Comparing her with Argante is not merely facetious: both are energetically pursuing men for frankly sexual purposes. And Spenser deliberately points to Britomart's similarity with Paridell in their titanic clash before Malbecco's castle. The differences between Britomart and these figures are also clear to us, all the more so because of the implied comparison.[13] Britomart's sexuality is directed towards marriage and the future father of a great dynasty. But her aim is sexual; and Spenser seems to see this paradoxical sexuality in chastity generally: one need only think of the sensuous description of Belphoebe and her powerful erotic effect on Braggadocchio. And she too enters with a javelin.

The spear, then, is a fitting symbol of the problematical nature of Britomart's quest, which involves not only chastity but an aggressiveness and combativeness inappropriate to the traditional role of a wife. When Britomart dismounts and relinquishes her spear to enter Busyrane's castle she leaves behind her the emblems of sexual and marital dominance normally the property of the male. When, mounted and armed, she does battle with Arthegall after Satyrane's tournament, she must be forced to relinquish these emblems again before a healthy accord can be reached. In their battle Arthegall accidentally wounds her horse and she is obliged to fight on foot. Whether or not

---

[13] As has already been shown to be the case in Paridell's claim that his ancestor Paris was one of the Nine Worthies.

this is a descent into nature, as T.K.Dunseath suggests, it is certainly a descent from her unnatural position of authority over Arthegall, whom she has already unhorsed.[14] As a result of this blow Britomart is forced to abandon her horse and is thus unable to continue to wield her spear; she

> her steed forsooke,
> And casting from her that enchaunted lance,
> Unto her sword and shield her soone betooke;   (IV.vi.14.6-8)

There is, no doubt, a foreshadowing of Britomart's loss of virginity to Arthegall in the loss of her spear at this point, as Hamilton suggests in his edition (p.468). But she is also now armed as she was when entering the house of Busyrane: she has been divested of the assumed attributes and emblems of male sexuality and authority, and is now suitably attired to return to the normal, subordinate role of the woman.[15]

2. Morddure

I

One of the few individuated weapons in *The Faerie Queene* is Prince Arthur's sword Morddure. This is described when the enchanter Archimago warns Pyrochles not to attempt to use it against the Prince:

> For that same knights owne sword this is of yore,
>   Which *Merlin* made by his almightie art
> For that his noursling, when he knighthood swore,
>   Therewith to doen his foes eternall smart.
>   The metall first he mixt with *Medaewart*,
>   That no enchauntment from his dint might save;
>   Then it in flames of *Aetna* wrought apart,
>   And seven times dipped in the bitter wave
> Of hellish *Styx*, which hidden vertue to it gave.
>
> The vertue is, that neither steele, nor stone
>   The stroke thereof from entrance may defend,

---

[14] *Spenser's Allegory of Justice in Book Five of 'The Faerie Queene'*, p.41.
[15] This is not, of course, the end of the story: Arthegall's difficulties in Book Five and the necessary reassumption of martial attributes and symbols in order to rescue him represent an important qualification in Spenser's attitude to the masculine dominance in marriage.

> Ne ever may be used by his fone,
> Ne forst his rightfull owner to offend,
> Ne ever will it breake, ne ever bend.
> Wherefore *Morddure* it rightfully is hight.   (II.viii.20; 21.1-6)

Two points immediately arise from this description. Firstly it confirms Spenser's usual practice of ignoring the ancient traditions concerning King Arthur's armour and weapons when equipping his Prince. Upton records with satisfaction,

> I cannot help observing how designedly Spenser here omits to follow either that silly romance called the History of Prince Arthur, which gives a long and ridiculous account of his sword, *Excalibur*, i.e. cut steel: or even Jeffrey of Monmouth, who says, his sword's name was Caliburn.[16]

Upton himself goes on to raise the second point, the new name 'Morddure'. As is often the case in *The Faerie Queene*, Spenser's phrasing invites us to interpret this name: 'Wherefore *Morddure* it rightfully is hight'. But how 'wherefore' and why 'rightfully'? Following Upton's suggestion, all critics seem to assume that the name means 'hard-biter'. A.C. Hamilton, one of the poem's most recent commentators, supports this interpretation by reference to two occasions on which the sword is said to bite.[17] But his own references reveal the deficiencies of this case, because one of them is mistakenly to a description of an entirely different sword, that of Cymochles (II.viii.44.8). Many swords bite hard in *The Faerie Queene*; but not all are called Morddure.

A more serious criticism of the standard interpretation of this name is that it leads nowhere and explains nothing. As Hamilton himself concludes, 'if one fully understood the poem's names, one would fully understand its allegory'.[18] 'Hard-biter' does not enable us to progress very far, and this seems particularly unsatisfactory when Spenser has made the naming of the sword so prominent. Whilst not rejecting the accepted interpretation altogether, we may suggest that it is a superficial meaning, and that there are others below, more complex, more significant, and more helpful to the reader.

Archimago names the sword at the end of his description of its manufacture and powers; and the implication of the word 'wherefore' is that the name derives from that description. In the stanzas quoted above Spenser concentrates on the sword's hardness: it penetrates steel and stone and will never break or bend. We are told that it gained its strength through immersion in the Styx; and the name

---

[16] *The Faerie Queene*, ed. John Upton, vol. 2, p. 474.
[17] *The Faerie Queene*, ed. A.C. Hamilton, p. 240.
[18] *The Faerie Queene*, ed. A.C. Hamilton, p. 15.

Morddure perhaps grows out of this hardening process: the Styx is the river of death. We may suggest that the meaning of Morddure is 'death-hard' or 'hardened by death', from *mors*, death, and *durus*, hard.

Arthur's sword is not unique in being tempered in this manner. In the *Aeneid* Turnus arms himself with the sword 'which the fire-ruling god [Vulcan] himself made for his father Daunus and dipped, glowing hot, in the Stygian wave'.[19] The phrasing of Spenser's 'dipped in the bitter wave / of hellish *Styx*' closely recalls Virgil's 'Stygia ... tinxerant unda'. The circumstances of the manufacture of Turnus's sword also resemble those of the Prince's: both are made by otherworldly figures with magical or divine powers. The principal difference is that Turnus's sword undergoes this baptism only once, whereas Arthur's is immersed seven times. As well as its significance as a number of perfection, the change to seven shows Spenser again 'overgoing' his sources.

As was noted in connection with Arthur's helmet, a reference to Turnus tends to point back a further stage in epic evolution to Achilles. In the non-Homeric legends, the child Achilles was dipped in the Styx by his mother Thetis in an attempt to render him invulnerable. But this action was only part of a general programme, the other elements of which are less widely known. Prince Arthur's sword is hardened in the fires of '*Aetna*'; and another of Thetis's techniques was to place her child in the fire each day.[20] There may also be a reference to Achilles in the strange herb '*Medaewart*' which Merlin is said to have mixed with the steel of the blade. Upton suggests that this is a reference to the herb *medica* mentioned by Virgil in the *Georgics* (IV.65), which has curative powers.[21] The effect of blending the herb with the steel would be to give the blade curative powers in addition to its hardness. A weapon that wounds and heals is, of course, well-known in Arthurian legend, the principal example being the spear used to heal the Maimed King; and such an analogy would strengthen the connections with Galahad noted in the first chapter. But it is now less well-known that these powers were also ascribed to Achilles's spear. The Elizabethans were certainly aware of this tradition. Thomas Wilson compares the wounds of love,

> With fatall woundes of *Telephus* alone,
> And say, that he, whose hand hath wrought my care,

---

19 *The Aeneid of Virgil*, ed. R.D.Williams; 12.90-91: 'ensem, quem Dauno ignipotens deus ipse parenti / fecerat et Stygia candentem tinxerat unda'.

20 *The Alexandra of Lycophron*, ed. and tr. George W.Mooney (1921), pp.20-21 (ll.178-79).

21 *The Faerie Queene*, ed. Upton, vol.2, p.474.

> Must eyther cure my fatall wounde, or none:
> Helpe therefore gentle *Love* to ease my heart,
> Whose paines encrease, till thou withdraw thy dart.
>
> *Hekatompathia* 68, 11.14-18

Watson helpfully explains to the reader that

> whereas the Author in the end of this passion, alludeth to the woundes of
> *Telephus*, he is to be understoode of that *Telephus*, the Sonne of *Hercules*,
> of whose wounde, being made and healed by *Achilles* onely, Ovid
> writeth.[22]

As was noted previously in connection with Arthur's spear, Spenser
has changed the weapon to which a particular quality belongs; but
the allusion to Achilles probably remains.

One further interpretation of Morddure should be mentioned. The
hardness implied in *durus* carries the sense of temporal duration, as
in the verb *duro*, to survive. The sword's name possibly suggests,
then, that it survives death. This could be taken to mean that the
Prince's fame outlives him; and the sword is sometimes an attribute
of Fame in the Renaissance.[23] Or one may read the name literally to
mean that the sword itself would survive after Prince Arthur's death.
In this case the name would imply the significant longevity mentioned
in the original description of his armour which, after his death, was
gathered up by the Faery Queen and brought to Faery Land, 'where
yet it may be seene, if sought' (I.vii.36.9). These two readings are
not, of course, mutually exclusive: the survival of Arthur's armour
may represent, among other things, the survival of his fame.

3. The Battle over Guyon's Body

I

Although I have suggested a meaning for the name Morddure, its
significance can only be understood in the context in which it is
named, the battle over Guyon's body. We must ask why Spenser did
not include the sword when he described the rest of Prince Arthur's
armour in Book One; and why he chose to reveal its nature at this
particular point in Book Two. In order to answer these questions we
must consider Arthur's battle with Pyrochles and Cymochles, and the
place of martial symbolism within it.

---

[22] *Poems*, ed. Edward Arber (1870), p.104. I am indebted to Professor Alastair
Fowler for drawing this poem to my attention.
[23] See Tervarent, col. 157.

Given C.S. Lewis's early judgement that Prince Arthur is too shadowy a figure to be interpreted satisfactorily, one should resist appropriating his term 'allegorical cores' for the rescues of the Red Cross Knight and Sir Guyon.[24] Nor would the appropriation of the term be entirely fair, for there is a real sense of distillation in the description of the Houses entered by the knights-patron in Books One and Two.[25] But in both cases the earlier rescue is something of a watershed: at the nadir of the fortunes of both these knights, a new perspective is introduced by the entry of Prince Arthur. The emblematic nature of his battles with Orgoglio and the sons of Acrates enables the reader to stand back suddenly from the individual episodes of the quest and perceive a pattern in the broad sweep of adventures. And this effect is not dissimilar to that Lewis saw in his allegorical cores, in which 'the theme of that book would appear disentangled from the complex adventures and reveal its unity'.[26] Furthermore, the outcome of these rescues projects the pattern into the future, reassuring the reader and allowing an element of humour to creep into the final confrontation of each knight-patron.

Arms and armour are in the forefront of both rescues. When Una first sees Prince Arthur she is carrying with her the Red Cross Knight's abandoned armour, 'the forlorne reliques of his powre' (I.vii.48.1). In the second book, the Palmer echoes both her thought and her phrasing when Pyrochles tries to disarm the unconscious Guyon, pleading with him to 'leave these relicks of his living might' (II.viii. 16.6). And as we shall see, throughout the battle with Pyrochles and Cymochles the weapons used are of the utmost significance in establishing Spenser's meaning.

Like Prince Arthur's rescue of the Red Cross Knight, the battle over Guyon's body is emblematic of the book in which it occurs. It sums up and recapitulates the previous seven cantos and foreshadows the eventual conclusion.

Expressed thus baldly, the reader could be forgiven for dismissing Spenser's repetitive structure in the way F.W. Bateson concludes his discussion of a Spenser sonnet: 'It is permissable to regret the diffuseness of Elizabethan poetry'.[27] Bateson criticises this sonnet, *Amoretti* LIX, for its 'non-committal tautologies' (p.30), its 'repetitions,

24 *The Allegory of Love* (OUP, 1936), pp.334 and 336.
25 In *English Literature in the Sixteenth Century Excluding Drama* (Oxford: Clarendon Press, 1954), p.381, the House of Holiness and the House of Alma are given as the 'allegorical cores' of Books One and Two. In *The Allegory of Love* the core of Book One is interestingly given as the Red Cross Knight's battle with Orgoglio.
26 *English Literature in the Sixteenth Century*, p.381.
27 *English Poetry and the English Language* (1934; 3rd edn., OUP, 1973), p.30.

glosses, and amplifications' (p. 29). In fact the sonnet's structure is somewhat analogous to that Spenser developed for *The Faerie Queene*, where the initial idea, or 'primary meaning' to use Bateson's words, is recapitulated in a variety of allegorical passages. Thus in Book One, for example, the Knight's battle with Errour is partially reflected in the three days of the final Dragon-fight; and both are summed up and contained within the Prince's battle with Orgoglio. Should *The Faerie Queene* be accused, with *Amoretti* LIX, of a 'disconcerting flatness and lack of emphasis' (p. 30)?

Bateson explains the tautologies of the sonnet as being the result of the poet's awareness of the unfixed nature of the language: one thought requires expression in a variety of different ways to ensure its intelligibility in future years. While this may be partially true, it is not an adequate description of Spenser's aims either in this sonnet or in *The Faerie Queene*. In both poems, each recapitulation and re-expression sheds a different light on the 'primary meaning', entailing the further exploration of the original idea. It is only by reducing the 'primary meaning' to the barest and least interesting of formulae that either poem can truly be called tautological. The theme of the sonnet, the Lady's 'settled mind', is complex; Spenser's meaning is by no means as obvious as Bateson suggests. By restating the theme in a variety of emotional and metaphoric contexts, Spenser develops and deepens our understanding of the Lady's psychological and moral state. Similarly in *The Faery Queene* the different allegorical expressions of a single theme enable the poet to expound it with greater resonance and clarity, a clarity depending not on simplicity but on a recognition of the true complexity of the subject.

We may see this technique in operation in Book One, where Spenser used martial symbolism in the battles with Errour, the Dragon, and Orgoglio to link these episodes in our minds. Furthermore, he uses the same martial symbolism to point the essential differences between them.

The turning point in the Red Cross Knight's battle with Errour is Una's admonition, 'add faith unto your force, and be not faint' (I.i.19.3). Her exhortation comes just at the crucial moment when Errour has 'lept fierce upon his shield' (18.6), the shield we know from the *Letter to Raleigh* to be that of faith. Una's words encourage her Knight to alter his attitude to human prowess and to God, to have faith in God rather than in his own strength. But in the battle with the Dragon, in which the monster at the decisive moment likewise 'did fiercely fall, / Upon his sunne-bright shield' (I.xi.40.8-9), the Knight's revivals and ultimate victory have nothing to do with his own attitudes. They are the result of God's grace gained inadvertently through the happy falls to lie beside the Well of Life and the Tree of

Life. Narratively, the conquests of Errour and the Dragon are similar; allegorically they are perhaps aspects of the same struggle, but different in this respect, that in one the struggle is seen from man's perspective, where human faith is the key to success; and in the other from God's perspective, where the gift of grace, enabling human faith, is seen as all-important.

The third of these episodes, Arthur's defeat of Orgoglio, also has its turning-point, this time the uncovering of the Prince's shield. As was seen in the first chapter, the diamond shield is symbolic of grace, and its sudden revelation conveys the entry of grace into the poem. But we also know that this is the shield of faith, perhaps the poem's pre-eminent shield of faith, and the uncovering of the Prince's shield suggests the entry of that virtue too. Thus in an emblematic scene, Spenser uses one action to convey the advent of both grace and faith; he unites in a single martial symbol the perspectives of both the earlier and later battles. And in doing so he further deepens our understanding by suggesting the essential unity of the two. The recapitulations bring with them not only the benefits of summary, but also fresh insights into Book One's central theme.

This technique is employed throughout *The Faerie Queene*: episodes in Spenser's poem are continually unfolding each other, while themselves being unfolded. One suspects that it is this interdependence which so forcibly suggests the existence of a structure to the reader, yet which paradoxically makes that structure so difficult to define.

II

In Books One and Two, the central emblematic recapitulation takes the form of Arthur's rescue of the titular hero. One of the distinguishing features of the emblem as a genre is its verse or written moral, which combines with the visual image to form a unified, larger statement or meaning. Continuing the analogy with an emblem, the battle over Guyon's body has the equivalent of such a verse. Firstly, the description of Arthur's sword, ironically spoken by Archimago, contains in embryo the general meaning of the episode. Secondly, the discussion that precedes the battle, in which the Prince tries with 'words well dispost' (II.viii.26.7) to calm the pagan brothers, develops the meaning of the sword and links that meaning with the actions of the combat.

Arthur's explanation of his attempt to reason with Pyrochles and Cymochles before the battle commences immediately recalls the description of Morddure:

> Words well dispost
> Have secret powre, t'appease inflamed rage.   (II.viii.26.7-8)

The secret power of words has already been ridiculed by Pyrochles when he seizes Arthur's sword:

> Foolish old man, said then the Pagan wroth,
> That weenest words or charmes may force withstond (22.1-2)

The sharp distinction evident here in their attitudes to and uses of words is constantly revealed throughout the opening stanzas of their encounter. Both Arthur and Pyrochles address old men; Arthur begins questioning the Palmer with 'Reverend syre' (24.1) and respectfully continues in a formal, rhetorical manner. Pyrochles, on the other hand, opens his reply to Archimago's warning with the contemptuous 'Foolish old man' (22.1). The difference is again pointed when Guyon reawakens after Pyrochles's death and addresses the Palmer with filial respect as 'deare sir' (53.7). But Spenser makes the contrast most forcibly in the complete silence and inarticulateness of Pyrochles and Cymochles in the face of Arthur's *politesse*:

> By this that straunger knight in presence came,
> And goodly salued them; who nought againe
> Him answered, as courtesie became,
> But with sterne lookes, and stomachous disdaine,
> Gave signes of grudge and discontentment vaine:[28]   (23.1-5)

Pyrochles and Cymochles have almost abjured the use of speech, communicating by brutish outward gestures alone. Pyrochles's manner also explicitly contrasts with the attributes Arthur sees as essential to a knight: having disdained words, 'that vertuous steele he rudely snatcht away' (22.6). But rudeness is what Arthur tells the Palmer is inconceivable in a true knight:

> Palmer, (said he) no knight so rude, I weene,
> As to doen outrage to a sleeping ghost: (26.1-2)

Tellingly in the context of the battle, the rudeness Arthur sees as impossible in a civilized man is the spoliation of arms and armour; and the Prince, in commenting on the theft of Guyon's equipment, unwittingly agrees with Spenser in condemning Pyrochles's rude seizure of Morddure. Spenser also makes the point that both the Prince and Sir Guyon are recognizably virtuous by their faces; but the chief contrast in this canto between the heroes and the Pagan brethren centres on their attitudes to words and weapons.

---

[28] 'Salued' in the sixteenth century seems to have been used primarily for verbal greetings; see *OED* Salue v1a.

In keeping with the references to speech before the battle, the Palmer subsequently describes it to Guyon as 'the whole debate' (54.6). The combat begins with the significantly unannounced assault on Arthur by Pyrochles, for which he is criticised for breaking 'the law of armes, to strike foe undefide' (31.7). With Cymochles's death the references to speech become almost parodic:

> He tombling downe on ground,
> Breathd out his ghost, which to th'infernall shade
> Fast flying, there eternall torment found (45.6-8)

As in the description of Arthur's sword, Spenser is relying on our knowledge of the conclusion of the *Aeneid*; Cymochles's death is closely similar to that of Turnus:

> But the other's limbs grew slack and chill, and with a moan life passed indignant to the Shades below.[29]

Spenser's 'breathd out his ghost' is close to the sense of *gemitu* in the *Aeneid*; but it lacks any of the reference to lamenting or groaning conveyed by the Latin. Unlike Turnus's audible last breath, Cymochles's is entirely silent.

Pyrochles's response, after a brief denunciation of Arthur, is to go literally berserk. The description of his desperate attack continues the parody. Arthur coolly watches Pyrochles exhaust himself; and wind or breath is the basis of the metaphor Spenser uses to convey his pointless and ineffective violence:

> As when a windy tempest bloweth hye,
> That nothing may withstand his stormy stowre,
> The cloudes, as things affrayd, before him flye;
> But all so soon as his outrageous powre
> Is layd, they fiercely then begin to shoure (48.1-5)

This metaphor contains another unrecognised allusion to Book Twelve of the *Aeneid*. Spenser has combined two similes describing Aeneas and Turnus in their final battle. Firstly Turnus is likened to

> the blast of the Edonian Northwind [which] roars on the deep Aegean, and drives the billows shoreward; where the winds swoop, the clouds scud through the sky[30]

---

29 *Aeneid* 12.951-52:
> ast illi solvuntur frigore membra / vitaque cum gemitu fugit indignata sub umbras.

30 *Aeneid* 12.365-67:
> ac velut Edoni Boreae cum spiritus alto / insonat Aegaeo sequiturque ad litora fluctus; / qua venti incubuere, fugam dant nubila caelo.

But later in the battle Aeneas is described as a great cloud dominating the winds:

> As when a tempest bursts, and a storm-cloud moves towards land through mid-ocean ... before it fly the winds.[31]

Spenser combines Virgil's two similes in one, using them to establish the difference between the ineffective wind and the more truly tempestuous and powerful rain-storm. Like his brother, and of course like Orgoglio (another empty windbag), Pyrochles is all air and no speech. Their incapacity to express themselves is mirrored by Pyrochles's inability to wield Arthur's sword; when Pyrochles, finding his windy turmoil useless,

> perceiv'd
> How that straunge sword refusd, to serve his need,
> But when he stroke most strong, the dint deceiv'd,
> He flong it from him   (49.1-4)

III

In the previous pages it has been noted that Spenser frequently alludes to the final stages of the *Aeneid*: as has often been said, Pyrochles's last words echo those of Turnus; we may now add that Cymochles's death also recalls the last lines of the *Aeneid*; and the storm simile wittily combines two of Virgil's. As we examine the battle over Guyon's body we become aware that these resemblances are not random, nor are they merely evidence of Spenser's adherence to epic convention. They are specific allusions designed to elucidate the meaning of this part of *The Faerie Queene*. Furthermore these allusions centre on the dominating symbols of this canto, the weapons used by Arthur and Pyrochles.

The extent to which these weapons govern the action has not been recognised. Arthur begins his defence of Guyon swordless, Morddure having been stolen by Archimago and seized by Pyrochles. The Prince defends himself with his spear, which is gradually destroyed by Cymochles, while Pyrochles finds that Morddure will not harm its rightful owner. The Palmer, rather tardily, gives Arthur Guyon's sword, with which he kills Cymochles and then Pyrochles, after the latter has thrown away Morddure in rage.

---

[31] *Aeneid* 12.451-55:
> qualis ubi ad terras abrupto sidere nimbus / it mare per medium; ... ferunt ad litora venti.

Two further allusions to the *Aeneid* should be noted briefly. Firstly the opposition of sword and spear is one Virgil makes in the final moments of the battle between Aeneas and Turnus, when he describes them as

one trusting to his sword, one fiercely towering with his spear.[32]

In *The Faerie Queene*, Arthur bears the spear, the weapon of the victorious Aeneas. Secondly, the difficulty Pyrochles experiences in using Morddure, how 'when he stroke most strong, the dint deceiv'd', is an allusion to Turnus's similarly misplaced trust in the sword he is using:

But the traitorous sword snaps, and in mid stroke fails its fiery lord.[33]

The epithet Virgil uses for Turnus, *ardentem*, particularly connects this hero with the literally fiery Pyrochles. The general resemblances between Pyrochles and Turnus have been noted previously.[34] But critics have not noticed the depth of Spenser's reference to the *Aeneid*, nor the particular allusions to the weapons wielded in its final stages.

In the line quoted above, 'one trusting to his sword, one fiercely towering with his spear', Virgil characterises his heroes by the weapons they use. His commentators went further, allegorising their arms and armour. Fulgentius, who sees the *Aeneid* as a *psychomachia*, interprets the battle, the participants, and the weapons they use. Turnus, as we would expect, emerges as something very close to Pyrochles:

In IX, X, & XI he [Aeneas] fights with his arms against Turnus. For Turnus is as to say in Greek *turonnus*, that is the furious sense.[35]

Like Pyrochles, Turnus represents ire and wrath undermining the good man. The weapons Venus gives her son are also interpreted:

then the arms of Vulcan, that is the defence against the fire of the senses, protecting against all wicked trials. For Vulcan [is] as if [to say] *bulencauson*, that is, spiritual counsel.[36]

---

32 *Aeneid* 12.789: hic gladio fidens, hic acer et arduus hasta
33 *Aeneid* 12.731-32:
    at perfidus ensis / frangitur in medioque ardentem deserit ictu
34 See the summary in James Nohrnberg's *The Analogy of 'The Faerie Queene'*, pp. 302-303.
35 *Fabi Planciadis Fulgentii V.C. Liber de expositione Virgilianae continentiae* (1589), p. 23: 'In IX, X, et XI, ipsis armis abjurus contra Turnum pugnat. Turnus enim Graece dicitur quasi *turonnus*, id est furibundus sensus'.
36 Fulgentius, p. 23: 'Deinde arma Vulcania, id est igniti sensus munimina adversus omne malitiae tentamentum induitur. Vulcanus enim *bulencauson*, id est ardens consilium dicitur'.

In the struggle between the good man and his undisciplined furious faculty, Virgil's real meaning in this passage according to Fulgentius, the defence from heaven is in the form of divine counsel or advice; Turnus represents the inflamed senses, and Aeneas's arms divine counsel.

With Fulgentius's interpretation in mind, we can now make more sense of Arthur's cryptic comment at the beginning of his defence of the helpless Guyon:

> Words well dispost
> Have secret powre, t'appease inflamed rage: (26.7-8)

Arthur relies on the 'secret powre' of his words to defeat the pagan brothers, as Aeneas uses his divinely given armour, symbolizing divine counsel, to overcome Turnus. The difference is, of course, that Arthur's words do not have their desired effect.

Spenser's battle, clearly, is different from Virgil's. In the *Aeneid*, the hero is able to defeat Turnus with his spear, whereas Arthur's spear is not sufficient in *The Faerie Queene*. There, the Prince is gradually losing, able only to defend himself, not to conquer his attackers, until the Palmer gives him Guyon's sword.

As soon as the battle opens, Arthur accomplishes all that Aeneas did, by wounding Pyrochles:

> With that his balefull speare, he fiercely bent
>   Against the Pagans brest, and therewith thought
>   His cursed life out of her lodge have rent:
>   But ere the point arrived, where it ought,
>   That seven-fold shield, which he from *Guyon* brought
>   He cast betwene to ward the bitter stound:
>   Through all those foldes the steelehead passage wrought
>   And through his shoulder pierst; wherwith to ground
> He groveling fell, all gored in his gushing wound.   (32)

The reference to the seven-fold shield through which he pierces connects this wound with that sustained by Turnus:

> Like black whirlwind on flies the spear, bearing fell destruction, and pierces the corslet's rim and the seven-fold shield's utmost circle: whizzing it passes right through the thigh.[37]

As with the allusions to Turnus's death, in which Pyrochles spoke Turnus's last words and Cymochles's spirit departed as the Latin prince's had done, so here Spenser has divided Aeneas's fatal blow

---

[37] *Aeneid* 12.923-25:
   volat atri turbinis instar / exitium dirum hasta ferens orasque recludit / loricae et clipei extremos septemplicis orbis.

95

between the two brothers. Pyrochles is wounded through the seven-fold shield, but in the shoulder; it is Cymochles who receives the spear in the thigh. This wound is more appropriate to him, a thigh wound being a mark of concupiscence.[38]

After Pyrochles has been wounded, Arthur is faced by Cymochles, who is able to achieve that which Pyrochles cannot, the unhorsing of Arthur. Furthermore, it is Cymochles who wounds the Prince and gradually destroys his spear. Herein lies another difference from the *Aeneid* in which there is no corresponding figure for Cymochles.

In the Book of Temperance, the unhorsing of Arthur should be read allegorically: the Prince has lost control of the horse of the passions, and it is Cymochles, the personification of the concupiscent faculty, who has undermined him. One assumes that Cymochles is able to challenge Arthur because of the latter's love for Gloriana; an ennobling love to be sure, but love by its nature is perilous and prone to excess.[39] The effect of concupiscence is to allow the other passions free rein; when Arthur has been unhorsed by Cymochles, Pyrochles is able to return to the fray, despite his wound, and with augmented fury: he rears

> himselfe againe to cruell fight,
> Three times more furious, and more puissaunt,
> Unmindfull of his wound, of his fate ignoraunt.   (II.viii.34.7-9)

And every time Arthur prepares the *coup de grace* for Pyrochles, and the latter wards the blow with Guyon's shield, the Prince's resolve vanishes:

> But ever at *Pyrochles* when he smit,
> Who *Guyons* shield cast ever him before,
> Whereon the Faery Queenes pourtract was writ,
> His hand relented, and the stroke forbore,
> And his deare hart the picture gan adore,
> Which oft the Paynim sav'd from deadly stowre.
>
> (II.viii.43.1-6)

And each time his hand relents he is assailed by Cymochles, who

> on the hauberk stroke the Prince so sore,
> That quite disparted all the linked frame,
> And pierced to the skin, but bit no more,
> Yet made him twise to reele, that never moov'd afore.   (44.6-9)

---

38 There are many examples of the association of such wounds with concupiscence. Perhaps one of the most interesting is Sir Perceval's self-inflicted wound in Book 14 of the *Morte D'Arthur*.

39 His love leads Arthur from the straight and narrow in his pursuit of Florimell, for instance (III.i).

Spenser's meaning seems to be that concupiscence is the key to control of the passions; until this temptation is mastered, the others cannot be restrained. For this reason Spenser links the fate of Pyrochles to that of his brother in a way that has caused problems for some critics. Spenser tells us that Pyrochles's end has come, and leads us to expect that his death will follow immediately:

> But him henceforth the same can save no more;
> For now arrived is his fatall howre,
> That no'te avoyded be by earthly skill or powre.　　(43.7-9)

But this expectation is not satisfied. What we then see is Cymochles's death.[40] By guiding our expectations in this way Spenser teaches us the interrelation of concupiscence and fury, demonstrating the need to conquer the former before the latter will become manageable.

Cymochles's power is demonstrated by his ability to destroy Arthur's spear, which Pyrochles cannot do. Gradually he reduces it to a useless stump.

Returning to Fulgentius, we can perhaps discover how to interpret this power. Fulgentius adds a second meaning for Aeneas's arms which accords with part of Arthur's role in the protection of Guyon:

against all fury the arms of wisdom and character struggle.[41]

As well as representing spiritual counsel, then, Aeneas's arms signify wisdom. Spenser perhaps has divided these two meanings, for in the first half of the battle Arthur uses only his spear. As hardly needs saying, the spear is an attribute of Minerva, goddess of wisdom as well as of chastity. In Arthur's hands it may indicate that his intervention should be seen as the use of wisdom to protect the good man against vice and intemperance.

But concupiscence can deprive unaided human wisdom of its power and ultimately destroy it. Even as Arthur gives Cymochles his symbolic thigh wound the latter begins to affect the Prince:

> through his thigh the mortall steele did gryde:
> He swarving with the force, within his flesh
> Did breake the launce, and let the head abyde:　　(36.5-7)

The spear is blunted and broken, and Cymochles progressively cuts it away, gradually reducing the power of wisdom.

'Against two foes of so exceeding might' (34.4), Arthur cannot conquer, only defend: 'nought could he hurt, but still at ward did ly'

---

[40] Cymochles dies by a wound to the head, corresponding with that he gave Arthur, which brought the latter down from his horse.
[41] Fulgentius, p.23: 'Contra omnem enim furiam sapientiae atque ingenii arma reluctant'.

(39.7). Although more than a match for Pyrochles, he cannot contend with both brothers at once using only his spear. At this point and in these terms we can begin to see the application of this emblematic restatement to the career of Sir Guyon. Relying on his temperance and human virtues, Guyon is able to resist all attacks on him in the first seven cantos of Book Two. But he is never able to destroy those things which militate against temperance. He cannot overcome Huddibras and Sans loy. His defeats of Furor and Occasion are temporary, and his separate battles with Pyrochles and Cymochles are inconclusive. Most of all Guyon can go through Mammon's realm unscathed but he is totally unable to challenge it. Finally his human, unaided virtue is insufficient, and he falls unconscious into the hands of the Pagan brothers.

This is the state represented by Arthur's temporary and diminishing power of self defence with the spear alone. Guyon's ultimate unconscious state is mirrored in Arthur's 'huge perplexity' (39.5) when he faces, effectively weaponless, the Pagan brothers.

IV

It will be recalled that in defining the meaning of Minerva's shield, Natalis Comes made a point similar to this concerning the inadequacy of human wisdom to overcome concupiscence. Comes there makes the loan of the shield to Perseus symbolic of the divine aid needed to defeat the Gorgon. That crucial assistance is signalled and further defined in the battle over Guyon's body by the Palmer's intervention, as has long been recognized; and indeed the Palmer himself virtually confirms this:

> Faire son, great God thy right hand blesse,
> To use that sword so wisely as it ought. (40.4-5)

But the gift of the sword also carries with it a more particular meaning. In the preceding sections we have noted many references to speech and words in this canto, the Palmer even calling the battle a debate. As we shall see at greater length in the following chapter, in terms of the Epistle to the Ephesians (the context to which Spenser directs us for the Red Cross Knight's armour in the *Letter to Raleigh*) the sword of the Christian warrior is 'the sword of the spirit, which is the word of God' (6.11). When the Palmer gives Guyon's sword to Arthur with God's blessing, allegorically it is God's word which is received by the man assailed by intemperance, and particularly by concupiscence. Until this point Arthur's weaponry has been confined to the spear, the symbol of wisdom but no more; subsequently, his arms also signify that spiritual counsel sent by God, as Aeneas's do for Fulgentius.

In the course of the preceding seven cantos, Guyon has progressively lost contact with his guide. The Palmer is left on the shore of Phaedria's lake, and his counsel is lacking when his charge meets Cymochles on her island and afterwards journeys through Mammon's realm. But at Guyon's moment of greatest need, after he has fainted, an angel comes to guard him and guides the Palmer to his side. It is this divine intervention which is represented emblematically in Arthur's receipt of the blessed sword from the Palmer.

The function of this sword connects with the naming of Morddure, which I have called the verse of this emblematic episode. The etymological meanings suggested, 'death-hard', 'hardened by death', or 'surviving death', all recall the role of Christ as saviour of mankind, who survived death and was paradoxically strengthened by it. Arthur's role as the rescuer of the Red Cross Knight and Sir Guyon has many times been compared to that of Christ. We may now suggest that the sword's name also refers to this. Support for the interpretation of Morddure as words or the Word may be gained through attention to Pyrochles's difficulty in wielding it. When Pyrochles first attempts to strike Arthur, Spenser emphasizes and re-emphasizes the weapon he is misusing:

> With that his hand, more sad then lomp of lead,
> Uplifting high, he weened with *Morddure*,
> His owne good sword *Morddure*, to cleave his head.
>
> (II.viii.30.5-7)

The perverseness of the action causes Spenser to reiterate the name; and to compare Pyrochles's hand to a 'lomp of lead'. But this comparison may do more than intensify the effect; it recalls a passage in Valeriano's *Hieroglyphica* which touches on some of the themes which have been traced in this account of the battle over Sir Guyon. Valeriano interprets the sword as symbolic of speech, citing Diogenes:

> Diogenes compares words to the sword, having seen a good young man devise dishonest things: 'Have you no shame (he said) to draw a sword of lead from a scabbard of ivory?'[42]

---

[42] Valeriano, f.314ᵛ: 'Diogenes verba gladio comparavit, cum adolescentem formosum admodum turpia quaedam fabulentem audivisset: Non te, inquit, pudet ex eburnea vagina plumbeum gladium exerere'.

The perversion of speech is common to the young man and to the Pagan brethren. But Pyrochles imitates the action in Diogenes's metaphor more precisely: before Archimago stole Arthur's sword, the Prince's

> mortall blade full comely hong
> In yvory sheath, ycarv'd with curious slights. (I.vii.30.6-7)

Both Morddure and the sword in the *Hieroglyphica* are taken from ivory sheaths. Spenser has transferred the leadenness to Pyrochles's hand; nevertheless the Pagan's action indicates that he too has appropriated speech or the Word and is attempting to misuse it.

IV: MARTIAL SYMBOLISM IN BOOK ONE

Martial symbolism occurs throughout *The Faerie Queene*, but it is perhaps most in evidence in the Legend of Holiness; and given Book One's explicitly religious theme, such symbolism takes on here a special character. From early in the development of Christian iconography, the struggle between good and evil was presented in terms of warfare; and the depiction of Christ with the attributes of a soldier is found as early as the Book of Revelations. From this beginning Christ the warrior, or Christ the victor, becomes one of the great traditional images of medieval art; and its popularity goes hand in hand with a progressive modulation into the forms and styles of chivalry.[1] The tradition and its images occur in literature too, most famously in English in Langland's vision of Christ's triumph over death as that of a knight in the lists:

> 'Is þis Jesus þe Justere', quod I, 'þat Jewes dide to deþe?
> Or is it Piers þe Plowman? who peynted hym so rede?'
> Quod Conscience and kneled þo, 'þise arn Piers armes,
> Hise colours and his cote Armure; ac he þat comeþ so blody
> Is crist wiþ his cros, conquerour of cristene.'[2]

But Will's uncertainty concerning the identity of the 'Justere' is a reminder that, in imitation of Christ, the individual Christian was also depicted as a soldier, as a *miles christi* in fact. He takes on the 'armes, ... colours, and ... cote Armure' of his Redeemer; and his martial equipment is the subject of ancient tradition, receiving extensive commentary and allegorization from the Epistle to the Ephesians onwards. St Paul's references there to the Christian man's armour were expanded upon and embellished in commentaries and sermons; for St John Chrysostom, one of the patristic writers most valued in the English Reformation, the relationship between the individual and Christ is that between the common soldier and his officer:

---

[1] See Gertrude Schiller, *The Iconography of Christian Art*, translated by Janet Seligman (Lund Humphries, 1972), vol.2, passim.

[2] *Piers Plowman: The B Version. Will's Visions of Piers Plowman, Do-Well, Do-Better, and Do-Best*, eds. George Kane and E.Talbot Donaldson (Athlone Press, 1975), Passus XIX, ll.10-14.

And for this reason we need strong armour, and also a noble spirit, and one acquainted too with the ways of this warfare; and above all we need a commander. The Commander however is standing by, ever ready to help us, and abiding unconquerable, and has furnished us with strong arms likewise.[3]

By the end of the Middle Ages the legionnaire of antiquity had become the questing or crusading knight; but the allegorization of his equipment continued. Ramon Lull, whose *Book of the Ordre of Chyvalry* was translated and published by Caxton, thus reaching and influencing Spenser's century, contains a sustained interpretation of the warrior's armour; and even Erasmus describes his *Enchiridion militis christi* as a 'lytel hanger' in the armoury of a good man.[4] Of more popular works, Jean Cartigny's *Wandering Knight* goes through a process of degradation into sin and thereafter education into virtue; and his spiritual state is signalled by the replacement of an armour of vice with that of virtue.[5]

The importance for *The Faerie Queene* of the traditions of Christian martial symbolism can hardly be overstated: the basic allegory of the poem depends upon the image of the knight on his quest, of an embattled man in progress towards salvation. The description of the Christian man's arms in Ephesians is the only source explicitly identified by Spenser, in the *Letter to Raleigh*; and immediately the poem opens we are confronted with a detailed account of the arms and armour Una gave to the 'clownishe younge man'. The knight and his symbolic equipment thus form our first impression of *The Faerie Queene*; and throughout Book One Spenser uses weapons and armour as a principal vehicle for his allegory. His hero becomes a type of the militant Christian on his perilous journey; and Spenser endows him with the classic device of the red cross on a silver or white background: the device of the *miles christi* throughout the ages, and of St George, the Crusaders, St Michael in the defeat of Satan, and Christ himself. Such is the centrality of that device that, although we come to know the knight as St George, Spenser continues to refer to him by his original, emblematic appellation: the Red Cross Knight.

Participation in this pervasive iconographical tradition is no drawback for Spenser. Unlike Lull or Cartigny, Spenser does not propose

---

3 *The Homilies of St John Chrysostom on the Epistle of S. Paul to the Romans* (1838; 3rd edition, revised, Oxford, 1887) [Library of the Fathers of the Holy Catholic Church], p.171.
4 *Enchyridion militis christi* (1533; facsimile reprint, Amsterdam: De Capo Press, 1969), sig. Ciiiir.
5 Jean Cartigny [or de Carthenay], *The Wandering Knight*, ed. Dorothy Atkinson Evans (Seattle: Washington UP, 1951).

many variations on the traditional meanings of each element in the armour of the Christian soldier; but the very commonness of his source material enables him to use the tradition wittily and ironically; and thus subtly to reveal the nature of his hero and the themes of this book in full confidence of the reader's comprehension. The initial description of the Red Cross Knight demonstrates this: the fundamental images of the *miles christi* and his characteristic device are obvious to all; but Spenser's lines also contain obscurities and puzzles which make this description resemble a riddle. The poet seems to challenge us to make sense of peculiar details: the shield, for instance, bears

> The cruell markes of many' a bloudy fielde;
> Yet armes till that time did he never wield   (I.i.1.4-5)

The battered arms of an experienced soldier; but a soldier without experience: we are teased by the poet to interpret this differentiation of 'arms and the man' in the very first stanza. And at the end of the knight's adventures Spenser is still using the punning style of a riddle in order to provoke in the reader a deeper understanding of the relationship between the individual and his armour, the relationship at the heart of this book, as in the significant repetitions of the invocation to canto xi, where Spenser asks for aid, 'that I this man of God his godly armes may blaze' (I.xi.7.9). Such serious play is only possible given the use of traditional Christian martial iconography.

Spenser's obliquely revealing style in such passages is reminiscent of the emblem and other forms of art which combine the visual and the verbal. In the previous chapter certain features of the battle over Guyon's body were compared briefly with the structure and processes of an emblem; Book One, because of the strength of the iconographical traditions behind it, can refer frequently and tellingly to Christian images. Often the wit of the poem, which reveals and enhances Spenser's meaning, is contained in a silent comparison between what is written on the page and an evoked iconographical scheme.

Because of its pervasive use of Christian iconography, then, Book One is anomalous within *The Faerie Queene* and is treated separately in this chapter as a special case. I first discuss the Dragon-fight which concludes the book, because there the theme of the Christian soldier and his armour as a single entity is christalized and brought to the forefront of our attention. This is followed by an examination of occasions on which the individual elements of the armour of the *miles christi* are used significantly and revealingly in this book. Finally a particular case of Spenser's allusion to an iconographical tradition is discussed.

Although in thus separating Book One I have stressed its singularity,

I do not mean to suggest that the lessons and education it contains for the reader are of no relevence to the rest of *The Faerie Queene*. Its position at the beginning of the poem renders Christian symbolism of considerable importance; and although the meanings assigned in this book to the arms and martial actions of the Knight may lose some of their overt prominence as the poem progresses, our reading of subsequent books is always conditioned and informed by Spenser's opening legend. And this is another reason why Book One merits sustained attention.

1. The Whole Armour of God

I

In setting the scene for Book One, Spenser informs us of the events preceeding the opening of the poem:

> a faire Ladye in mourning weedes [entered], riding on a white Asse, with a dwarfe behind her leading a warlike steed, that bore the Armes of a knight, and his speare in the dwarfes hand. Shee falling before the Queene of Faeries, complayned that her father and mother an ancient King and Queene, had bene by an huge dragon many years shut up in a brasen Castle, who thence suffred them not to yssew: and therefore besought the Faery Queene to assygne her some one of her knights to take on him that exployt. Presently that clownish person upstarting, desired that adventure: whereat the Queene much wondering, and the Lady much gainesaying, yet he earnestly importuned his desire. In the end the Lady told him that unlesse that armour which she brought, would serve him (that is the armour of a Christian man specified by Saint Paul v. Ephes.) that he could not succeed in that enterprise, which being forthwith put upon him with dewe furnitures thereunto, he seemed the goodliest man in al that company, and was well liked of the Lady.[6]

Although Spenser mentions other authors in the *Letter to Raleigh* he supplies no other 'sources' for his allegory. He specifies here the context for armour, at least in Book One; and he makes the bringing of the armour, Una's offering of it to the young man, its being a prerequisite for success against the Dragon, and the armour's transforming of its bearer into 'the goodliest man in al that company', the most significant information necessary to be provided for the reader. And in the course of Book One, the Red Cross Knight's armour

6 *Var* I, p.169.

104

fulfils its promise as the central symbol: in the Knight's defeat by Orgoglio for instance, his propensity for sin is conveyed by his disarming; his defeat by the return of his 'reliques sad' (I.vii.24.9) to Una; and the arrival of a saviour by her presentation of them to Prince Arthur as the 'heavie record of the good *Redcrosse*' (I.vii.48.8).

Spenser's citation of St Paul seems to provide us with a simple context whereby to interpret this symbolic armour; and the Epistle to the Ephesians, with its famous itemization of the 'whole armour of God' (6.11), itself is clear and straightforward. But when we begin to apply this context to the interpretation of the poem problems appear: by the end of Book One the identification of the Red Cross Knight's armour with that of Ephesians seems incompatible with the role it has played.[7] Perhaps most incongruous is the roasting of the Red Cross Knight inside his armour on the first day of the final Dragon-fight, which has led the best critic of this episode, Carol V. Kaske, to comment, 'such treacherous armor can hardly represent "the armour of a Christian man" of the Letter to Ralegh, the "armes" extolled above the "man" in the invocation to this canto'.[8]

Kaske is right: the armour has 'served' the Red Cross Knight in a way unintended by Una's words in the *Letter to Raleigh*. And the doubts raised here are doubly serious, in that as well as questioning the stated meaning of armour they also call into question the overall relevance and reliability of the *Letter*, Spenser's only direct comment on his poem. Yet the final Dragon-fight is precisely the 'enterprise' for which the Ephesians armour should be appropriate and it is also the culmination of the Knight's adventures. The armour's failure to protect its wearer on the first day of that battle seems to place an intolerable strain on the Pauline interpretation.

However, the apparent incongruity noted by Kaske is founded on only a partial understanding of St Paul's martial metaphor: closer study of the Dragon-fight and of St Paul's use of the image of the Christian soldier reveals a solution to these problems. The allegorical description of armour in the Epistle to the Ephesians is only the climactic, triumphant exhortation concluding a subtle and perceptive exploration of the trials and defeats of the Christian man conducted through the image of warfare and centring on his martial equipment.

---

[7] Spenser encourages us to see the armour as an active participant in the action of the poem. In the last analysis, it is not the Red Cross Knight who kills the Dragon but his personified sword:

> The weapon bright
> Taking advantage of his open jaw,
> Ran through his mouth   (I.xi.53.5-7)

[8] Carol V.Kaske, 'The Dragon's Spark and Sting and the Structure of Red Cross's Dragon-Fight: *The Faerie Queene* 1.xi-xii', *SP* 66 (1969), p.621.

An awareness of St Paul's wider use of the martial metaphor enables us to see Spenser manipulating the reader's attention to narrative detail, and thus to the symbolic connotations of the arms and weapons which figure in the combat. As a result we can see that the Red Cross Knight's difficulties in wielding his arms, but his ultimate victory using them, are entirely consistent with St Paul's use of the metaphor of armour. We also see that these arms participate symbolically in *The Faerie Queene* in a coherent account of the Christian's path to salvation; and that the Knight's varying performance takes us to the heart of the mystery of the relationship between Christ and the *miles christi*.

St Paul uses the metaphors of armour and warfare particularly in the Epistles to the Romans and to the Ephesians. In both he is concerned with the transformation of the individual from the Old Man of the pre-Christian era to the New Man of Christianity. This change, potential not automatic, requires an effort on the part of the individual to overcome his own propensities for evil. And it is in connection with the Christian's internal struggle that the martial metaphors are used.

The central statement of this theme, apart from the itemization of the Christian's weapons in Ephesians, is Romans, Chapter 6, where St Paul associates the Christian's weapons with his body:

> Let not sinne reigne therefore in your mortal bodie, that ye shulde obey it in the lustes thereof.
> Nether give ye your membres as weapons of unrighteousnes unto sinne: but give your selves unto God, as they that are alive from the dead, and give your membres as weapons of righteousnes unto God.[9]

(Rom. 6.12-13)

In terms of this metaphor, the limbs of the body are seen as weapons, potentially employable for good or ill, for or against the individual of whom they form part. The use to which they are put depends on the motivation of the bearer. This is an important qualification in St Paul's use of the metaphor of armour; and with this in mind, 'the armour of the Christian man' given to the Red Cross Knight can already be seen to be more complex than is initially apparent.

St Paul's use of the metaphor of armour to express the equivocalness of the body should not be seen in isolation but as part of his complete theology. The body is central to his thought concerning man's redemption; as John A.T.Robinson comments, 'one could say without exaggeration that the concept of the body forms the key-

---

9 All quotations from the Bible follow the *Geneva Bible: A Facsimile of the 1560 Edition*, ed. Lloyd E.Berry (Madison, Milwaukee: Wisconsin UP, 1969).

stone of Paul's theology'.[10] The apostle sees the body as undergoing changes as mankind progresses towards salvation. Before the advent of Christ it is the body 'of sinne and death'.[11] As a result of the Incarnation, when Christ assumed our flesh, we can share substance with Him, 'for by one Spirit we are all baptized into one bodie' (I.Cor.12.13); although we are still liable to temptation and sin. Finally, through Christ's death and resurrection, the process of becoming one in body with Him can be perfected at the Last Judgement, when 'we [shall] all mete together ... unto a perfite man' (Eph.4.13). And this perfect man, of whom Christ is the head, will be immortal: when 'this mortal hathe put on immortalitie, then shall be broght to passe the saying that is written, Death is swalowed up into victorie' (I.Cor.15.54). In short, the body is itself transformed and has three distinct modes corresponding to the phases of human history: before the Incarnation; between that and the Last Judgement; and thereafter.

Commentators on St Paul, from the early patristic writers to Spenser's own period, recognized his stress on the initially amoral and equivocal state of the body, and developed the Apostle's metaphor of armour to express this. St John Chrysostom explains,

> The body then is indifferent between vice and virtue, as also instruments are. But either effect is wrought by him that useth it... For the fault is not laid to the suit of armour, but to those that use it to an ill end. And this one may say of the flesh too, which becomes this or that owing to the mind's decision, not owing to its own nature.[12]

St John Chrysostom recognizes the use of the metaphor to represent the body and develops particularly the sense of ambivalence and the individual's responsibility to use his 'instruments' virtuously. In Spenser's own time, Hieronymous Lauretus agrees with this interpretation of the Epistle, and solidifies the metaphor into a symbol:

> The arms of justice and iniquity which is to say our bodies and our limbs.

Lauretus provides other biblical authorities as well; but his principal source remains the Epistle to the Romans.[13]

---

[10] John A.T.Robinson, *The Body: A Study in Pauline Theology*, (SCM Press, 1952), p.9. My comments on St Paul are greatly indebted to Bishop Robinson's work.

[11] Marginal gloss in the Geneva Bible to Romans 7.24.

[12] *The Homilies of St John Chrysostom on the Epistle of S. Paul to the Romans*, p.169.

[13] Hieronymous Lauretus, *Sylva allegoriarum totius sacrae scripturae*, 2 vols, (Venice, 1575). Vol.1, p.122: 'Arma justitiae et iniquitatis dicuntur corpora nostra et membra'.

It is immediately noticable that the Red Cross Knight's battle with the Dragon follows a pattern similar to that noted in St Paul's theology of the body. As in that theology, the battle is divided into three stages, the divisions being marked by the Knight's two falls: firstly into *'the well of life'* (I.xi.29.9); and secondly to sleep blissfully beneath *'the tree of life'* (I.xi.46.9).

The result of these falls is not just the regeneration of the Red Cross Knight to his original state, but the strengthening and enhancing of both man and armour. After his baptism in the well, the renewal of the Knight is conveyed by a simile drawing attention to his outward appearance and attributes:

> As Eagle fresh out of the Ocean wave,
> Where he hath left his plumes all hoary gray,
> And deckt himselfe with feathers youthly gay,
> Like Eyas hauke up mounts unto the skies,
> His newly budded pineons to assay,
> And marveiles at himselfe, still as he flies:
> So new this new-borne knight to battell new did rise.
>
> (I.xi.34.3-9)

The repetitions of the alexandrine stress the newness of the Knight, who is now able to wound the Dragon seriously for the first time.

Adopting an ignorant persona, Spenser tentatively suggests several reasons for the Knight's success, beginning with his arms:

> I wote not, whether the revenging steele
> Were hardned with that holy water dew,
> Wherein he fell, or sharper edge did feele   (I.xi.36.1-3)

Although presented as a speculation, the transformation of the armour is a result of immersion in the *'well of life'*. This transformation closely corresponds to the first alteration in the nature of the body resulting, according to St Paul, from baptism. As Robinson summarizes,

> The resurrection of the body starts at baptism, when a Christian becomes 'one Spirit' (*i.e.*, one spiritual body) with the Lord (I Cor.6.17), and 'puts on (the body of) Christ' (Gal.3.27), 'the new man', which 'hath been created' (Eph.4.24) and 'is being renewed ... after the image of him that created him' (Col.3.10).   (p.79)

The emphasis is on renewal, regeneration, and transformation, rather than outright substitution. Like the Red Cross Knight's armour, the same body remains, but it is transformed and possesses new powers and capacities.

On the second day of the Dragon-fight, the battle centres on the Knight's armour. And it is only on this second day that the armour can bear interpretation as the Christian armour of Ephesians. On the first day, as Kaske notes, the armour defies such a reading. But we should not, as a result, seek a completely different interpretation for the armour in the initial phase of the battle. we must merely see the Ephesians passage in the context of St Paul's overall use of the martial metaphor. Until the Red Cross Knight is baptised and thus becomes a Christian, he clearly cannot wield the weapons of the Christian soldier. Reading the armour with St Paul as representing the body, the Knight's limbs cannot become weapons of righteousness, weapons in the battle for salvation, until they are transformed from the body 'of sinne and death' through baptism; in St Paul's words, until he has become 'as they that are alive from the dead'. Up to this point the body remains ambivalent: easily infected with sin and lust, it is a weapon rapidly turned against the individual.

The crucial test of any interpretation of the first day of the Dragon-fight is located in the stanzas describing the Knight's reaction to the 'flake of fire' unleashed by the monster. Spenser first describes the Red Cross Knight's immediate physical state and response:

> The scorching flame sore swinged all his face,
> And through his armour all his bodie seard,
> That he could not endure so cruell cace,
> But thought his armes to leave, and helmet to unlace.

$$(I.xi.26.6-9)$$

Ironically, as Spenser points out, the agony comes 'through' the armour: infected by the Dragon's searing fire, the armour has itself become the torturer of the wearer. And the Knight's response is to seek to remove that which is torturing him. Two stanzas later, Spenser covers the same ground again, but this time dwells on the spiritual state of Una's champion:

> Faint, wearie, sore, emboyled, grieved, brent
> With heat, toyle, wounds, armes, smart and inward fire
> That never man such mischiefes did torment;
> Death better were, death did he oft desire,
> But death will never come, when needes require. (I.xi.28.1-5)

Occuring to either side of an epic simile, these two passages describe the Knight's reaction to the Dragon's 'flake of fire'. They are different in that the former expresses a physical desire to remove the armour, the latter a spiritual desire for death. But this difference only exists if we read stanza twenty-six literally. Read with an awareness of the Pauline martial metaphor, the Knight's attempt to remove his armour may be seen as expressing figuratively the explicit death-

109

wish of stanza twenty-eight. The armour he 'thought ... to leave' represents a body which, infected with sin and death, has become intolerable. The close association of armour and body in the second line quoted, 'and through his armour all his bodie seard', supports this interpretation.

This reading gains strength when we consider St Paul's closely similar plea for death in the Epistle to the Romans (a passage to which Kaske also points): 'O wretched man that I am, who shall deliver me from the bodie of this death!' (Rom.7.24). The Geneva Bible's gloss on body leaves us in no doubt of its meaning: 'this fleshlie lump of sinne and death'. St Paul wishes to be free of the body in its unredeemed state. The closeness of the Romans passage suggests that it is the body itself that the Red Cross Knight wishes to abandon, and that this is represented in his desire to remove his armour.

The interpretation of the armour as representing the body in Book One allows us to make more coherent sense of the action on the first day of the combat with the Dragon. It also allows us to understand one of Spenser's peculiar riddling lines, lines which often seem to contain the meaning, as well as the ironically conveyed pathos, of events in the poem. Commenting on the Red Cross Knight's torture within his scorching armour, Spenser draws attention to his paradoxical predicament, through an internal rhyme:

> That erst him goodly arm'd, now most of all him harm'd.
>
> (I.xi.27.9)

The witty, punning quality of the line heightens the sense of paradox, a paradox which is pointless unless we have understood the symbolism of the armour. The underlying irony Spenser expresses is that the body was 'created according to the image of God'; that is, 'in righteousnes, and true holiness' (Eph.4.24 and marginal gloss; compare Genesis 1.26 and gloss. The Red Cross Knight is, of course, the patron of Holiness). The body, which was created in the likeness of God and thus in perfection, has become through the Fall the chief weapon in the armoury of sin and death: our limbs have become 'weapons of unrighteousnes'. Thus it is on the first day that, before the Red Cross Knight's symbolic baptism, the armour which should have protected him acts as the instrument of his torture.

On the first day of the Dragon-fight, then, we are shown the Red Cross Knight failing to harm his enemy and finally being vanquished through his burning armour. In non-figurative terms, the Knight is vanquished because he is in the pre-Christian state. He is reliant on his own resources, and they are insufficient. Ultimately his body is itself infected with sin and it is through the body that he is defeated.

As a result of his baptism in the well of life the Knight becomes a more serious opponent for the Dragon. The simile comparing the 'new-borne knight' to an eagle, quoted earlier, confirms that on the second day he is no longer reliant solely on his own powers. A.C. Hamilton refers us to Spenser's probable source for this simile, Isaiah 40.31:

> But they that waite upon the Lord, shal renue their strength: they shal lift up the wings as the egles: they shal runne, and not be wearie, and they shal walke and not faint.[14]

Apt though this is, the previous verse is perhaps even more instructive, because it (and the Geneva Bible gloss) confirm that the change in the Knight concerns his self-reliance:

> Even the yong men shal faint, and be wearie, and the yong men shal stumble and fall.   (40.30)

The 'yong men's' fall has close similarities with that of the Red Cross Knight; even verbal similarities, in the use of 'faint' and 'wearie'. And the Geneva gloss pinpoints the source of their feebleness:

> They that trust in their owne vertue, and do not acknowledge that all cometh of God

are those intended by the young men. The Red Cross Knight's previous career has provided evidence of just this presumptuous confidence, implicitly in his adventures after the initial act of *hubris* in judging and abandoning Una, and explicitly in his first battle. When he approaches Errour's cave, he arrogantly dismisses Una's warning of danger by asserting the self-sufficiency of his own, unaided spiritual strength: 'Vertue gives her selfe light, through darknesse for to wade' (I.i.12.9). Spenser humorously deflates the Knight, and particularly any thoughts of the invincibility of his armour, by describing how 'his glistring armor made / A litle glooming light, much like a shade' (I.i.14.4-5). Later, when he is being crushed in the 'endlesse traine' of Errour, it is only through Una's exhortation 'Add faith unto your force, and be not faint' (I.i.19.3) that he manages to break free. Only then does the Red Cross Knight 'acknowledge that all cometh of God' and thus gain the strength to overcome Errour. This process, of becoming Christian, of gaining faith, and of thus being able to rely on more than solely human powers in the struggle against evil, is represented during the final battle in the Knight's baptism in the well of life and the simile of the rejuvenated eagle.

---

[14] *The Faerie Queene*, ed. A.C. Hamilton, p.150.

Although the Red Cross Knight is able to wound the Dragon seriously on the second day of his battle, he still cannot deliver the *coup de-grace* but instead falls a second time. This fall too can be understood in the light of St Paul's theology of the body and the symbolism of armour.

The second fall is quite different in character from the first. The Knight is no longer burning in his armour, the Dragon does not brush him aside contemptuously with its tail: instead the Knight stumbles while undertaking a tactical withdrawal to avoid the effects of the fiery breath, the very weapon that had forced him into panic-stricken defeat on the previous day. But now, the mood is entirely different:

> The heate whereof, and harmfull pestilence
> So sore him noyd, that forst him to retire
> A little backward for his best defence,
> To save his bodie from the scorching fire,
> Which he from hellish entrailes did expire.
> It chaunst (eternall God that chaunce did guide)
> As he recoiled backward, in the mire
> His nigh forwearied feeble feet did slide,
> And downe he fell, with dread of shame sore terrifide.   (I.xi.45)

That phrase, 'A little backward for his best defence', is sufficient to illustrate the difference from the Knight's uncontrolled frenzy at the end of the first day. And the parenthesis in the sixth line confirms the Knight's new dependence on God for his safety.

That parenthesis contrasts with one in which Spenser commented on the Knight's first fall: 'It fortuned (as faire it then befell)' (I.xi. 29.1). The second authorial comment stresses the presence of the guiding hand of God, as opposed to the earlier reliance on fortune. The difference expresses the almost universal change that has come about through the Knight's baptismal fall into the well of life.

Further comparison of the first two days of the battle reveals telling differences concerning the arms and armour worn by the Red Cross Knight. As mentioned above, Carol V. Kaske complained that on the first day the armour could not be that 'of a Christian man specified by Saint Paul v. Ephes.'. We have already seen that theologically this is necessarily true, since the Knight, in the context of this three-day battle, has yet to become Christian. And close attention to the details of the combat confirms that although the Red Cross Knight possesses armour in the first trial of strength with the Dragon, that armour is carefully presented by Spenser in such a way as to omit all reference to the arms and weapons specified by St Paul in the Epistle to the Ephesians. For most of the opening day, the Red

Cross Knight's principal weapon is his spear, nowhere mentioned by St Paul; and the Dragon demonstrates this weapon's inadequacy when

> he snatcht the wood,
> And quite a sunder broke [it] . (I.xi.22.2-3)

But more important than the spear's weakness as an offensive weapon is the Red Cross Knight's inability to defend himself. His defensive arms are worse than useless: when the Dragon looses its 'flake of fire', St George has no protection and makes no attempt to ward off the consequences. Paradoxically, it is essential here to bear in mind the allegorization of the Christian man's armour in the Epistle to the Ephesians, and to note Spenser's ironic omission of the crucial weapon. The action of Spenser's Dragon in emitting fiery breath is specifically foreseen in St Paul's epistle:

> Above all, take the shield of faith, wherewith ye may quench all the fyrie dartes of the wicked. (Eph.6.16)

But on the first day of the Red Cross Knight's battle, this paramount element in the Christian man's armour is never mentioned: it is, to all intents and purposes, absent. When the 'fyrie dartes' threaten the Knight, he is without the protection of the shield of faith. But on the second day the shield assumes the prominence accorded to it by St Paul; and it is as the all-important element in the Christian man's armour that it is fought over by the combatants.

Indeed, on the second day, the whole battle revolves around the shield. The Dragon, recognizing its importance, tries to wrest it away; and as a result of the struggle for it, the Knight wounds the monster severely. But of greater significance than any single event in the battle is the shield's mere presence: by registering that, we can perceive the reasons for the Knight's previous inadequacy. Before baptism in the well of life St George cannot wield the Christian's weapons; particularly, the protection of faith is not available to him. Even more, the few weapons he has can be turned disasterously against him. But on the second day, because of his new state, the Dragon's 'scorching fire' has become manageable: the Knight must still retreat, but not in disarray. The second fall is fortunate, arranged by God; and the Knight's shield, to which the Dragon paid such great attention, remains with him.

Yet he falls. Despite his regeneration and the change from the body of sin and death to that of a baptised Christian, the process by which he becomes one in Christ is not yet completed. As St Paul says, it will only be completed at the Last Judgement:

Beholde, I shewe you a secret thing, We shal not all slepe, but we shal all be changed,

In a moment, in the twinkling of an eye at the last trumpet: for the trumpet shal blowe, and the dead shal be raised up incorruptible, and we shal be changed ...

So when this corruptible hath put on incorruption, this mortal hathe put on immortalitie, then shal be broght to passe the saying that is written, Death is swalowed up into victorie.   (I.Cor.15.51-54)

Robinson comments, 'the completion of this transformation must wait upon the day of the *Parousia*' even for the faithful (p. 80). Although a Christian warrior on the second day, the Red Cross Knight remains a mortal, and mortals by definition cannot defeat death: as the Geneva gloss says of St Paul's rebellious body in Romans 7.23, 'Even the corruption which *yet* remaineth' (my italics). But his second fall leaves him below the '*tree of life*' which seems to symbolize not only the tree of the Garden of Eden, but also the cross of the crucifixion, of Christ's victory and resurrection. On the final day, after the second transformation, the Knight is in this perfected state and is able to despatch his enemy with little difficulty. Significantly, the Knight fatally wounds the Dragon through its mouth: as it approaches 'him to have swallowd quight' (I.xi.53.2), the Dragon is itself 'swalowed up into victorie'.

Interpreted thus, the Red Cross Knight is never equated with Christ, even on the final day. Despite A.C. Hamilton's praise that Carol V. Kaske 'raised to a new level of understanding' the debate about the Knight's ultimate standing, her final formulation that the Knight is 'Christ the perfect man' seems unsubtle and curiously inverted.[15] As Rosemond Tuve remarked, 'Red Crosse "figures" Christ, but is never equated with Him'.[16] If we read the battle using the symbolism of armour and in terms of St Paul's theology of the body,

---

[15] *The Faerie Queene*, ed. A.C. Hamilton, p. 26. Throughout this discussion of the Red Cross Knight's battle with the Dragon I have used Professor Kaske's stimulating and erudite article as a sounding-board, as a statement with which to disagree. In general, she documents her argument superbly, but does not supply any contemporary evidence for the interpretation of the armour on the first day as the Mosaic Law of the Old Testament (pp. 622-23). Indeed, her own authorities, St Paul and Lauretus, have been seen to propose the symbolism of the armour as the body on which I have based my account. Professor Kaske is right to draw attention to the ambivalence of the Knight's armour; and as the first attempt at a detailed explication of the battle, her discussion highlights the demands made upon any reading. However, her own interpretation is undermined by its need to isolate the events of the first day rather than discover a consistent meaning for the armour which accommodates its fluctuating value for the Knight.

[16] Rosemond Tuve, *Allegorical Imagery*, p. 404.

114

we may suggest that the Knight, as a result of Christ's death and resurrection, has become part of Christ the perfect man: not Christ, but 'in Christ', to use St Paul's phrase.[17] The Red Cross Knight does not lose his identity as St George; instead that identity is enhanced and transformed, as is signified by the transformations of his armour in the course of the battle. As Nature says of things affected by Mutability, by change his being has dilated until he reaches perfection (VII.vii.58). Perfection for man is to become in Christ as the Red Cross Knight does on the third day of his final battle.

IV

Although particularly applicable to the final Dragon-fight, the Pauline context for the Red Cross Knight's armour may be of significance elsewhere. An obvious instance is when Sir Guyon takes up the cause of Ruddymane; doing so, he lifts up the armour of Mortdant, the child's father:

> But his sad fathers armes with bloud defilde,
> An heavie load himselfe did lightly reare   (II.ii.11.3-4)

Confirming the Pauline metaphor, the ambiguity of 'himselfe' tells us, as Alastair Fowler has noted, that the arms are an allegory of 'his own flesh with its unavoidable sin and decay'.[18]

But a more difficult passage to interpret is the enchanter Archimago's assumption of an imitation of the Red Cross Knight's arms in order to deceive Una:

> But now seemde best, the person to put on
> Of that good knight, his late beguiled guest:
> In mighty armes he was yclad anon,
> And silver shield: upon his coward brest
> A bloudy crosse, and on his craven crest
> A bounch of haires discolourd diversely:
> Full jolly knight he seemde, and well addrest,
> And when he sate upon his courser free,
> *Saint George* himself ye would have deemed him to be.   (I.ii.11)

Una is fooled by the imitation; but later Archimago is defeated and sorely wounded by Sans loy:

---

[17] On the significance of this phrase for St Paul, see Robinson, p.46.
[18] 'The Image of Mortality: *The Faerie Queene*, II.i-ii', *HLQ* 24 (1960-61), p.104.

> But that proud Paynim forward came so fierce,
>> And full of wrath, that with his sharp-head speare
>> Through vainely crossed shield he quite did pierce
>
> (I.iii.35.1-3)

When Archimago is such a convincing copy of the Red Cross Knight, why is his shield 'vainely crossed'?

The answer lies perhaps in the description of his 'transformation', the wording of which recalls certain passages in which St Paul urges the transformation of the Christian. The phrase 'put on', which occurs nowhere else in *The Faerie Queene* in this sense, is used by St Paul in particular to convey the three interrelated processes which I have suggested lie at the heart of Spenser's meaning in the Red Cross Knight's armour: the change from the Old Man to the New; the process of becoming one with Christ; and the taking of the armour of the Christian warrior. We are exhorted to 'put on the whole armour of God' (Eph.6.11), to 'put on Christ' (Gal.3.27), and finally, to

> put on the new man, which after God is created in righteousnes, and true holines. (Eph.4.24)

At the very beginning of the poem, the Knight is named as 'the Patron of true Holinesse' (I.i.Arg.1) (a reference which seems to have escaped the poem's editors). And, in the *Letter to Raleigh*, the 'clownish person' is transformed into a potential hero when 'that armour which she brought' is 'put upon him'. Spenser's phrasing echoes that of the Epistle; and the irony of its second use for Archimago's deception points the difference between the enchanter's action and that of a true Christian. As we expect of Hypocrisy, the enchanter takes merely the outward show: there is grim humour in the discrepancy between what Archimago means by 'the person to put on / Of that good knight' and what the phrase means to the true Christian. Archimago, with his beads and carelessly strewn Ave Marias, is false Holiness. His is an external imitation, possessing none of the transforming, transformed inner reality; and hence his shield is 'vainely crossed'.

This episode confirms the point made concerning the 'treacherous armour' of the first day of the Dragon-fight. Spenser announces the beginning of the battle by arresting the narrative in order to invoke the assistance of his Muse. This invocation is peculiar in a number of ways, not least in the ambiguity of the poet's final statement of his theme,

> That I this man of God his godly armes may blaze. (I.xi.7.9)

The line contains, as was noted earlier, a puzzling, riddling quality in the repetitiousness of 'God' and 'godly'. In retrospect, it also seems

116

incongruous, as Carol Kaske says: on the first day these so-called 'godly armes' cause the Knight's downfall. But the foregoing study of the symbolism of armour in this passage, and its association with the body, allows us to comprehend Spenser's meaning: as St John Chrysostom said, both body and armour are 'indifferent between vice and virtue' and become 'this or that according to the mind's decision'. Spenser's teasing pun alerts us to the need to assertain the spiritual state of the Knight before we condemn his arms as useless. Before he becomes a 'man of God' his arms cannot be 'godly'; hence 'the armour of a Christian man specified by St Paul v. Ephes.' does not appear in the first day's combat.

But this very fact contributes to the 'blazing' which Spenser says he is to undertake. The invocation makes it clear that the aim of the canto is to proclaim or blaze the arms, not the man; although for reasons we now understand, Spenser's word-order and expanded genitive allow a momentary ambiguity. On the first day, the arms are shown to be virtually useless; but these are pre-baptismal weapons. Their inadequacy acts as a contrast against which the virtues and powers of the true Christian armour, seen on the second and third days, stand out. The failure of the Red Cross Knight's arms on the first day can thus be seen as essential to the reader's ultimate awareness of the value of the Pauline, 'godly' arms.

The invocation to this canto contains other peculiarities: unusually, it is placed several stanzas in from the beginning, for instance; and it also contains an elaborate self-denigration by the poet. It has already been noted that, when suggesting the transforming powers of the well of life, Spenser adopts a curiously ignorant persona; and this ignorance and inadequacy without the aid of his Muse constitutes a theme started in the invocation. Though this may seem no more than conventional modesty, the terms used and particularly a latent comparison between the poet and his champion in the narrative cast Spenser in a role not unlike that of the Red Cross Knight: as a 'clownishe younge poet', perhaps. Just as the Knight requires divine aid throughout his battle, so the poet requires inspiration in order to tell a tale beyond his normal capacities. And this inspiration, indirectly from God, is conveyed through a Muse who also inspires warriors:

> O gently come into my feeble brest,
>   Come gently, but not with that mighty rage,
>   Wherewith the martiall troupes thou doest infest,
>   And harts of great Heroës doest enrage ...
>
> But now a while let downe that haughtie string,
>   And to my tunes thy second tenor rayse   (I.xi.6.1-4; 7.7-8)

The same Muse inspires the Christian poet and the Christian soldier. Spenser gives the poets the second string; but, if the pun can be forgiven, they are on the same lyre. The fact that both poets and soldiers, with the aid of the Muse, rise above their normal selves suggests that the two groups are here in some way connected.

This is not to suggest that *The Faerie Queene* is in any way an allegorized autobiography. But it does suggest that Spenser sees analogies between the role of the Christian warrior and that of the Christian poet. In attempting to achieve his own goal, which the poet frequently compares with a quest, Spenser too runs risks, often falling on the way, and only manages to tell of the final battle through external, supernatural aid. The analogy between knight and poet, quest and poem, is perhaps explicit in this invocation; but it has perhaps been implicit since the beginning of the Red Cross Knight's quest. The Knight's first opponent, his own Errour, does not spew out misused weapons as we might expect:

> Her vomit full of bookes and papers was.   (I.i.20.6)

2. Elements of Armour

I

In the preceeding section the discussion of martial symbolism in Book One centred on the armour as a single entity: on the 'whole armour of God' and its overall meaning. But as has already been mentioned, the individual elements of the Christian's armour, his helmet, for instance, or his shield, each possess their own more specific meaning. During the battle with the Dragon, although our attention is fixed primarily on the symbolism of the whole armour, Spenser draws notice to particular elements of the Red Cross Knight's armour in order to achieve greater depth and subtlety in conveying the nature of the Knight's struggle. And this is also true of the rest of the Legend of Holiness.

The central text for the understanding of the symbolism of the different parts of the Christian man's armour is that cited in the *Letter to Raleigh*, St Paul's Epistle to the Ephesians:

> Put on the whole armour of God, that ye may be able to stand against the assaults of the devil ....
> For this cause take unto you the whole armour of God, that ye may be able to resist in the evil daye, and having finished all things, stand fast.
> Stand therefore, and your loines girde about with veritie, and having on

the brest plate of righteousnes,
    And your fete shod with the preparation of the Gospel of peace.
    Above all, take the shield of faith, wherewith ye may quench all the
fyrie dartes of the wicked,
    And take the helmet of salvation, and the sworde of the Spirit, which is
the worde of God.   (Eph.6.11-16)

In using this text Spenser follows in the footsteps of many allegorical writers before him. But unlike some of these, Spenser manages to integrate these weapons into his own work of literature: St Paul's metaphors become his metaphors as he breathes fresh life into them. One may compare *The Faerie Queene* with Jean Cartigny's *Wandering Knight*, which has been suggested as a source for Book One.[19] Cartigny equips his hero first with an evil armour of vices; then, on his hero's repentence, he rearms him, more or less in the Pauline armour. But the arms are mere labels; they exist, that is all. Cartigny's hero never used or loses them and they remain lifeless attributes. But as we have already seen, the Red Cross Knight's weapons almost become participants: they are fought over, removed, or misused, and are continually involved in the action and the allegory of the poem.

The integration of the weapons in the poem can be seen in the first encounter between two knights. The Red Cross Knight's battle with the Pagan, Sans foy, only becomes truly comprehensible if we study the blows received and the weapons used. At first the combat is described generally, as honours are shared, until the Pagan pauses to curse the Knight:

> Curse on that Crosse (quoth then the *Sarazin*)
> That keepes thy body from the bitter fit;   (I.ii.18.1-2)

In locating the source of the Knight's strength in his armour, Sans foy becomes the first interpreter of martial symbolism in the poem: his curse brings the armour to the forefront of our attention by alluding to its non-physical attributes. And immediately he has done so the pace of the combat changes: it is as if the poet can now, having alerted us through Sans foy, bring into play the detailed symbolism of the arms. The blows cease to be generalized and become instead specific: having uttered the curse,

> Therewith upon his crest
> With rigour so outrageous he [Sans foy] smitt,
> That a large share it hewd out of the rest,
> And glauncing downe his shield, from blame him fairely blest.
>   (I.ii.18.6-9)

[19] Jean Cartigny [or de Carthenay], *The Wandering Knight*, ed. Dorothy Atkinson Evans. See particularly Evans's comments, pp. xliii-xlvii.

Roused, the Red Cross Knight delivers the final blow; he

> at his haughtie helmet making mark,
> So hugely stroke, that it the steele did rive,
> And cleft his head. (I.ii.19.3-5)

These are the only detailed blows of the battle and critics have rightly seen them as crucial to an understanding of this encounter. A.C. Hamilton has suggested that this exchange relates to the earlier description of the Red Cross Knight's anger with Una: 'Sans foy's blow hews a large share from his helmet — his eye of reason being blinded'.[20] This is an interesting possibility, but it is noticeable that Hamilton can adduce no evidence from the poem to support the connection between the Pagan's blow and the earlier line, 'the eye of reason was with rage yblent' (I.ii.5.7). One is left to infer that he sees an association between the reasoning faculty and the helmet as the protection for the head.

In the context of Spenser's careful use of martial symbolism elsewhere such an arbitrary association seems unlikely, and also somewhat unnecessary. Beside the other faults the Knight has displayed in the first two cantos, rage is a mere peccadillo. But Hamilton is right in pointing to the significance of the helmet. Recalling St Paul's allegorization, we recognize that the Red Cross Knight is probably wearing the 'helmet of salvation' or, as this is expanded in I Thessalonians, of the 'hope of salvation' (5.8). It is this that Sans foy attacks so vigorously.

But it is not enough to identify, as though one were reading Cartigny. The description of the blow combines with the symbolism of armour to take us deeper into Spenser's meaning. The 'share' hewn out of the helmet has as its primary meaning a 'part' or 'piece'.[21] The loss of a share of the helmet of salvation may carry the same sense as this passage from the Book of Revelations:

> God shal take away his parte out of the Boke of life, and out of the holie
> citie (Rev.22.19)

The Saracen's blow expresses symbolically the diminished spiritual quality of the Red Cross Knight subsequent to his loss of faith in and abandonment of Una. Indeed, this whole encounter with Sans foy may be read as depicting the Knight's spiritual struggle: the Pagan is not an external force which the Knight happens to encounter; rather,

---

20 A.C.Hamilton, *The Structure of Allegory in 'The Faerie Queene'*, p.64. In his edition of the poem, Hamilton revises his opinion somewhat, but persists in this unsupported association of the helmet and the 'eye of reason' (p.48).
21 *OED* Share sb31.

the Red Cross Knight's meeting with him is a direct result of his slide away from faith into an increasingly faithless state. And as that faith is lost, so the Knight's 'hope of salvation' is also diminished. The Pagan can attack the helmet of salvation successfully, not because of the Knight's rage, but because of the much larger and more radical fall from grace that has been depicted already in the poem.

The relationship between the Red Cross Knight and Sans foy, between a lessening faith and utter faithlessness, is confirmed by the similarities between their injuries: Sans foy's blow shears away part of the Knight's helmet; the Knight's return blow is exactly similar, being aimed at the crest. But his is much more effective: he splits his opponent's helmet and skull. The difference, however, is one of degree, not of kind: although diminished, the Knight retains just enough faith, in the shape of his Pauline shield which 'from blame him fairely blest', to ward off death. But by definition, Sans foy cannot possess this shield; and without faith, he has no 'hope of salvation' and his helmet accordingly affords no protection.

The manner of Sans foy's death, however, again enforces the relationship between these two figures, making him seem more and more an exaggerated and distorted reflection of the Red Cross Knight:

> He tumbling downe alive,
> With bloudy mouth his mother earth did kis,
> Greeting his grave: (I.ii.19.5-7)

His death is, we later realise, almost a parody of the Red Cross Knight's birth and discovery. In canto ten, the Knight is told that the Faery who abducted him,

> thee brought into this Faerie lond,
> And in an heaped furrow did thee hyde,
> Where thee a Ploughman all unweeting fond,
> As he his toylesome teme that way did guyde,
> And brought thee up in ploughmans state to byde,
> Whereof *Georgos* he thee gave to name; (I.x.66.1-6)

As is well known, Spenser probably derived this interpretation of the name from the *Golden Legend*, which explains that

George is sayd of geos, which is as moche to saye as erthe; and orge, that is tilyenge. So george is to saye as tilyenge the erthe, that is his flesshe.[22]

---

[22] *The Golden Legend* in the appendix to Andrew Barclay, *The Life of St George*, ed. William Nelson (OUP for EETS, 1955), p.112. I have modernized the punctuation.

As the name George alludes to his being found as if born of the earth, so Sans foy's death is a return to 'his mother earth'. It is perhaps significant that the first time the Red Cross Knight is called St George is immediately prior to this encounter (I.ii.11.9; 12.2).

II

The symbolism of the helmet noted here in the battle with Sans foy occurs elsewhere in Book One. During the first day of the battle with the Dragon, for instance, the Red Cross Knight 'thought his armes to leave, and helmet to unlace' (I.xi.26.9). Previously this desire to remove his arms was connected with the Knight's despairing desire for death; and it is significant that the only element in his armour which Spenser mentions is the helmet: despair indicates an absence of hope and results in the loss of salvation. Confirmation of this is to be found in the earlier encounter with personified Despair in the ninth canto. Before arriving at the latter's 'darkesome cave' (I.ix.35.1), the Red Cross Knight and Una see Sir Trevisan fleeing, and they 'perceive his head / To be unarmd' (I.ix.22.1-2). Before Trevisan has a chance to explain his predicament, his uncovered head has conveyed his fault: he is in despair since he lacks his 'helmet, the hope of salvation' (I Thess.5.8). Spenser implicitly relies on the reader's knowledge of the Pauline armour, for without such knowledge the absence of the helmet would be meaningless.

When they reach Despair's cave there is further mention of arms and weapons. Sir Trevisan had accepted a rope as his means of self-destruction, a rope being the traditional symbol of despair following the suicide of Judas Iscariot. But the Red Cross Knight refuses a rope, once he begins to succumb to the rhetoric of Despair, and takes, like the dead Sir Terwin, a knife.

This is an appriopriate weapon in two ways. Firstly, as in the absence of the 'armour of a Christian man' on the first day of the Dragon-fight, it is important to realise that St Paul nowhere mentions a knife in the Epistle to the Ephesians. A knife forms no part in the arms the Red Cross Knight should be wearing and wielding in his enterprise on behalf of Una. His choice of it as a weapon reveals how far he is from his Christian ideal. Furthermore, knives are also regarded as unfit for use by any knight, Christian or not; they are associated with treachery and guile, as in Chaucer's grim image, in *The Knight's Tale*, of 'the smylere with the knyf under the cloke' (1.1999). Such a weapon is hardly that of an heroic Christian soldier.

The choice of weapon in this instance seems designed to underline the incongruity between the Red Cross Knight's intended suicide and his proper quest: the weapon he chooses shows just how far he has fallen from the chivalric ideal.

The knife is also twice described as 'rusty' (I.ix.29.9; 36.8). A.C. Hamilton assumes that Spenser means by this that the knife is bloody; and he is obviously right to some extent.[23] But the simple substitution of one word for another is reductive and fails to take account of the symbolic and moral connotations of rusty weapons.

In earlier poetry, both Chaucer and Hoccleve seem to imply moral corruption in their use of the word 'rust'. Hoccleve's irresponsible cleric 'recketh never how rusty bene his schepe';[24] and Chaucer's narrator in *The Canterbury Tales* remarks,

> For if the preest be foul, on whom we truste,
> No wonder is a lewed man to ruste;   (Gen. Prol. 501-2)

Both poets imply corruption, and specifically religious corruption, by the word. In the sixteenth century, the evil connotations of rust appear in the Countess of Pembroke's version of Psalm CXL:

> Preserve me, Lord, preserve me, sett me free
>   From men that be
> Soe vile, soe violent:
> In whose entent
> Both force and fraud doth lurk
> My bane to work:
> Whose tongues are sharper things
> Then adders stings,
>   Whose rusty lipps enclose
> A pois'nous sword, such in the aspick growes.[25]

In this splendidly terse and intense rendering, the translator seizes on the natural redness of lips, as Spenser does of blood, to introduce the evil, corrupting connotations of rust. Interestingly, the Psalmist draws on the Old Testament use of the metaphor of the armour of God (the basis of St Paul's) later in this Psalm, apostrophizing Him as 'the strength of my salvation, thou hast covered mine head in the daie of battel'.[26] The Psalmist, like St Paul, associates the helmet and salvation.

---

[23] *The Faerie Queene*, ed. A.C.Hamilton, p.125.
[24] 'The Regement of Princes', in the *Works of Thomas Hoccleve*, 3 vols, ed. Frederick L.Furnival and Sir Israel Gollancz. Vol.3 (EETS ES 73, 1897), p.52.
[25] *The Psalms of David*, tr. Sir Philip Sidney and the Countess of Pembroke (1823), p.269.
[26] Geneva version, Psalm 140, verse 7.

We are accustomed to finding rusty weapons elsewhere in *The Faerie Queene* without these connotations. When Prince Arthur and Sir Arthegall arrive at Mercilla's court, they see that

> at her feet her sword was ... layde,
> Whose long rest rusted the bright steely brand;   (V.ix.30.6-7)

The rust here is a sign of virtuous disuse. But disuse can have less favourable associations. It can either reflect a just peacefulness and tranquility, as at Mercilla or Elizabeth I's courts; or it can indicate a culpable failure to act.[27] In Despair's cave this latter sense is implied: Una, finding her champion knife in hand, reproaches him:

> Fie, fie, faint harted knight,
> What meanest thou by this reprochfull strife?
> Is this the battell, which thou vauntst to fight
> With that fire-mouthed Dragon, horrible and bright?
>
> (I.ix.52.6-9)

Her cause for complaint is the Red Cross Knight's failure to act as he had engaged to do. And her stress on his failure to perform his mission is particularly fitting in the cave because of the connections perceived in the Middle Ages and the Renaissance between sloth and despair.[28] And just this connection between sloth and a rusting blade is made in Lydgate's translation of Deguileville's *Pilgrimage of the Life of Man*. The Net-Maker tells the Pilgrim,

> So as a swerd (I dar expresse,)
> Yffadyd ys off hys bryhtnesse,
> And off hys clernesse ek also,
> Whan men take noon hed ther-to,
> But rusteth and ffareth al amys,
> Ryght so a man that ydel ys,
> And kan hym sylff nat occupye,
> (By resemblaunce thow mayst espye,)
> In-to hys sowle (thus I be-gynne)
> The rust off vyces or off synne

---

[27] See William Nelson, 'Queen Elizabeth, Spenser's Mercilla, and a Rusty Sword', *Renaissance News* 18 (1965), pp.113-17.

[28] See Ariel Sachs, 'Religious Despair in Medieval Literature and Art', *Medieval Studies* 26 (1964), pp.231-256, especially pp.234-37. For the general iconography of despair, see Adolf Katzenellenbogen, *Allegories of the Virtues and Vices in Medieval Art* (Warburg Institute, 1939). Webster notes the corrupting effects of sloth and uses the image of rust to express them: 'If too immoderate sleep be truly said / To be an inward rust unto the soul' (*Duchess of Malfi* I.i.77-78). Nelson in his article notes the connection between rust and sloth but finds no uses of this in *The Faerie Queene* (p.114).

Doth a-way (with-oute gesse)
Offe alle vertu the clernesse;[29]

As when the Red Cross Knight entered Errour's den at the beginning of Book One, the Net-Maker links virtue and the brightness of arms and armour (Una's reference to the Dragon's being 'horrible and bright' may also refer to this ironically). The dulling effect of rust on the blade, signifying moral degeneration and disuse, also suggests the psychological paralysis associated with despair. As well as conveying the bloodiness of the blade, then, the rust on the knife offered to the Red Cross Knight conveys much of the character of the sin into which he is falling; and it thus combines with the symbolism of this weapon to express the moral state of St George and the grounds for Una's complaint.

III

Although his armour is, as we have seen, of prime importance to the Christian soldier, it is not all that is required for success in the combat with evil. As the Red Cross Knight makes clear in the war of words with Despair, military posture is also important: he interjects only once in Despair's long, persuasive speech to state the case against suicide:

> The knight much wondred at his suddeine wit,
> And said, The terme of life is limited,
> Ne may a man prolong, nor shorten it;
> The souldier may not move from watchfull sted,
> Nor leave his stand, untill his Captaine bed.   (I.ix.41.1-5)

The Red Cross Knight extends the martial metaphor into the relationship between the common soldier and his commander, following the tradition noted at the beginning of this chapter. Furthermore, the wording of the final couplet, particularly in the wordplay on 'sted' and 'stand', recalls the beginning of the exhortation to the Christian soldier in the Epistle to the Ephesians, of which the description of the 'whole armour of God' forms part. The exhortation begins, 'Stand therefore'; and this is repeated (Eph. 6.11; 14) St Paul's phrase is picked up by biblical commentators, again most notably by St John Chrysostom, who greatly develops the analogy between moral preparedness and the bearing of the Christian warrior:

[29] *The Pilgrimage of the Life of Man*, ed. Frederick L. Furnival, 3 vols (EETS ES 77, 83, 92; 1899), pp. 312-13.

Stand therefore, saith he. The very first feature in tactics is, to know how to stand well, and many things will depend on that ... He that stands well, stands upright; not in a lazy attitude, not leaning upon anything. Exact uprightness discovers itself by the way of standing, so that they who are perfectly upright, they stand. But they who do not stand, cannot be upright, but are unstrung and disjointed. ... He who knows how to stand will from his very footing, as from a sort of foundation, find every part of the conflict easy to him.[30]

This interpretation brings out the full analogy between the posture of the soldier and the moral readiness and watchfulness of the Christian.

Although the Red Cross Knight himself states the case for 'standing' and uprightness in his disputation with Despair, he fails in this respect on several crucial occasions. The prime example, of course, is when Orgoglio surprises him. Here Spenser is quite specific about the Knight's physical position throughout this episode. When Orgoglio is first heard, the Red Cross Knight is 'pourd out in loosnesse on the grassy grownd' (I.vii.7.2); he has been lying next to Duessa by a fountain. Although he 'upstarted' at the noise (7.8), he remains 'inwardly dismayde, / And eke so faint in every joint and vaine' (11.6-7) that his resistence is ineffective. As St John Chrysostom says, the Knight's moral ill-preparedness is reflected in the act of not standing, in the Knight's lack of physical cohesion. He is literally disintegrated and unmade as a warrior. The giant's first blow, although it fails to hit him, creates sufficient wind to cast him to the ground:

> Yet so exceeding was the villeins powre,
> That with the wind it did him overthrow,
> And all his sences stound, that still he lay full low.   (I.vii.12.7-9)

He thus returns to the position, prone on the ground, in which he started the battle. The unreadiness of the Knight, his physical and moral unpreparedness for combat, is symbolized by his inability to stand.

Furthermore, when dallying with Duessa he was 'disarmed all of yron-coted Plate' (I.vii.2.8). As well as abandoning his military bearing, he has 'put off' the weapons he was exhorted to bear as a Christian solider. The lack of armour and weapons, his proneness, and a certain fluidity are all summed up in the line, 'pourd out in loosnesse on the grassy ground'. The dangerous fluidity of the Knight's state is often referred to: he and Duessa 'bathe in pleasaunce' (4.2),

---

[30] St John Chrysostom, *Commentary on the Epistle to the Galatians and Homilies on the Epistle to the Ephesians* (Oxford, 1879) [Library of the Fathers of the Holy Catholic Church], pp.363-64.

and his 'chearefull bloud in faintnesse chill did melt' (6.8). The Knight is 'dismayde' in mind and body, lacking the moral and muscular integrity necessary for combat. In his pun on 'dismayde', alluding to both the physical and psychological or spiritual state of the Knight, Spenser provides a miniature of his development of the martial metaphor. Ironically, this is the very trope the Red Cross Knight uses to counter Despair's arguments; it is typical of Spenser that he should make the Knight ennunciate the very metaphor he has so signally failed to enact.

This riposte to Despair's arguments may serve as the explanatory verse to a number of other episodes in *The Faerie Queene*. The combination of disarming, abandonment of martial stance, and fluidity reminds one immediately of those instances noted previously when such knights as Scudamour, Cymochles, and Mortdant have given way to lust. With these we may compare Malecasta's entreaty to Britomart,

> Her to disarme, and with delightfull sport
> To loose her warlike limbs and strong effort.   (III.i.52.4-5)

Here, the distinction between the physical relaxation, the loosening of the limbs through the removal of armour, and the moral laxity implied by the abandonment of spiritual defences has almost disappeared. By contrast, in Busyrane's castle, Britomart's prudent watchfulness is conveyed by her careful arrangement of her weapons. Lying behind this figurative use of armour in Book Three, I have suggested, is the general symbolism of virtue; but we may now add that, although there is no specific mention of the 'armour of a Christian man' in this book, the lessons of the Red Cross Knight's armings and disarmings contribute to and inform our understanding of the events concerning Britomart's martial equipment.

IV

The most prominent part of the Red Cross Knight's equipment, his shield, has been mentioned in passing in the course of this chapter. It emerges as the preeminent symbol of St George and in particular of his faith, in accordance with the allegorization of the Epistle to the Ephesians. But in that Epistle St Paul does not mention a device for the shield; and the red cross is itself irrelevant to the meaning of faith. It is, as a device, closely connected with St George, with England, and with the Christian questing activities of the Crusaders;

but it is also, as Spenser makes clear in his description of it, symbolic of the Passion of Christ:

> But on his brest a bloudie Crosse he bore,
>> The deare remembrance of his dying Lord,
>> For whose sweete sake that glorious badge he wore,
>> And dead as living ever him ador'd:
>> Upon his shield the like was also scor'd,
>> For soveraine hope, which in his helpe he had: (I.i.2.1-6)

As we shall see, the association of the red cross and the Passion underlies certain episodes in Book One in which shields play a prominent part.

For our purposes, the most interesting point concerning the device of the red cross is that it appears on the shield and the breastplate of the Knight; that is, it appears in an heraldic context. Moreover, in the course of Book One, this device is implicitly compared with several others: not just that of the Knight's rescuer, Prince Arthur; but also those of his Pagan opponents, Sans loy, Sans joy, and, in particular, Sans foy.

The red cross is frequently found associated with the Passion as an heraldic symbol; one need only think of the many images of the Harrowing of Hell in which Christ bears a pennant with this device. But the association of the red cross and a shield occurs specifically in the iconographical traditions of the *arma christi*, the instruments of the Passion, including such items as the Crown of Thorns, the Spear of Longinus, even the nails used to fix Christ's body to the wood. But the central image is that of the Cross itself. And in this complex of traditions the instruments represent not only the suffering of Christ, but act also as 'symbols of [Christ's] triumph and authority'.[31] This latter meaning is no doubt the origin of the heraldic use of the *arma christi*; as Gertrude Schiller remarks, '*arma* also means 'arms' and in fact they were also seen as Christ's arms and were represented in the form of a shield or coat-of-arms'.[32] The Red Cross Knight bears the red cross in an heraldic context too: this device appears on his shield as the 'glorious *badge*' of his 'dying Lord' (I.i.2.2-3; my italics).

In establishing the meanings of the *arma christi* Gertrude Schiller cites numerous works of art; and again in exploring the martial symbolism of Book One discussion has returned to Spenser's affinities with visual representations. Throughout this book, one senses the presence of the iconography of Christ's Passion and resurrection, and

---

31 Schiller, vol. 2, p.184.
32 Schiller, vol. 2, p.184.

of the Christian solider. This iconographic background, however, does not remain inert or passive; instead it is involved in a continuous, implied dialogue with the episodes of the Red Cross Knight's adventures: throughout, the *miles christi* is compared in his progress with his Commander. Spenser relies on this body of traditional images, using his readers' awareness of Christian iconography and their recognition of the disparity between the Knight's imitation and the original as represented in visual art. And because of the dominant presence of the cross in the iconography of Christ, we may expect St George's shield to play an important part in the allusion, frequently ironic, to images of his Commander.[33]

For instance, the red cross as the heraldic device of Christ may be significant to the interpretation of the battles between the Knight and the Pagan brothers, Sans foy and Sans joy. Having defeated the former, the Red Cross Knight rides off in pursuit of Duessa,

> Bidding the Dwarfe with him to bring away
> The *Sarazins* shield, signe of the conqueroure.   (I.ii.20.6-7)

The Red Cross Knight's right to spoil the dead is in doubt in *The Faerie Queene*.[34] But there is a more serious moral ambiguity in these lines: the phrase 'signe of the conqueroure' literally means that the taking of Sans foy's shield is indicative of the Knight's victory over him. But Spenser's word order implies that the '*Sarazins* shield', normally a sign of the individual to whom it belongs and is appropriate, is itself the sign of the victor; in other words, there is a latent sense in which the 'great shield' on which 'was writ ... *Sans foy*' (I.ii. 12.7-8) is an appropriate emblem for the winner of the battle. It has previously been argued that the details of the preceding combat

---

[33] In stating this I may seem to be covering some of the same ground as Patrick Grant in *Images and Themes in Literature of the English Renaissance* (Macmillan, 1979). However, important qualifications must be made to his use of christian iconography. He discusses parts of Book One of *The Faerie Queene* in relation to the living cross scheme, which he calls the 'effectus passionis'. But the distinguishing feature of this tradition, as Grant summarizes, is that it contains 'the *animated* arms of a red cross' (p.37; my italics). Gertrude Schiller defines the tradition thus: 'By "Living Cross" we mean a Cross of Christ of which the four extremities end in moving hands that do not belong to the figure of Christ' (vol.2, p.158). Nowhere in *The Faerie Queene* does such a cross appear; and Grant's suggestion thus seems somewhat far-fetched (unnecessarily so). In adopting various iconographical schemes in order to explicate Spenser's poem we must pay close attention to the extent to which they are genuinely appropriate.

[34] Compare his action with the Palmer's later condemnation of Pyrochles and Cymochles: 'To spoile the dead of weed / Is sacrilege, and doth all sinnes exceed' (II.iii.16.4-5).

between these knights, and especially the blows to their helmets, establish a relationship between them; and that on one level the battle is an externalization, in the manner of a *psychomachia*, of the Red Cross Knight's internal struggle to remain faithful. The blow to his helmet, shearing away 'a large share', indicates that it was a struggle in which he was only partially successful. This sense of the Knight's slide away from his adherence to the truth is confirmed by the events subsequent to his apparent victory: he takes up the heraldic attributes of the figure he has just defeated, and makes them his own. He pursues Sans foy's paramoure Duessa, instead of Una; and takes the Pagan's shield as 'signe of the conqueroure', supplanting the *crux invicta*, the 'glorious badge' of the eternal conqueror, Christ. Hitherto the Knight has borne as his only device the symbol of Christ's victory; now he also bears its reverse.

The inversion of correct values involving the shields culminates at the House of Pride. The Red Cross Knight and Sans joy participate in a formal joust, in which the prizes are Duessa and Sans foy's shield. In the duelling area,

> in all mens open vew
> *Duessa* placed is, and on a tree
> *Sans-foy* his shield is hangd with bloudy hew:
> Both those the lawrell girlonds to the victor dew. (I.v.5.6-9)

Just as in the careful positioning of Prince Arthur and Sir Arthegall to either side of Mercilla's throne, Spenser's deliberate phrasing here alerts us to the possible significance of the spatial interrelation of the prizes. And if we visualize this scene, we recognize in general outline the familiar organization of certain images of the crucifixion: beneath the Cross (often represented as a tree, the *arbor crucis*) stands Ecclesia, the personification of the Church of the New Covenant; hanging on the Cross is either Christ or the *arma christi* as symbolic of Him.[35] Arranged before the lists at the House of Pride, then, is a tableau referring to the central event of creation and salvation, the Crucifixion.

But the version presented here, in detail, is the absolute inverse, a terrible parody of Christ's sacrifice. Below the tree stands Duessa, a figure associated throughout Book One with Synagogue, not Ecclesia. On the tree is hung, not the crucified Christ nor any symbol of Him, but the emblem of faithlessness. Even the mention of 'lawrell girlonds' may be part of this ironic allusion to the common Christian scheme, since the Crown of Thorns was regarded in the *arma christi*

---

35 On the Cross, the 'arbor crucis', and the figures standing beneath it, see Schiller, vol. 2, p. 135. See also her illustrations, e.g. plates 443 and 450-1.

tradition as Christ's victory wreath.[36] And the relationship between wreaths in general and the Crown was widely accepted: as Marilyn Stokstad has said, 'the ambiguity of twisted branches is typical of medieval visual imagery'.[37] The reference to wreaths may join the other features of the scene in alluding to common images of the Crucifixion, forming a deliberately ironic comment on the Red Cross Knight's progress, a comment contained in the silent allusion to Christian visual art.

The association of the red cross with Christ's heraldic device is the key to the interpretation of this episode. Bearing the *crux invicta*, an instrument of the Passion and a symbol of Christ's triumph over evil, the Knight proceeds to invert the correct role of his device by using it in an attempt to gain and possess the attributes of faithlessness and duplicity, attributes inimical to his own virtue. Tracing the perversion of his shield and its emblem to this scene of their prostitution enables us to perceive how far St George has strayed from the path of truth. Following the martial symbolism of the three days of the Dragon-fight permits us to comprehend the process by which such a representative of flawed humanity can achieve the ultimate success, the victory over sin and death of his Commander.

[36] Schiller, vol. 2, p. 185.
[37] *Gardens of the Middle Ages*, eds. Marilyn Stokstad and Jerry Stannard (Lawrence, Kansas: Spencer Museum of Art, 1983), p. 209. Her remarks come in a discussion of plate 61, a dindanerie plate showing a seated woman holding a coronet, encircled by 'twisted, clipped and pruned branches'; although the primary allusion here is to the thorny path to love, the ambiguous reference to the Passion is present, as she says.

V: THE ORDER OF MAIDENHEAD AND
SATYRANE'S TOURNAMENT

1. Chivalry and 'The Faerie Queene'

In the preceding chapters details of the knight's conduct and equipment have been considered and meanings suggested for them. But apart from the Christian knighthood of Book One, the specifically chivalric associations of the armour, weapons, and martial actions of *The Faerie Queene* have not yet been examined. In this and the following chapter I shall consider these associations, centring my discussion on the consciously chivalric festivals of the poem, the tournaments of Satyrane and Marinell. In these the symbolism of chivalry becomes of major significance; and an understanding of Spenser's meaning depends on our recognizing allusions in general to the institution of knighthood and in particular to the Order of the Garter.

But before embarking on this discussion we must briefly consider chivalry itself and its relation to *The Faerie Queene*. How seriously can we take the poem's chivalric milieu? It is a question which, in a sense, underlies much of this book. The descriptions of knights and battles in *The Faerie Queene* have been seen as more than ornamental; but this has not established any significance for the concept of chivalry. The standard view is that this concept was effectively dead by Spenser's day, that chivalry survived as a literary convention, as little more than a source for pageant costumes. Arthur B. Ferguson, in his influential *Indian Summer of English Chivalry*, states this case persuasively:

> theirs was a really nostalgic, truly romantic, at times even a frivolous attempt to recreate the spirit of an irretrievable past.[1]

Chivalry, on this estimation, was the medieval plaything of a new renaissance society.

---

[1] Arthur B. Ferguson, *The Indian Summer of English Chivalry: Studies in the Decline and Transformation of Chivalric Idealism* (Durham, North Carolina: Duke UP, 1960), p. 226.

However, doubts about this view begin to arise once we probe deeper: it is not just Elizabethan chivalry which is nostalgic; nostalgia is essential to the ethos of chivalry and virtually every literary portrait of the good knight seems to be tinged with it. Two hundred years before the writing of *The Faerie Queene*, in what Ferguson would have us believe to have been the genuine chivalric age, Chaucer's 'worthy knight' is presented as a relic of the past, as having fought (anachronistically) in battles of long ago, and as meriting the affection we reserve for things admirable but outmoded. Seemingly at any date, chivalry is an attempt to recreate the past. Its heroes are always distanced by time: even Sir Philip Sidney had to die before his elevation to the chivalric pantheon.[2]

A subtler and more perceptive account than Ferguson's of chivalry and the reasons for its persistence is given by Jacob Huizinga:

> But *was* it only a question of literature, this third path to the sublime life, this flight from harsh reality into illusion? Surely it has been more. History pays too little attention to the influence of these dreams of a sublime life on civilization itself and on the forms of social life. The content of the ideal is a desire to return to the perfection of an imaginary past. All aspiration to raise life to that level, be it in poetry only or in fact, is an imitation. The essence of chivalry is the imitation of the ideal hero, just as the imitation of the ancient sage is the essence of humanism.[3]

Although Huizinga's comments apply primarily to the late middle ages, his account of the psychological attractions of chivalry is equally valid for that curiously mixed period in which Spenser was writing. The fact that we, with confident hindsight, judge the ideal to have been an insubstantial dream does not necessarily exclude the possibility that it was perceived as attainable at the time.

Huizinga's placing of chivalry in a psychological context leads to a second point: more than in any one action or set of actions, chivalry resides in a manner of seeing and interpreting the world. He suggests that 'the conception of chivalry constituted ... a sort of magic key, by the aid of which they explained to themselves the motives of politics and of history' (p.66). This comment implies a far deeper meaning for chivalry than that allowed by Ferguson's definition of it as a purely 'military ideal' (p.124). The latter's oversimplification is revealed in his own quotation from a tournament proclamation of

---

[2] See Roger Howell, *Sir Philip Sidney: The Shepherd Knight* (Hutchinson, 1968), especially pp.1-12.

[3] Jacob Huizinga, *The Waning of the Middle Ages* translated by F.Hopman (1924; reissued, Penguin, 1979), p.37. See also Frances Yates's more specific account of the survival of the Order of the Garter in the Elizabethan period, where she makes similar points (*Astraea*, pp.108-11).

Edward IV's reign, which amply supports Huizinga's description. In this proclamation chivalry is defined as that

by which our mother Church is defended, Kinge and Princes served, Realmes and Countreyes kept and maintained in Justice and peace.[4]

Such a definition gives chivalry a role far beyond the purely military, placing it in the centre of the political and social structure of the state. That it did not, in twentieth-century estimation, really occupy this place is neither here nor there. And as to the military nature of the ideal, it would perhaps be nearer the truth to say that the chivalric mode of thought finds its characteristic literary expression through the medium of idealized military action.

The word chivalry has a variety of meanings and we should clarify the sense in which it is used here. Ferguson, for instance, fails to distinguish between these meanings and thus becomes confused. After Sir Thomas Elyot's generation, he writes,

it was impossible to revive the medieval knight — the man-at-arms whose primary duty was the simple protection of society, the *preux chevalier* in the service of holy church, of his lord, and of his lady, the debonair adulterer, the 'errant' in search of adventure and renown, the landowner who left all but the lighter forms of learning to clerks — without the exercise of a conscious and historically deceptive archaism.   (pp. 220-21)

This is indeed a remarkable list. The various qualities of Ferguson's medieval knight are confused and conflicting. His conception shifts from the life-like portrait of the ignorant land owner; to the lady-killing errant of the romances; and finally includes the loyal defender of the ecclesiastical and political status quo, this last being drawn from the theoretical manuals of chivalry, often religiously inspired. These versions of chivalry must be kept separate if we are to achieve any understanding; and we may question whether the first element of Ferguson's definition, the everyday, often boorish and crude behaviour of those of knightly class in the period, can be included in the semi-philosophical concept of chivalry at all.

The literary chivalry of the romances and the quasi-religious chivalry of the theoretical manuals have points in common. Nevertheless they are differentiated by the varying emphasis they place on either the physical adventures of the knight or on his moral, political, and religious responsibilities. This difference can be seen most clearly when a writer deliberately contrasts the two, as for instance during the tournament of the Black and White Knights in the *Queste de*

---

[4] Ferguson, p.16.

134

Saint Graal.[5] Like a good romance knight, the knight of the literary ideal, Sir Lancelot joins the underdogs, the weaker and ultimately defeated Black Knights; only to learn subsequently that in this theologically orientated work his correct course would have been to have aided the White Knights of celestial chivalry. In order to point the differences between the two chivalries, the writer of the *Queste* has had Sir Lancelot stumble painfully and unsuccessfully into a foreign genre; and the reader accompanies the knight in the process by which he learns that, in this work, standards other than those of the romances apply.

The *Queste* is an extreme case: Spenser was not a Cistercian as the earlier writer probably was and the contemplative withdrawal at the heart of his work is explicitly denied the Red Cross Knight at the Mount of Contemplation. Yet it is to the genre of theoretical, rather than purely romance, chivalry that *The Faerie Queene* ultimately belongs.

Spenser's ideal knight was to have been perfect in personal virtue; and carrying this integrity into the social context, loyal to church and monarch, lovingly protective towards the weak and the poor, and justly condemnatory of evil in all its forms. This integration of personal and social virtue is central to the tradition of theoretical chivalry. Huizinga summarizes Philip de Mézières's influential regulations for a proposed order of knighthood:

> The three monastic vows are to be modified for practical reasons: instead of celibacy he only requires conjugal fidelity. Mézières adds a fourth vow, unknown to preceding orders, that of individual, moral perfection, *summa perfectio.*
> (p.84)

Huizinga may be right that no order had officially required moral perfection before Philip de Mézières's; but it was certainly required in the manuals of chivalry at least a century before. Ramon Lull first discusses the physical conduct of a knight, but then continues:

> al these thynges afore said apperteyne to a kny3t as touching his body; in lyke wise justice, wysedom, charite, loyalte, verite, humylite, strength, hope, swiftnes, and al other vertues semblable apperteyne to a kny3t as touchyng his soule; and therfor the kny3t that useth the thynges that apperteyne to thordre of chyvalry as touchyng his body and hath none of these vertues that apperteyne to chyvalry touchyng his soule is not the frende of thordre of knygthode.[6]

---

5 *The Vulgate Cycle of Arthurian Romances* vol.6, *Les Aventures del Graal*, pp.100-103.
6 Ramon Lull, *The Book of the Order of Chyvalry* translated by William Caxton, ed. Alfred T.P.Byles (OUP for EETS, 1926), pp.31-32. I have normalized the punctuation of this quotation and of that which follows.

Lull then goes on to state that the virtues cannot be separated from the actions of the knight. If that were true,

> it shold signefye that the body and chyvalrye were bothe two to gyder contrarye to the soule and to these vertues and that is fals. (p.32)

It is clear from these quotations that chivalry is not prized only as a vehicle for allegory by Lull and Mézières but also as an ideal order in which virtue and action combine to the benefit of a society centred on God.

It is worth repeating that this is not to deny the decline in the actual political role of the knight. As Huizinga comments,

> the reason of this disproportion lies in the fact that long after nobility and feudalism had ceased to be really essential factors in the state and in society, they continued to impress the mind as dominant forms of life. (p.54)

In other words, chivalry as a structure within the mind persisted long after its demise in the workings of society. This much is confirmed by the existence of Caxton's translation of Lull's *Book of the Order of Chyvalry* two centuries after its composition and at the end of the disillusioning Wars of the Roses. Nonetheless, to judge by his admonitory preface, Caxton certainly thought of chivalry as a worthwhile and valuable institution for his modern world. In fact the sixteenth century saw an upsurge of interest in chivalry, and not just in its more frivolous trappings. As we shall see, the register of the Order of the Garter, the *Liber Niger*, compiled anonymously in the reign of Henry VIII and one of the most significant chivalric documents of the age, concentrated its account of the Order on the moral and religious benefits derived from it by the nation.[7] At the end of the century and in the early years of the seventeenth century the scholarly and erudite works of such as Favyn and Selden still share this attitude to the values and origins of chivalry.[8] It is an attitude succinctly summed up by the chronicler of the Garter's greatest rival, the Order of the Golden Fleece: in defining knighthood, Guillaume Fillastre, the second chancellor of the Golden Fleece, briskly states that 'en vertue consiste noblesse'.[9]

---

7 *The Register of the ... Order of the Garter*, ed. and tr. John Anstis (1727); see especially pp. 2, 15, and 23-24.
8 See Andrew Favyn, *The Theater of Honour and Knighthood* [anonymously translated from the French] (1623), Book One, Chapter One; and John Selden, *Titles of Honor* (1614), Preface, sigs. b3r-c1r especially.
9 Guillaume Fillastre, *Le Premier [-Second] Volume de la Toison d'Or* (1516), fiir. The notion was not, of course, confined to antiquarians and heralds: Spenser's headmaster Richard Mulcaster wrote, 'For to become a gentleman is to bear the cognisaunce of virtue, whereunto honour is companion'. (*Positions*, abridged and edited by R. L. De Molen [New York, 1971]).

The stated intention of *The Faerie Queene* is the education of a 'gentleman or noble person in vertue and gentle discipline'; and this goal is to be achieved by means of the examples contained in the poem, particularly that of Prince Arthur and his virtue of magnificence, the 'perfection of all the rest'. This perfection 'in the twelve private moral vertues' resembles the *summa perfectio*, the personal integration of all the virtues required of the knight by the chivalric theorists. And the process by which this education in virtue is to be accomplished is the same as that 'imitation of the ideal hero' seen by Huizinga as 'the essence of chivalry'.

Chivalry in *The Faerie Queene* is not mere romantic colouring therefore: its central image, the good knight, is the paradigm of the virtuous and noble life Spenser advocates. This much is indicated in Spenser's use of 'virtue' and 'knighthood' as near synonyms when introducing and concluding Marinell's tournament. At its opening the poet informs the reader that he will avoid inessential detail, despite its attractions; instead,

> for so much as to my lot here lights,
> That with this present treatise doth agree,
> True vertue to advance, shall here recounted bee.   (V.iii.3.7-9)

'True vertue' is his theme, not the colourful trappings of pageant and entertainment. But when he draws the moral at the end of the tournament, and expresses his aim once more, this time the promotion of 'true vertue' is couched in chivalric terms. Braggadocchio, the false knight, has been 'baffled':

> So ought all faytours, that true knighthood shame,
> And armes dishonour with base villanie,
> From all brave knights be banisht with defame:
> For oft their lewdnes blotteth good deserts with blame.
>
> (V.iii.38.6-9)

'True knighthood' has been advanced and vindicated in the course of this canto, substituting for the 'true vertue' which was to have been its subject.

This prominence for the chivalric ideal is consistent with Spenser's remarks on Prince Arthur in the *Letter to Raleigh*. There, the Prince is not interpreted as a good man, or even a perfect man. When Spenser does identify his hero, his chivalric role does not disappear as the mere vehicle for the allegory: Arthur is 'the image of a brave knight'; that is, he expresses the essence of 'brave knighthood'. In other words, although the trials and adventures of *The Faerie Queene* may be allegorical, chivalry itself is not: it remains an ideal to be striven for. Viewed in the light of this statement, the tournaments of

Book Four and Five, with their insistent references to the institutions of chivalry, deserve closer attention than they have yet received.

2. The Orders of Maidenhead and the Garter

The primary expression of the chivalric ideal is the institution of knighthood; and as the works of Philip de Mézières and Guillaume Fillastre indicate, the specific orders of knighthood embody that ideal in a more exalted, more concentrated, and more considered form. It comes as no surprise, then, that Spenser creates for his poem an entirely new order with Gloriana as its sovereign. But despite its originality and close connection with the Faery Queen herself, the Order of Maidenhead receives few mentions in the criticism of *The Faerie Queene*: scholars have usually taken either the line or the tone of Kitchin, who remarks, 'Spenser probably only meant that all who entered the Queen's service became champions of her purity'.[10] But such comments undervalue the Order of Maidenhead and seriously underrate Spenser's use of chivalric institutions and their symbolism. In particular, despite the lead of such scholars as C. B. Millican and Edwin Greenlaw in the 1930s, the Order of Maidenhead's close similarities with the Elizabethan Order of the Garter have gone largely unremarked. Yet the Garter was the principal chivalric institution of England, and arguably of Europe; and it was a crucial element in the pageantry and state propaganda of Spenser's period.

Only a few critics accord the Order of Maidenhead any real function in *The Faerie Queene* and those who do comment on its role frequently display misunderstandings of its basic features. For instance, Angus Fletcher notes that the 'Knights of Maidenhead are a recollection of the Round Table'.[11] This is certainly the case. He further comments that the Order occupies a significant place in the overall structure of the poem: 'the Faerie Queene will eventually marry Prince Arthur, at which time all nature in her kingdom will have been redeemed by the various quests of her Knights of Maidenhead' (pp. 97-98). But this latter statement reveals an underlying confusion: Fletcher appears to believe that all the titular knights of the poem, the questing knights who are patrons of each book, are

10 *Var* 2, p. 280.
11 Angus Fletcher, *The Prophetic Moment: An Essay on Spenser* (Chicago: Chicago UP, 1971), p. 108.

members of the 'transcendental family structure' of the Order of Maidenhead (p.178). This cannot be right: Britomart is not a member, nor is the Red Cross Knight, that 'clownishe younge man' just arrived at Gloriana's court. A more serious misapprehension seems to lurk in Fletcher's assumption that the Order of Maidenhead's effects are purely beneficial: he does not take into account the disruptive element among these knights, the Paridells and Satyranes.

John E. Hankins's comments on the Order improve on Fletcher's in that they countenance the possibility of its imperfection. Hankins considers the Order to be central to the Books of Chastity and Friendship, and he suggests that it is prominent because the Knights of Maidenhead represent 'the forces persuading [a woman] not to surrender her virginity'.[12] He explains that these forces prompt opposition both to illegal lust and to the valid claims of the marriage bed; and that they are therefore not entirely positive. Thus it is that the Order is confronted not only by the philandering Paridell but also by the honourable husbands and lovers, Cambell and Triamond (pp.145-46).

This interpretation of the Order of Maidenhead has considerable merit. But once Hankins begins to mention specific knights we again become aware of confusions and contradictions. He takes as members of the Order of Maidenhead only those who fight with Satyrane at the tournament for Florimell's girdle. But Satyrane's force is routed by Arthegall, who is earlier described as one of the two preeminent members of the Order (II.ix.6.9). Similarly, Paridell fights for the opposition; but he is certainly included in 'all the noble knights of *Maydenhead*' (III.viii.47.7) with whom Satyrane mourns the loss of Florimell. Although they correctly sense the prominence of the Order of Maidenhead in the poem, the detailed interpretations of both Fletcher and Hankins founder on the treacherous rock of membership: the fact that Arthegall, Satyrane, Guyon, and Paridell are all Knights of Maidenhead, whereas Britomart and the Red Cross Knight are not, demands that we seek a more complex interpretation of the Order.

A clearer picture of the Order of Maidenhead's meaning in *The Faerie Queene* is possible if one considers its chivalric context. Angus Fletcher commented that the Order of Maidenhead was reminiscent of the Round Table; and even without any further evidence we might speculate on the possibility that it is associated with that other pseudo-Arthurian institution, the Order of the Garter. Indeed, it has frequently been noted that there are fleeting references to the Garter

---

[12] John Erskine Hankins, *Source and Meaning in Spenser's Allegory: A Study of 'The Faerie Queene'* (Oxford: Clarendon Press, 1971), p.145.

on several occasions in *The Faerie Queene*. However, an examination of these references and of others hitherto unseen reveals that they centre on Spenser's invented chivalric institution, the Order of Maidenhead, and on that part of the poem in which it is most prominent, the tournament held by Satyrane.

As usual with Spenser, it is important first to grasp the significance of the Order's name. John E. Hankins begins his discussion of the Order of Maidenhead with a sensitive commentary on its possible meaning:

> The term [maidenhead] is used for maidenhood .... But Spenser is aware of 'maidenhead' in its anatomical sense, referring to the hymen as the sign of a girl's virginity.   (p.145)

The associations he proposes, maidenhood and the hymen, are undeniably present and are particularly applicable in Books Three and Four. But in this lies a problem: the Order functions throughout the first five books (at least); and such is its prominence that its name may be expected to relate to the poem as a whole.

There is a strong possibility that the use of the name 'Maidenhead' for a chivalric order is intended to remind us immediately of the Order of the Garter. This latter order was founded by Edward III in 1348 with a tournament at Windsor Castle, where the Garter's headquarters, in St George's Chapel, have remained ever since. So strong is the association of the Garter with Windsor and its surrounding area that the writer of the *Liber Niger* (among others) even contrives (in order to impart a spurious aura of antiquity to Edward III's creation) to imply that the castle was one of the principal residences of King Arthur, in imitation of whose Round Table the Garter was established there (p. 21). The geographical connection between the Garter and the locality is sufficiently strong for Shakespeare to rely on his audience's awareness of it to comic effect in *The Merry Wives of Windsor*.[13] And this strong geographical association may lie behind the naming of Spenser's order in a similar way: the nearest town to Windsor, a little way up the Thames, is called Maidenhead. It is possible that, as well as containing the anatomical associations proposed by Hankins, Spenser's use of the name Maidenhead serves to alert the audience, through its topographical associations, to an

---

13 *Merry Wives of Windsor* IV.iii and v, for instance. See also William Green, *Shakespeare's 'Merry Wives of Windsor'* (Princeton: PUP, 1962), for a discussion of the play's many references to the Elizabethan Order of the Garter and to the Order's earlier history.

analogy between this invented Order and that existing at the court of Elizabeth.[14]

This is all the more likely given that the traditional civic heraldry of this part of the Royal County of Berkshire displays prominently the device of a maiden's head and shoulders, thus resembling those shields of Maidenhead borne in *The Faerie Queene* by Sir Satyrane and Sir Guyon.[15] The arms of Reading, confirmed in 1566, show five maidens' heads, one crowned; and this motif was found on the Common Seal of the town as early as 1365. Maidenhead was only granted its own civic bearings by the College of Arms in 1947; but the ancient Common Seal, showing the maiden's head, is recorded in the heraldic visitation by Henry Chitting and John Philipott on behalf of William Camden in 1623.

Bearing in mind this possible topographical allusion we should examine other aspects of the Order of Maidenhead with care. The relationship with the Garter is subsequently confirmed by references to the establishment of this Order and to St George as its principal patron-saint in the train of events leading up to Satyrane's tournament, the point at which the Order is most prominent in the poem. These references begin with Satyrane's simple action of finding Florimell's girdle.

Satyrane discovers Florimell's lost girdle on the seashore and uses it to tie up and thus pacify the Hyena which had been pursuing her. As has been noted by previous critics, this action closely resembles the defeat of the dragon in the *Golden Legend*'s 'Life of St George'. Having wounded the dragon, St George

> after sayd to the mayde, delyver to me your gyrdell, and bynde it aboute the necke of the dragon, and be not aferde. Whan she had done soo, the dragon folowed her as it had be a meke beest and debonayre.[16]

The use of the maiden's girdle and its effect on the beast recur in Satyrane's battle with the Hyena:

[14] Camden in fact uses the same etymology as Hankins to explain the town's name, which he derives from 'the superstitions [sic] worshipping of I wote not what British *Maidens-head*' (*Britannia*, p. 286).

[15] See C. Wilfred Scott-Giles, *Civic Heraldry of England and Wales* (1933; revised edition, Dent, 1953), pp. 52-53; Geoffrey Briggs, *Civic and Corporate Heraldry: A Dictionary of Impersonal Arms of England, Wales, and Northern Ireland* (Heraldry Today, 1971), pp. 250-52 and 319-20; *Official Guide to Reading* [Gloucester: BPC for Reading District Council, 1977], p. 10; and, for the Maidenhead seal, *The Four Visitations of Berkshire*, ed. W. Harry Rylands, Harleian Society vols LVI and LVII (1907, 1908), vol. LVI, p. 64.

[16] *The Golden Legend* in *The Life of St George*, p. 114. I have normalized the punctuation.

> The golden ribband, which that virgin wore
> About her sclender wast, he tooke in hand,
> And with it bound the beast, that lowd did rore
> For great despight of that unwonted band,
> Yet dared not his victour to withstand,
> But trembled like a lambe, fled from the pray,
> And all the way him followd on the strand (III.vii.36.1-7)

Despite critical awareness of this allusion to the *Golden Legend*, no explanation has been given of Spenser's reasons, if any, for linking Satyrane and the Hyena with St George and the dragon. Indeed these reasons remain obscure until the arrival of Sir Paridell, whose comments specify the context in which the battle should be seen. The latter informs Satyrane that all the knights of Gloriana's court have left in search of Florimell. In saying this, and in describing their adventure as a 'quest' (III.viii.50.8), Paridell redefines the combat with the Hyena in chivalric terms. Satyrane accepts and adopts this chivalric context, telling Paridell that,

> dead, I surely doubt, thou maist aread
> Henceforth for ever *Florimell* to be,
> That all the noble knights of *Maydenhead*,
> Which her ador'd, may sore repent with me (III.viii.47.5-8)

The finding of Florimell has become the quest of 'all the brave knights, that doen in armes excell' (III.viii.46.7).

In this chivalric context the allusion to St George and his dragon may be comprehended. St George is both the patron-saint of England and specifically the patron of the Order of the Garter. His defeat of the dragon is the Order's most striking image, being represented on its principal badges, the Great and Lesser Georges. The many portraits of Garter knights prominently displaying their badges and particularly the astonishing portrait of Elizabeth I holding up to the onlooker the Lesser George are testimony to the image's prestige and peculiar significance.[17] As Roy Strong says, the image of St George was clearly regarded as a 'sacred badge or hieroglyph', a fact all the more remarkable given the saint's near-eclipse as a mere anonymous 'armed knight' in Edward VI's proposed revision of the Garter insignia.[18]

With Paridell's introduction of a chivalric context the allusion to St George becomes an allusion in particular to that saint as patron of the Order of the Garter. Again, we must wait until the tournament to see the full significance of this comparison. But in the meantime we may indicate some of the local, yet telling points perceived through

---

[17] See Roy Strong, *Portraits of Queen Elizabeth I*, catalogue no. P. 28.
[18] Roy Strong, *The Cult of Elizabeth*, p.185.

an awareness of the reference to St George. In Chapter Three I briefly interpreted the struggle with the Hyena as representing Satyrane's battle with his own concupiscence. In Tudor allegoriz-ations of the Garter badge this is precisely the meaning drawn from the combat with the dragon. The *Liber Niger* confirms this, albeit grudgingly surrendering St George to allegory:

> I shall not contradict those who will make an Allegory of ... [the badge], so they do not deny the Certainty of this History. Suppose every one *George*, who being cloathed with the Virtue of Baptism and Armor of Faith, keeps his earthly Body in Subjection by the due Exercise of Religion and Piety; and by the Armour of the Spirit overcomes, and by true spiritual Arts, crushes and confounds the Serpent's Poison, the Snares of the old Dragon, and his diabolical Arts and Stratagems.   (p.39)

The anonymous author falls easily and naturally into the style and forms of martial symbolism when interpreting the badge, his phrasing obviously echoing that of the Epistle to the Ephesians. This interpret-ation of the combat with the dragon confirms the account of Satyrane's struggle: both he and St George are fighting against their own propensity towards evil, and particularly against the lusts of the flesh.

The interpretations of badge and battle strengthen the connections between them. But of greater significance is the crucial difference highlighted through this comparison. For whereas St George subdues and ultimately kills the dragon, saving the Lady, Sir Satyrane fails in all respects: the Hyena escapes and Florimell is lost, presumed dead. This difference is significant in both the immediate moral allegory and in the effect of the allusions to the Order of the Garter. Satyrane is shown unable to achieve the perfection of St George (for whom he was also an inadequate substitute in Book One). But as a result of this episode and of his wearing of the lost girdle, he assumes the leadership of the Knights of Maidenhead at the tournament. He does so, despite the fact that his failure to control the Hyena is in direct contrast to the successful act depicted on the badges of the Garter, the Order of Maidenhead's counterpart in the Elizabethan world. This contrast is our first indication that the Order of Maidenhead is not the ideal chivalric institution we might expect in *The Faerie Queene*. The imperfection of Satyrane and of the Order is confirmed at the tournament which results from the finding of the girdle.

After the escape of the Hyena, Satyrane takes up the girdle and wears it, giving rise to hostility among his fellow knights. As the Squire of Dames explains,

> Full many knights ...
> Thereat did greatly grudge, that he alone

143

That lost faire Ladies ornament should weare,
And gan therefore close spight to him to beare:
Which he to shun, and stop vile envies sting,
Hath lately caus'd to be proclaim'd each where
A solemne feast, with publike turneying,
To which all knights with them their Ladies are to bring.

(IV.ii.26.2-9)

Tournaments for trophies were common. But in the details of the Squire of Dames's account the Elizabethan reader would have recognized specific allusions to the popular version of the Order of the Garter's origins. As John Selden recounts, for instance, the Order arose out of the response to the wearing of a lady's lost garter (significantly, as we shall see, a circular garment):

> Some and the most part affirme, that the King dancing with the Queen, or rather the Countess of *Salisburie* (whom he much affected) a Garter fell from her. The King took it up, and ware it on his leg, and, whether upon the Queens jelousie, or his Lords merrie observing it, told them *Hony soit que mal y pense*. And that he would make it the most honourable Garter that ever was worn. (p.362)

Edward III went on to establish the Order of the Garter at Windsor with a solemn feast and tournament.

The resemblances between Satyrane's problems with the girdle and Edward III's with the garter are clear. Both discover and wear a circular garment connected with chastity which has been lost by a lady. The wearing of each garment causes ill-feeling. Satyrane and Edward III both seek to obviate this by elevating the garment into a symbol or relic and both hold tournaments at which to celebrate their devotion. Edward does this by issuing a challenge on behalf of his new Order of the Garter; and Satyrane by doing the same, leading the members of the Order of Maidenhead as challengers. Step by step, the origins of Satyrane's tournament follow the pattern set in the establishment of the greatest of chivalric institutions, the Order of the Garter.

The name of the Order; the battle with the Hyena; the finding and wearing of the girdle; and the occasion of Satyrane's tournament: the resemblances in these four areas are the grounds for suggesting that the Order of Maidenhead is based much more closely than hitherto perceived on the iconography and legends of the Order of the Garter. We may further add that the sovereign of each is a virgin queen: Gloriana in *The Faerie Queene* and Elizabeth in the world beyond. And subsequent to Satyrane's tournament, Scudamour retrospectively applies the motto of the Garter to the events that took place there:

> Shame be his meede (quoth he) that meaneth shame. (IV.vi.6.1)

144

In order to appreciate the significance for *The Faerie Queene* of the connection between Maidenhead and the Garter we should briefly note the prominence of the latter at Elizabeth's court. Membership of the Garter was the highest accolade in the land and the Order formed the apex of the system of honour. It was not only the dominant chivalric institution in England, but was preeminent among European orders of knighthood. William Camden proudly informs us that twenty-two foreign emperors and kings had been members up to his day.[19] Membership was indeed highly coveted, both at home and abroad: to gain the honour the Duke of Wurttemberg made a trip to England, pleaded and lied, bribed and threatened over a period of ten years; and was finally admitted only after the queen's death.[20] Elizabeth wisely kept all the orders of knighthood select, thus retaining their elitist allure: hence her fury at the so-called 'Essex knights', the many creations of the dangerous Earl which devalued the honours he dispensed.[21] In particular Elizabeth limited the creation of the Garter knights: in 1592 ten of the twenty-five stalls were vacant, not for want of candidates.[22] The exclusiveness of the Garter enabled it to remain highly prized, unlike the constantly diluted orders of chivalry of other European countries.

The Garter's preeminence was reflected in the attitude of the populace. Its rituals and ceremonies attracted vast crowds and the Order became a potent weapon in the queen's propaganda armoury. For instance the election of new knights and the various rituals merit frequent mention in the news which Philip Gawdy, a scion of the gentry and minor figure at court, sends home to his brother and nephew, successive heads of his family.[23] The Garter was a favourite motif for artists and sitters, and for poets in praising the queen and her court.[24]

In Spenser's poem the Order of Maidenhead occupies a similar

---

[19] Camden, *Britaine*, pp. 287-88.
[20] Strong, *Cult of Elizabeth*, p.178.
[21] See H.H. Leonard, *Knights and Knighthood in Tudor England*, unpublished PhD dissertation, University of London (1970), pp.120-25.
[22] Leonard, pp.176-77.
[23] See *The Letters of Philip Gawdy*, ed. Isaac Herbert Jeayes (Roxburghe Club, 1906), pp.51, 70, 78, and 81-82.
[24] See, for instance, Peele's 'The Honour of the Garter' and the portrait of Elizabeth I holding the Lesser George; and the portraits of the Earl of Nottingham and Lord Burghley in the National Portrait Gallery (Strong, *Tudor and Jacobean Portraits* [HMSO, 1969] 2 vols, catalogue nos 4434 and 362). As late as 1713 the Garter remains a sufficiently potent image for it to be used satirically in 'The Blue Garter no more a Sign of Honesty than a Gilded Bush is of Good Wine'!

position at Gloriana's court, being the highest rung on the ladder of honour. Guyon tells Prince Arthur,

> But were your will, her sold to entertaine,
> And numbred be mongst knights of *Maydenhed*,
> Great guerdon, well I wote, should you remaine,
> And in her favour high be reckoned,
> As *Arthegall* and *Sophy* now beene honored.   (II.ix.6.5-9)

The status of the Order of Maidenhead at Gloriana's court and of the Garter at Elizabeth's should make us question what use Spenser makes of his Order and the purposes behind his allusion to its counterpart in Elizabethan England.

3. Satyrane's Tournament

I

Satyrane's tournament has received little critical attention and there has been little agreement concerning its interpretation. T.K. Dunseath describes it as 'chaos', with all the participants (except Britomart) tarred through the animal imagery with the same bestial brush.[25] On the other hand Alastair Fowler has seen it as 'a poetic imitation of a *balletic* tournament, of a kind which actually took place in the sixteenth century'.[26] Fowler discovers subtle numerological patterns which seem to establish differences, denied by Dunseath, between various figures and actions (pp.178-180).

Both critics have their points. Dunseath rightly indicates the ferocity and brutalized nature of the fighting, which contrasts wildly with the courtly tilting of the 'balletic' tournaments of the day, in which successful blows and serious injuries were comparatively rare. Yet Fowler places the tournament in its essential context for the reader; just as the full appreciation of many Elizabethan tournaments, with all their colour and glitter, required of the onlooker a developing interpretation, so that of Satyrane must also be read with an eye for meaning as well as movement.[27] For this exercise, Spenser's original audience would have been well prepared, not merely enjoying the tournament for the exciting description of combat. Keeping

---

25 *Spenser's Allegory of Justice*, pp.32 and 36.
26 *Spenser and the Numbers of Time*, pp.179-180.
27 Of the many writers on this subject, see Jean Wilson's introduction to *Entertainments for Elizabeth I* (Woodbridge: D.S. Brewer, 1980), pp.31-38.

his family informed once more, Philip Gawdy retails news of all the latest tournaments; and on one occasion he expresses his disappointment. But this is not because of any lack of valour displayed; instead Gawdy complains that the intellectual standard has dropped:

> Uppon Saterday was the running of the tilt very well performed, thoughe not so full of devises and so riche as I have seene. (p. 25)

Martial skill was — at best — half the point. Gawdy's priorities are reflected in the *Arcadia*, where Pyrochles, describing the Iberian tournament, confesses that 'the delight of those pleasing sights have carried me too far into an unnecessary discourse'; but he has only briefly recounted one passage of arms, the rest of his extended description being taken up with the costumes and their interpretation.[28]

Arthegall appears at Satyrane's tournament in the well-known guise of a Savage Knight; and Savage Knights are also found in Sidney's Iberian tournament and, Frances Yates suspects, in the Accession Day Tournament of 1584.[29] Such coincidence might lead us into a hasty pigeon-holing of Spenser's tournaments as the counterparts of Sidney's or those of Elizabethan England. But Arthegall's is the only armour described at Satyrane's tournament; and this indicates the different emphasis in Spenser's poem. Where others are primarily concerned with the delightful ceremonial and individual brilliance of dress and wit, Spenser subordinates these to the requirements of his overall allegory. He foregoes the set-piece of description in order to achieve clarity of meaning.

Spenser's knights are also unlike those of the *Arcadia* or of real Elizabethan tournaments in that they do not understand the allegory in which they take part. They recognise devices only as means of identification, not as requiring interpretation.[30] It is the reader who interprets as allegory that which seems to the combatants purely physical. In this sense the analogy with actual tournaments must be qualified. Unlike Sidney's, Spenser's tournaments are not really very similar, in detail, to those of the Elizabethan court; but Spenser requires us to understand his tournaments by using some of the same interpretative methods as his contemporaries did when watching the stately spectacles of the late sixteenth century.

---

[28] *New Arcadia*, p. 355.
[29] *Astraea*, p. 91.
[30] The exception that proves the rule is, of course, the device of the red cross shared by St George and Sir Burbon, which is identified as 'his deare Redeemers badge' (V.xi.53.5).

To begin to understand Satyrane's tournament requires that we again stress its context. It is the occasion on which the Order of Maidenhead is most prominent in *The Faerie Queene*. And furthermore this tournament alludes to the similar event at which Edward III, it was believed, established the Order of the Garter.

Edward's supposed reasons for establishing a chivalric order are reported in the *Liber Niger*. The anonymous writer states that Edward,

> saw what a vast Increase of Piety, Nobility, and Virtue would accrue from thence; how our Countrymen would the easier accord amongst themselves, and Foreigners likewise be joined in the same Bond of Peace and Friendship with us. And that he might the sooner and more firmly gain this End, he suited Vests and Ornaments with Names proper for the Order, that every one might know, that all these Things tended to Virtue, Friendship and Concord. (pp. 24-25)

In passing it is noticeable again that, according to this writer at least, Edward III was well aware of martial and chivalric symbolism in the selection of 'Vests and Ornaments with Names proper for the Order'. Whatever Edward III's real views, it is clear that by the sixteenth century the Order of the Garter was considered a fount of virtue in national life. And the virtue most closely connected with it is that of 'Friendship and Concord', exactly the virtue celebrated and explored in Book Four of *The Faerie Queene*, the book in which Satyrane's tournament takes place.

The 'Vests and Ornaments' of the Order include, of course, the Garter itself. And the author of the *Liber Niger* goes on to stress that this garment particularly is symbolic of friendship, unity, and concord:

> For by that honourable and orbicular Garter ... the Knights were reminded, whatever they undertook to go thorow it with Piety, Sincerity, and Friendship, Faithfulness and Dexterity: That they should not undertake, or attempt any Thing contrary to the Oath and Institution of their Order ... That they should not stir a Foot contrary to their Fidelity, or what their Union and Band of Friendship required And that one Friend should not in the least derogate from another. (p. 26)

The garter symbolizes the ties of friendship and concord between the knights of the Order. We should also notice that the salient quality of the garter, the quality allowing it to bear this interpretation, is its circularity: it is 'orbicular' and can thus signify a 'Band of Friendship'.

The sense of the garter as binding together in a continuous circle reappears in later comments on the Order. Camden says that the Garter is, the bond of a most inward society, in token of concord and unity, that there might bee among them a certaine consociation and communion of vertues.[31]

Again we note that the Order of the Garter entails the integration of the virtues, the *summa perfectio* of Ramon Lull and Philip de Mézières; and especially it requires the virtue of concord. Finally, we may cite Elias Ashmole, perhaps the greatest of writers on the Garter, who reiterates that the garter was 'a Badge of *Unity* and *Concord*'.[32]

Such a context is obviously appropriate for Satyrane's tournament. It takes place to reestablish good relations among the various knights following Satyrane's contentious wearing of the lost girdle. Spenser stresses its potential for creating concord out of discord when the invocation of the mere prospect of the tournament is sufficient to pacify various fractious knights. The Squire of Dames mentions it to reunite (at least on the surface) Paridell and Blandamour (IV.ii.25-27). Cambina similarly calms Blandamour, Paridell, Triamond, and Cambell on their way to take part (IV.iv.5; 12). Finally, the tournament takes place in the Book of Friendship and in its fourth canto. As Alastair Fowler has pointed out, such placing should render it the very heart of concord in the poem.[33] The tournament then, which is the showcase for the Order of Maidenhead, should provide that institution with the perfect opportunity to imitate its model in the establishment of order, concord, and virtue.

It opens with a formal procession, and this again recalls the Elizabethan Order of the Garter. During Elizabeth's reign the procession of the Knights of the Garter was greatly developed as a spectacle and was extremely popular.[34] In that procession, as at Satyrane's event, 'the knights in couples marcht' (IV.iv.14.9) as can be seen in contemporary illustrations.[35]

This initial procession introduces the expected sense of potential concord and order in Book Four. Processions of participants in which the allegorical burden of the display was revealed were a major feature of Elizabethan tournaments, as in the Accession Day Tournament of 1590 when Sir Henry Lee resigned his role as Queen's Champion.[36] Satyrane's procession, although not containing the detailed meaning of the tournament, indicates the direction it is to

31 Camden, *Britaine*, p. 278.
32 Ashmole, p. 183.
33 Fowler, *Spenser and the Numbers of Time*, pp. 24-33; see also pp. 175-82.
34 See Strong, *Cult of Elizabeth*, pp. 168-173.
35 As in the engraving by Marcus Gheeraerts the Elder of the Garter procession of 1576 (reproduced in Strong, *Cult of Elizabeth*, plates 80-83).
36 Yates, *Astraea*, pp. 102-104.

take: Alastair Fowler has shown that the grouping of figures in the procession gives it a tetradic structure, further contributing to the symbolism of concord (p.177).

But the unity thus signalled is disrupted by the presence of Brag-gadocchio, who,

> rather chose,
> For glorie vaine their fellowship to lose,
> That men on him the more might gaze alone.   (IV.iv.14.4-6)

His self-isolation upsets all numerological calculations here, as Fowler suggests it does also in the total number of contestants involved in the tilting (p.179). And we notice that it is 'fellowship' or friendship that is lost by his egotistical isolation, the theme of the book and of the chivalric order. There are other indications that the harmony implied in the procession is superficial: to group themselves for it, incomers 'did divide / Them selves asunder' (IV.iv.14.1-2). Spenser's division of the phrase by the line ending may deliberately make concrete the latent discord and disunion disguised by the apparent concord of the procession.

There is a further source of disquiet in the description of the opening of the tournament. The procession's ceremonial is excessive and suspect:

> Then first of all forth came Sir *Satyrane*,
>   Bearing that precious relicke in an arke
>   Of gold, that bad eyes might it not prophane:
>   Which drawing softly forth out of the darke,
>   He open shewd, that all men it mote marke.
>   A gorgeous girdle, curiously embost
>   With pearle and precious stone, worth many a marke;
>   Yet did the workmanship farre passe the cost:
> It was the same, which lately *Florimel* had lost.
>
> The same aloft he hong in open vew,
>   To be the prize of beautie and of might;   (IV.iv.15; 16.1-2)

The problem here is both a matter of decorum and of religious principle. There is, firstly, a disproportion between the object, Flori-mell's girdle, and the reverence with which it is treated. But more seriously, Satyrane's conduct, hiding the girdle from the profanation of the eyes of the unworthy and then solemnly revealing it, is reminiscent of Roman Catholic ritual: the girdle is a 'precious relicke' hidden mysteriously within an 'arke of gold'. There is more than a whiff of Papistry in this behaviour.

If we are right in sensing excess — or worse — here, a further irony is to be found in the relationship between Sir Satyrane and St George. According to the *Golden Legend*, the reason for the latter's martyrdom was his refusal to participate in idolatry, to worship 'precious relickes'.[37] The silent comparison with St George again undermines Satyrane's standing as a virtuous knight.

But Satyrane's questionable devotion to the 'relicke' sheds a further interesting, and complicating, light on the analogy with the Order of the Garter's history in the sixteenth century. The Garter was itself regarded as religiously suspect following the Reformation: its elaborate and mysterious ceremonies; its organization derived from and so reminiscent of a monastic order; its 'Vests and Ornaments', with their clear and acknowledged symbolism; all these seemed to indicate the habits of mind of the old religion, Roman Catholicism. And after Henry VIII's death, the more radically reformist administration confronted the issue: Edward VI's reign saw a series of determined attempts to set the Garter to Protestant rights. The preamble to the boy-king's abortive revision of the Order's statutes speaks of its 'pristine and auncyent fundation':

> Our most noble progenitors, kinges of Englande, studiyinge and consider-ing with themselfes of the duetie they ought to shewe towardes God, their contrye, and those that be under their obeysaunce, They sone founde that nothyng dyd so much bilonge to their office as to advance to honor and glory good, godly, valiant, well couraged, wise and noble men for their notable desertes, and to nourishe a certaine amytie, fellowship, and agrement in all honest thinges among all men, but specially among equalles in degre, for they do judge honor, as surely it is, the rewarde of vertue, and concorde the fundation and enlarger of common weales.[38]

Edward's version is immediately recognizable as containing many of the standard elements of works in praise of the Garter, albeit these elements are dressed in the 'godly' terminology of the more radical reformers. But the king goes on to assert that the Garter has been polluted and diverted from its original course:

> which ordre, being of all mens mouthes commended, that serpent Satan, adversary to mankinde, dyd seeke holly to distroye, whenne he beheld it inkindeled men so much to vertue.[39]

And the Devil's method was to stuff 'the statutes of this fellowship with many doubtefull, superstitious, and repugnant opinions' (p.184).

Edward and his advisors, William Cecil prominent among them (his autograph appears on the manuscripts as well as that of the king),

[37] *Golden Legend* in *The Life of St George*, pp.114-16.
[38] Edward Maude Thompson, 'The Revision of the Statutes of the Order of the Garter by King Edward the Sixth', *Archaeologia* LIV (1894), p.184. See also Strong, *Cult of Elizabeth*, p.166.
[39] P.184. Thompson demonstrates the king's own 'painful tinkering' with these statutes (p.198).

attacked primarily the vestiges of the cult of saints: the name of St George was to be expunged, 'lest the honor which is onely dew unto God shulde be thereby abused'; and the image of the saint slaying the dragon to be replaced by 'the picture of an armed knight on horsbake with a sweard, with a garter of gold enamel' (p.186). And, in case this was still not clear, the statutes continue explicitly:

> seeing this honor is taken from Sainct George, that he shalbe no lenger Patrone of thordre, the knightes shall weare no more that picture [of George and the dragon] after the feast of Whitsontid next comming.
> (p.186)

These revisions to the Garter statutes were worked on from around the third year of Edward's reign; but they were never finalized and died with him in 1553. However, the religious scruples which had caused his concern did not vanish and there were criticisms of the more papistical trappings of royal pagenatry and court life throughout Elizabeth's reign: the queen had to ward off successive attempts by her own hierarchy of bishops to deprive her of the candlesticks, vestments, and saints' images of her private chapels.[40] In Edward VI's revisions of the Garter statutes there is clear embarrassment at the vestment-like garments of the Order, 'Mantles only' at one point being substituted, in the king's hand, for 'Roobes' (p.188). The same scruple arose in Elizabeth's reign when Frederick II of Denmark refused to accept the insignia of the Garter for a time in 1582 because they smacked of Roman Catholicism. As a correspondant of Sir Francis Walsingham reported from Copenhagen, the king doubted the godliness

> especially of the robes, being a thing so contrary to his nature to have any strange attire or superstitious to come on his back, 'as by no means he can away with it,' in such sort that he protests that he cannot be 'at quiet' till he is assured that my lord [Elizabeth's ambassador] will 'dispense with' him herein. I let the [king's] ambassador understand that the habit was of an ancient and grave fashion, very comely and full of reverence, neither anything, as he suspects, papistical therein.[41]

Eventually the king accepted the George and garter only, refusing the robes. Satyrane's procession of the girdle, with its mystery and ritual paraphernalia, is open to exactly the same attacks as was its counterpart, the Garter.

---

[40] For a recent account of Elizabeth's struggles with the Anglican hierarchy over her ecclesiastical paraphernalia, see Patrick Collinson, *Archbishop Grindal (1519-1583): The Struggle for a Reformed Church* (Cape, 1979), pp.167-176; especially p.167.

[41] W.Waad to Walsingham; *CSP Foreign Series, May – December 1582* (HMSO, 1909), p.215. See Strong, *Cult of Elizabeth*, p.178.

Once the fighting at the tournament begins, all attempts to preserve order and concord are abandoned and our doubts concerning
the moral quality of some of the combatants amply confirmed. In
seeing the tournament as giving expression to the faults of many of
the participants I agree with T.K. Dunseath; but we must be careful
to understand the precise way in which Spenser leads us to condemn
them, and here Dunseath's argument requires refinement.[42]

Although Satyrane emerges victorious from the first day's battle,
his triumph is rendered suspect by the terms in which it is described.
Spenser tells us that, as *victor ludorum*,

> *Satyrane* that day was judg'd to beare the bell.　　(IV.iv.25.9)

'The bell' in this line may refer to the prize given at races or contests
in classical times. But the form of the phrase here recalls that of the
saying, 'to bear the bell', which derives from 'the bell worn by the
leading cow or sheep ... of a drove or flock'.[43] Dunseath, as has
already been remarked, sees in the extensive use of animal imagery at
the tournament evidence of the dehumanized nature of the contestants. This phrase applied to Satyrane would seem to confirm his
view, since it makes the knight outstanding on the first day only as
the leading animal, the bell-wether at the head of the herd. Furthermore, the same phrase is used to describe the victory of the false
Florimell in the cestus competition of the following canto (IV.v.13.6).
To be thus associated with the personification of the false and
sexually incontinent reflects no credit on Satyrane.

Overall, however, Dunseath's argument seems anachronistic unless
it is qualified. Spenser uses animal imagery elsewhere in *The Faerie
Queene* without derogatory overtones; and its presence in battle
scenes without pejorative connotations is sanctioned by epic
tradition.[44] Nonetheless the animal imagery is worthy of attention
because it reveals, not the common bestiality of the combatants, but
differences between them, between groups of characters during the
tournament.

Spenser's intention and effect can be seen when he allows us to
compare Satyrane with the second day's victors. Satyrane is defeated

[42] Dunseath, pp.31-39.
[43] *OED* sb1 III 7. See also Morris Palmer Tilley, *A Dictionary of Proverbs in
England in the Sixteenth and Seventeenth Centuries* (Ann Arbor: Michigan
UP, 1950), B.275; and Bartlett Jere Whiting and Helen Wescott Whiting,
*Proverbs, Sentences, and Proverbial Phrases from English Writings Mainly
Before 1500* (Cambridge, Mass.: Harvard UP, 1968), B.230.
[44] See for instance the *Aeneid* 12. 715-721.

by Cambell, which Dunseath sees as merely confirming their similarity:

> Cambell, in envying Satyrane's glory as the ruler of beasts, becomes animal-like in turn. (p.34)

And of both Cambell and Triamond he says,

> Their style of battle is appropriate and not out of keeping with the standards established by Satyrane. (p.34)

Even before analyzing Dunseath's grounds for this suggestion one must hesitate to agree with him, since he disregards the obvious virtue, stressed by Spenser, displayed by these two knights, the friendship celebrated in the book of which they are jointly patron. And these reservations are justified when one comes to study the animal imagery, which, far from establishing the similarities between Satyrane and Cambell (or Triamond), enables us to distinguish between them. Satyrane is compared to a bull and to the leading animal of a herd. Cambell is compared to a lion, as Arthegall is later in the tournament; and Cambell and Triamond are compared to a pair of wolves. The obvious difference is that Satyrane is compared to domesticated, herd animals, albeit as the leader of a herd; whereas Cambell, Triamond, and Arthegall are all compared to animals which prey on the herd.

One simile may serve to elucidate this point. The fighting of Cambell and Triamond is such

> As when two greedy Wolves doe breake by force
> Into an heard, farre from the husband farme,
> They spoile and ravine without all remorse,
> So did these two through all the field their foes enforce.
> (IV.iv.35.6-9)

Were Spenser's concern the degradation of humanity into beast-like ferocity, Cambell and Triamond would be damned indeed (as Satan is as a result of just such a simile in *Paradise Lost* [IV.183-87]). But to interpret Spenser's simile thus would be to mistake vehicle for tenor; and besides, the context should lead us to expect a reversal of normal attitudes. Instead of forcing entry into a defenceless herd, Cambell has been taken prisoner and he, with Triamond, is fighting his way out. Their situation, in fact, is the exact reverse of that of the wolves. Spenser's point does not lie in the fact that they are bestial but in the relationship between wolves (and later lions) and the 'heard': Cambell and Triamond are wolf-like because they oppose and fight against the herd of the Order of Maidenhead. Cambell and Arthegall are compared to lions for the same reason. It is through the

154

animal imagery that they are differentiated from the Order on this occasion.

It will be noticed immediately that the three combatants thus distinguished from the 'heard' are the three knights-patron who take part in the tournament before the arrival of Britomart. Unlike previous critics, we can now suggest that these two groups, the Knights of Maidenhead and the knights-patron, are not one and the same. Although there is some overlap in membership, at Satyrane's tournament they appear in total opposition to each other.

This opposition is not arbitrary. The knights-patron fight against the Order of Maidenhead, as it is manifested in this tournament, because it is corrupt. Just as Satyrane's deficiencies are highlighted by the implied comparison with St George, so the Order of Maidenhead is revealed as imperfect through the analogy with the Garter. As has been seen, the ritual of the tournament is religiously suspect; and there are among the Knights of Maidenhead individuals who do not fulfil those expectations of virtuous and honourable living, and particularly of friendship and concord, aroused by allusions to the Garter and by the placement of the tournament in the poem. And these individuals include Satyrane, who on this occasion acts as the leader of the Order.

The Order of the Garter's principal aim was the promotion of concord. The coincidence of this virtue with the subject of Spenser's fourth book makes the failure of the tournament to promote, or even preserve, friendship among the knights of the 'heard' all the more catastrophic. The discord reigning among the Knights of Maidenhead, which breaks out openly and violently at the cestus competition, is indicative of their more general failure in terms of the *summa perfectio*. And Spenser underlines their disharmony and lack of virtue by having them opposed in chief by the dual patrons of the virtue of friendship, Cambell and Triamond.

After their victory on the second day of combat, these two knights enact a perfect demonstration of their virtue; and in so doing they raise it from the purely human quality of friendship to kinship with the universal virtue of divine concord. In deference to the other, each refuses to accept the prize as the second day's best warrior:

> Then all with one consent did yeeld the prize
> To *Triamond* and *Cambell* as the best.
> But *Triamond* to *Cambell* it relest.
> And *Cambell* it to *Triamond* transferd;
> Each labouring t'advance the others gest,
> And make his praise before his owne preferd: (IV.iv.36.3-8)

Characteristically, their victory enables the many-headed multitude to speak with one voice, to achieve 'one consent'. And although there are only two figures involved in the action, Spenser wittily contrives to allude to one of the poem's dominating iconographical schemes. The representation of the names in the text —

> *Triamond* and *Cambell*
> *Triamond* to *Cambell*
> *Cambell* it to *Triamond*

— suggests the pattern of the Three Graces:

> two of them still froward seem'd to bee,
> But one still towards shew'd her selfe afore;   (VI.x.24.7-8)

And as in the dance of the Graces, the reciprocity of Cambell and Triamond is never ending, since 'the doome was to another day differd' (IV.iv.36.9), a day which never comes in the poem as we have it. But Spenser's elegant allusion is not a redundant finesse; when we reach the description of Mount Acidale in Book Six we realise that Cambell and Triamond have acted out one of the blessings attributed to the Graces:

> These three on men all gracious gifts bestow ...
> As comely carriage, entertainement kynde,
> Sweete semblaunt, *friendly offices that bynde*,
> And all the complements of curtesie:
>
> (VI.x.23.1-6; my italics)

The friendly offices of Cambell and Triamond in the mutual resignation of the prize show them to be possessed of the heavenly concord of the Graces.

The difference between the knights-patron of Friendship and the Knights of Maidenhead is humourously pointed when Spenser parodies his own verse and the pattern of the Graces in the lustful quarrel that erupts over the possession of the false Florimell:

> Thereat exceeding wroth was *Satyran*;
> And wroth with *Satyran* was *Blandamour*;
> And wroth with *Blandamour* was *Erivan*;
> And at them both Sir *Paridell* did loure.   (IV.v.24.1-4)

This too is a kind of reciprocity. Aptly the parody ends with Sir Paridell, the descendent of that Paris who caused the Trojan war and had to decide the fate of the apple of discord (the lust of the goddesses for that prize is perhaps the iconographical scheme underlying the acrimony of the cestus contest). Paridell, though presented humourously, is treated seriously by Spenser as a perverter of the chivalric ideal; his story is one of 'knighthood fowle defaced by a faithlesse knight' (III.ix.1.9). Yet he is a member of the Order of Maidenhead. Instead of friendship, concord, and the desire to give, the Knights of Maidenhead are concerned only with the possession of the worthless false Florimell; those knights-patron present refuse to have anything to do with her. The tournament, instead of concluding as a celebration of harmony and order, ends in chaos.

The events of the third day of the tournament may be thought to invalidate these conclusions concerning the role of the knights-patron in opposition to the Order of Maidenhead. Britomart, another knight-patron, rescues the knights of the Order from total defeat at the hands of Sir Arthegall. But our assessment of her role must include our awareness that she is an outsider, not of Gloriana's court and, in particular, not a member of the Order of Maidenhead. She is, furthermore, a woman and an unknown. In the course of the fighting she is never likened to an animal, either of the wild or of the 'heard'. In fact her position is metaphorically superior to that of all present; and she acts to prevent an excessive or inflamatory outcome. Spenser likens her to

> A watry cloud [that] doth overcast the skie,
> And poureth forth a sudden shoure of raine,
> That all the wretched world recomforteth againe.   (IV.iv.47.7-9)

Continuing the metaphor, Spenser states that she relieves, not one party or the other, but 'all brute beasts ... [which] doe hunt for shade' (IV.iv.47.3-4).

Britomart's victory suspends the defeat of the Knights of Maidenhead. She acts, as her superior position suggests, as a kind of *dea ex machina* descending to prevent the wholesale rout of the Order at the hands of the other titular knights. Why such a suspension is necessary is perhaps explained by reference to the only suit of tournament armour Spenser describes. Although the poet does not follow contemporary practice in endowing each of his knights with an outlandish costume, he does expect his audience to apply their minds to the interpretation of Arthegall's guise of the Salvage Knight:

> all his armour was like salvage weed,
> With woody mosse bedight, and all his steed
> With oaken leaves attrapt, that seemed fit
> For salvage wight, and thereto well agreed
> His word, which on his ragged shield was writ,
> *Salvagesse sans finesse*, shewing secret wit.   (IV.iv.39.4-9)

Arthegall's disguise confirms the division expressed by the animal imagery: the Salvage Knight is an outsider like the wolves and the lions. But this much is obvious and cannot be the explanation of the 'secret wit' of the costume, especially of the motto. Arthegall's 'salvagesse' seems clear enough; and the crux, perhaps, lies in the fact that he is 'sans finesse'. 'Finesse' is normally interpreted as refinement; but it can also mean fineness or the ability to make subtle distinctions.[45] In the tournament, Arthegall's destruction of the Order of Maidenhead threatens to be absolute and indiscriminate:

> his sword he drew,
> The instrument of wrath, and with the same
> Far'd like a lyon in his bloodie game,
> Hewing, and slashing shields, and helmets bright,
> And beating downe, what ever nigh him came   (IV.iv.41.3-7)

This has all the finesse of a blunt instrument. Wielding his 'instrument of wrath' like the avenging angel, Arthegall slashes, beats, and hews in a career of wholesale destruction, presented in disturbingly vivid verse by Spenser. Arthegall's victory is liable to be too absolute: the virtuous as well as the vicious will be annihilated, and the positive aspects and possibilities of the chivalric institution will disappear together with their inverse. Britomart, the knight of wisdom and prudence as well as chastity, introduces the necessary tempering, the necessary 'finesse', needed to stabilize the outcome of the tournament. The Order of Maidenhead is preserved from absolute destruction, though defeated; but it is not preserved by its own power, for that would confirm it in its corruption. Instead the third day's combat is won by Britomart, who stands outside both the warring groups: intervening from a position of superior wisdom, she prevents Arthegall from completely abolishing that which is perhaps capable of reformation.

45 *OED* Finesse sb2.

VI: THE EMBLEMS OF KNIGHTHOOD AND MARINELL'S TOURNAMENT

Satyrane's tournament is deeply unsatisfactory: it ends in shambles; and the following cestus competition serves only to reveal more clearly the vices which unite and divide the various Knights of Maidenhead. The conclusion effected by Britomart's intervention is temporary and resolves none of the problems of the Order.

We have to wait until the tournament celebrating the spousal of Marinell and Florimell to see a fitting conclusion to the themes of the earlier event. The second tournament obviously recalls, and is intended to recall, the first in many of its details: its three-day structure, for instance, and the presence of such characters as Braggadocchio and the false Florimell, whose joint triumph summed up all that was wrong with Satyrane's event. But by contrast Marinell's tournament has a conclusive air: it is the terminus for the story of Braggadocchio; his snowy consort melts into thin air; the real Florimell and her husband are united by Arthegall's intervention and then are never mentioned again; and Spenser even reactivates and resolves an all-but-forgotten unfinished element in the history of Sir Guyon, before letting that knight once more retreat into the background.

Few commentators perceive this event as in any way conclusive, despite these examples. But while not claiming dominance for Marinell's tournament in Book Five, let alone in a wider view, even the series of resolutions noted above makes the tournament stand out as a moment of rare transition in the poem, in which one set of narrative lines, which have persisted for several books, is concluded and gives way to another.

The unusual decisiveness of this episode extends beyond the various strands in the narrative, however, into the chivalric symbolism briefly noted in the previous chapter as existing in the genesis of Satyrane's tournament. And in order to comprehend the peculiar standing of the spousals tournament this play on symbols must be confronted and explained. The combat itself receives little attention from Spenser; instead the action centres on a number of weapons and other attributes, all of which possess chivalric significance, and all of which are repossessed from unfit owners. Their prominence enables the poet to encapsulate and resolve, at least in outline, his theme of knightly worthiness.

159

1. Braggadocchio's Degradation and the Return of the Emblems of Knighthood

I

At Satyrane's tournament, there was a gradual and unemphatic emphasis on the spear as the dominant weapon. Satyrane himself, when he opens the fighting, takes

> in hand
> A huge great speare, such as he wont to wield.   (IV.iv.17.1-2)

Triamond's anger at Braggadocchio's cowardice is expressed through an action involving the same weapon:

> But *Triamond* halfe wroth to see him staid,
> Sternly stept forth, and raught away his speare   (IV.iv.20.5-6)

Finally the tournament is concluded by the arrival of the 'Knight of the Hebene Speare':

> for no powre of man
> Could bide the force of that enchaunted speare,
> The which this famous *Britomart* did beare;   (IV.iv.46.3-5)

Spenser provides no commentary to enable us to state confidently that this apparent prominence of the spear is more than fortuitous; or if it is significant, what is signified. However, we may speculate that the essence of the poet's meaning is contained in Triamond's action: he, one of the patrons of the book, deprives the falsest of the pretenders to knighthood, Braggadocchio, of one of the principal attributes of a warrior.

This interpretation is highly speculative. But the suggested importance of Braggadocchio's dispossession by Triamond gains in credibility once one reaches Marinell's tournament, for at this event much of the action is taken up by the display and return of various weapons and emblems. In particular the forcible confiscation of a number of attributes forms the climax of the episode. And all of these attributes have one thing in common, that they are associated symbolically with the institution of knighthood.

II

The most obvious action involving the emblems of knighthood is that with which Marinell's tournament ends, the public disgrace of Braggadocchio: following the judgement of Arthegall, Talus enacts the formal degradation of the boaster from the office and dignity of a knight.

Braggadocchio is one of the most troublesome characters in *The Faerie Queene*, and not only for those who encounter him within the poem. Beginning his career as an insubstantial figure of fun, a stock *miles gloriosus*, his metamorphosis into the sinister, maleficent agent who attempts to blast the spousals tournament seems initially unthinkable; and some critics view this transformation as a failure.[1] Be that as it may, by Book Five it is Braggadocchio, not Paridell or Blandamour, who is the subject of the ritual violence meted out at the instigation of the Knight of Justice:

> First he his beard did shave, and fowly shent:
> Then from him reft his shield, and it renverst,
> And blotted out his armes with falshood blent,
> And himselfe baffuld, and his armes unherst,
> And broke his sword in twaine, and all his armour sperst.
>
> (V.iii.37.5-9)

The punishment is a detailed version of chivalric degradation. Upton attempts to explain its appropriateness, commenting that 'cowards in the lists were proclaimed false and perjured, their armour taken from them, beginning from their heals upwards, and then ignominiously flung piece by piece over the barriours: they were likewise dragged out of the lists and punished as the judges decreed'.[2] Although the chivalric context is correctly stressed here, Upton's confining of the punishment to those convicted of cowardice in tournaments is too restrictive and thus misleading. John Guillim's summary of the occasions of degradation defines more correctly the context in which Braggadocchio's fate should be seen:

> Degrading of Knights is not very customary, Examples being seldom found, it is used only for great and notable Facts and Offenses against Loyalty and Honour; as abscenting themselves dishonourably from their King's service; for leaving their Colours, and flying to the Enemy; for betraying Castles, Forts, and the like heinous Crimes.[3]

A knight was to be degraded, not for cowardice simply, but for crimes which denote unworthiness, for the lack of nobility they betoken. The rarity of the action increases its force when it is used.

Spenser follows the standard pattern of the chivalric degradation, a ceremony if anything more impressive than the creation of a

---

[1] See, for instance, John M. Hill, 'Braggadocchio and Spenser's Golden World Concept: The Function of Unregenerative Comedy', *ELH* 37 (1970), p. 317.

[2] *The Faerie Queene*, ed. John Upton, Vol. 2, p. 617.

[3] *A Display of Heraldry* (1610; 7th edition, 1724), p. 232.

knight. Guillim's account of the 'Manner of Degrading a Knight' can again be used as an example:

> When a Knight had been found thus disloyal and corrupt, he was to be apprehended, and armed Cap-a-pe, as if he was going to the Wars, was to be placed upon a high Scaffold made for the Purpose in the Church; and after the Priest had sung some Funeral Psalms, as are used at Burials, as though he had been dead, first they take off his Helmet to shew his Face, and so by Degrees his whole Armour: Then the Heralds proclaiming him a disloyal Miscreant, with many other Ceremonials to declare him Ignoble, he was thrown down the Stage with a Rope; and this was done about the time of King *Arthur*.   (p.232)

As Guillim states, degradation was rare. But it could still occur when a knight was convicted of 'great and notable Facts and Offenses against Loyalty' in Spenser's time. In 1569 the Earl of Northumberland was stripped of his membership of the Order of the Garter *in absentia* having been convicted of high treason:

> for the which detestable offence and high treason the said Thomas hath deserved to be disgraded of the said most noble Ordre, and expelled out of the said companye; and not worthy that his armes, ensigns, and hachements, shuld remayne amongst virtuous and approved Knights of the said most noble Ordre. Wherefore our most righteous Quene, supreme and Soveraigne of this our most noble Ordre, with the Companions now present of the same, wyll and command that these armes, ensigns, and hatchments, of the said Thomas, be taken away and throwne downe, and he be cleane put from this Ordre, & from henceforth to be none of the number thereof.[4]

A manuscript account of this degradation describes how the earl's arms were thrown down 'violently from the tabernacle whereon they hong, into the body of the quyre' of St George's Chapel, and after further indignities came to rest ignominiously in 'the dyke without the castell gate'.[5]

The account of the traitorous earl's expulsion conveys the value placed on its various symbols by chivalry. Not only is the man himself dishonourable, but his 'armes, ensignes, and hachements' have themselves become unworthy to 'remayne amongst virtuous and approved Knights'.

---

4   John Nichols, *The Progresses and Public Processions of Queen Elizabeth*, 3 vols (2nd edition, 1823), Vol.1, p.263.
5   BL Harley MS 304, f84v. Further details of degradings are given by Selden, pp.337-39.

III

It is important to recognize the reasons for Braggadocchio's fate. His degradation does not follow upon his cowardice in the lists; indeed, he takes no part in the fighting at the second tournament. Nor is it a result of his fraudulent claims to victory or his verbal assault on Florimell. The crucial prelude is the discovery of his theft of Guyon's horse.

Guyon's reappearance and the recovery of his property have been seen as evidence of the close connection between the virtues of Books Two and Five of *The Faerie Queene*. James Nohrnberg states that,

> Justice is now done to temperance: the golden girdle is restored to the lady who can wear it, and the horse with the golden bridle is returned to the knight who can manage it. The analogy here is the analogy of government. Braggadocchio's incontinence has consisted in his inability to resist appropriating the attributes of more noble natures.[6]

While Nohrnberg's explanation has much merit, the transformation of Braggadocchio's opportunistic exploitation of his chances into kleptomania is overwrought. Certainly, his unsuccessful lunge at Belphoebe can be described as intemperate; but it does not necessarily follow that Braggadocchio must always be tarred with this particular brush. After all, despite Nohrnberg's implication, the boaster has been able to ride Guyon's passionate horse well enough for three books, if a little uncertainly at times, and thus has not been conspicuous in his intemperance.

The sense of strain in this account derives from the desire to equate Guyon's horse consistently with the horse of the passions. But individual attributes, like individual characters, do not always retain a constant signification in *The Faerie Queene*. According to the context any of the latent meanings of an attribute can be brought into play. We recognize this readily enough in the case of more frequently used symbols, such as arrows: Cupid's arrows are different from Belphoebe's or Maleger's. But beyond the range of 'parallels the critic happens to be acquainted with', as Herbert Grabes puts it while making a similar point, we are less able to accept the need to be guided by context.[7] The theft of Guyon's horse is a good example of the dangers of assuming that the meaning we know for a symbol is necessarily appropriate on all occasions. It has been convincingly

---

6 Nohrnberg, p.356.
7 *The Mutable Glass: Mirror Imagery in Titles and Texts of the Middle Ages and English Renaissance* (Cambridge: Cambridge UP, 1982), p.7.

argued that Guyon loses the horse of the passions, control of which is required for the virtue of Temperance.[8] But it is by no means clear that, in terms of its symbolism, this is the same horse as that acquired by Braggadocchio. Spenser's description of the theft, and of the boaster's motivation, appears to define a different context altogether:

> The whiles a losell wandring by the way,
> One that to bountie never cast his mind,
> Ne thought of honour ever did assay
> His baser brest, but in his kestrell kind
> A pleasing vaine of glory vaine did find,
> To which his flowing toung, and troublous spright
> Gave him great ayd, and made him more inclind:
> He that brave steed there finding ready dight,
> Purloynd both steed and speare, and ran away full light. (II.iii.4)[9]

No connection, explicit or implicit, is made between the horse and the passions. What is more, we now realise that it is not just the horse that was stolen: Braggadocchio steals the spear also, not mentioned by Nohrnberg or others. Unlike the horse, the spear has no connection with temperance.

Reading this stanza without preconceptions we become aware that the theft of both horse and spear is associated above all with courtliness and honour (or their lack), the context suggested by such terms as 'glorie', 'honour', and 'bountie'. Braggadocchio's right to the horse and spear is not disdained because he is intemperate, but because he is utterly ignoble.

Although characterized temporarily by lust in his encounter with Belphoebe, intemperance does not dominate the presentation of Braggadocchio. His characterization centres primarily on his chivalric unworthiness; and in the course of the poem he accumulates a number of attributes which are symbolic of knighthood. As well as the armour, 'sperst' by Talus, Braggadocchio possesses or steals, and later loses, three things in *The Faerie Queene*: the horse, the spear, and the shield which Arthegall uses, and later reclaims, at Marinell's tournament. All have general connections with the courtly world of honour and nobility and are specifically symbolic of knighthood.

Little need be said of the shield's chivalric meaning beyond recalling the general conclusions of the first chapter. As Favyn remarks, 'the Scutcheon or Shield ... is the essential note of a Nobleman, as also of an Esquire and Knight'; and he later notes that 'the Shield

---

8 See *The Faerie Queene*, ed. A.C.Hamilton, pp.184 and 548, for a summary.
9 This quotation follows the Oxford English Texts edition of *The Faerie Queene* (1909) by J.C.Smith, whose retention of the second 'vaine' in line 5 follows the edition of 1596. See the similar repetition in *Amoretti* LXXV.5.

was the principall part of Armes for a Knight'.[10] It is in recognition of this symbolic role that Braggadocchio's shield bears the brunt of Talus's attentions, being reversed and having the device blotted out. This action is again drawn from the ritual dishonouring of those unworthy of knighthood; as John Guillim says, 'Also about the Degrading of Knights these Things have also been used; as the reversing of their Coat of Arms' (p. 232).

The kind and degree of significance attached to such treatment of a shield in *The Faerie Queene* can be gauged by comparison with the description of Verdant's armour in the Bower of Bliss:

> his brave shield, full of old moniments,
> Was fowly ra'st, that none the signes might see;
> Ne for them, ne for honour cared hee,
> Ne ought, that did to his advauncement tend   (II.xii.80.3-6)

Verdant's shield has lost the evidence of his nobility, office, and station. That which marked him out as a knight and of gentle birth has been erased. The fate of his shield represents symbolically the fall from nobility and honour in the man himself. His armour's destruction emblematizes the first stage of decline into Grill-like bestiality, in which humanity, not just nobility, is ultimately lost; and as a result the fate of Verdant's arms signifies more than idleness. In like manner Braggadocchio's degradation represents more than cowardice: rather it implies total unfitness for the responsibilities and honours of knighthood.

The fundamental significance of the shield to a knight is emphasized explicitly when Arthegall reprimands Sir Burbon for abandoning his red cross shield:

> Hard is the case, the which ye doe complaine;
> Yet not so hard (for nought so hard may light,
> That it to such a streight mote you constraine)
> As to abandon, that which doth containe
> Your honours stile, that is your warlike shield.   (V.xi.55.2-6)

At Marinell's tournament Braggadocchio loses the shield containing his 'honours stile' because he has no right to the honour it symbolizes. As in the case of Sir Burbon, it is Arthegall who states this explicitly:

> That shield, which thou doest beare, was it indeed,
> Which this dayes honour sav'd to *Marinell*;
> But not that arme, nor thou the man I reed,
> Which didst that service unto *Florimell*.   (V.iii.21.1-4)

---

[10] Favyn, pp.12 and 13.

The shield, as a symbol of the honour gained by the victor of the tournament, belongs to Arthegall, as surely as do the wounds received in the fighting.

The interpretation of the shield as a symbol of honour generally and as a symbol of knighthood in particular is reinforced when we consider the spear stolen by Braggadocchio, and repossessed by Triamond. To return to Favyn, 'the principall Armes of the French Chevaliers, was the Lance and Shield' (p.17). And not only the French, as Ashmole reminds us. He finds the donation of a spear and shield to be the principal sign of knighthood in all the Germanic races:

> among whom [the Germans], as *Tacitus* affirms, the *Shield* and *Launce* were accounted the grand *Badges* of *Military Honor*, or *Knighthood*.(p.27)

In *The Faerie Queene* this tradition is most obviously pertinent to Britomart's arming, which symbolizes her assumption of the role of a questing knight. Spenser's description distinguishes the shield and spear by repetition:

> Both speare she tooke, and shield, which hong by it:
> Both speare and shield of great powre, for her purpose fit.
> (III.iii.60.8-9)

As in much epic poetry, the formulaic conjunction of spear and shield becomes symbolic of the warrior or knight in *The Faerie Queene*. Although Braggadocchio gains his spear and shield on different occasions (indeed we are never told the origin of the shield) these two attributes are linked through their common fate: Talus 'from him reft his shield' after Arthegall's judgement; and the spear is 'raught away' from Braggadocchio by Triamond, another of the knights-patron, when the boaster hesitates to join in the previous tournament. In both cases the attributes act as symbols of the knighthood to which Braggadocchio pretends, symbols repossessed by representatives of true chivalry.

As with shield and spear, Braggadocchio's stolen horse is seized at a tournament. While the crowd stands amazed at the disappearance of the false Florimell,

> Sir *Guyon* as by fortune then befell,
> Forth from the thickest preasse of people came,
> His owne good steed, which he had stolne, to clame;
> (V.iii.29.3-5)

In this context, the return of Guyon to claim his horse draws attention to another chivalric symbol. Many writers comment on the central position of the horse in chivalric symbolism, alluding to the words for 'knight' in other European languages: 'Ritter' or 'chevalier', for example. The chivalry of the Christian era was frequently associated with the Roman equestrian order; in which, as its name suggests, the horse was accorded pride of place as a symbol:

> The *Equestrian Order* among the ancient *Romans* was conferr'd by particular Ceremonies, to wit, the donation of a *Horse*, or giving of a *Ring*.
>
> (p.21)

But, as Ashmole goes on to say,

> as the donation of a *Horse* was the ancienter badge of *Knighthood*, so were those to whom it was given, saith *Justus Lipsius, most anciently, properly, and alone in times past called* Equites.
>
> (p.21)

Selden also notes that for a warrior to be connected with a horse was a great honour in the ancient world, as it was in later Europe:

> As all these in this Western part expresse a speciall honor implying abilitie of martiall service with horse: so the old Greeks attributed not to a great man a better name then what truly was the same with every of those. That is, ιωωοτυς; whence Hecuba calls *Polymestor* King of *Thrace*, Θρρικι Θιωποτυς, and in Homer ιωωοτα *Nestor*. So the chief men and of best worth in *Chalcis* were known by the Title of *Hippobatae* i. Equites. (p.333)

Like the spear and shield, the horse is one of the primary symbols of knighthood.

In the course of *The Faerie Queene* Braggadocchio acquires these three attributes. At the two tournaments, and especially at the second, he is deprived of them. In each case he loses these symbols of a knight as a result of revealing his baseness by unchivalric behaviour. All three symbolic attributes are repossessed by knights who are also patrons of books of *The Faerie Queene*. The connection between his behaviour, these symbols, and the institution of knighthood is finally made in the presentation of his formal degradation from the office and station of a knight.

The various attributes unworthily possessed by Braggadocchio may have diverse meanings in other contexts. But their congregation around the boaster and the circumstances of their loss during the tournaments suggest that we should seek the common ground between them in the institution of knighthood. At Marinell's tournament in particular we see the attributes in the process of returning to their worthy owners: Guyon reclaims his horse, Arthegall the shield of victory; and finally Talus deprives Braggadocchio of the last physical signs of chivalry.

The primacy of the chivalric meaning of these symbols is recognized in Arthegall's dismissal of Braggadocchio. He condemns the boaster

> Hence [to] fare on foot, till he an horse have gayned.
>
> (V.iii.35.6)

This is not, except very incidentally, a reference to temperance; instead Arthegall draws directly on chivalric symbolism. The false *chevalier* must be expelled from the order of knighthood, and that explusion is signalled by the seizure of his horse, by sending him away 'on foot'. In using this punishment Arthegall follows the ancient traditions of degradation once more: Guillim states that the dishonouring of a knight was achieved

> by seizing of their Equipage (except one Horse) *ne qui dignitate factus est Eques cogatur pedes incedere.* (p.232)

Arthegall's judgement leaves Braggadocchio without even the single horse of Guillim's parenthesis; and in order to obtain reentry to the chivalric world, the boaster must earn his right to this principal symbol of a knight. With this final indignity Braggadocchio marches, on foot, from the poem as we have it.

At the end of Marinell's tournament Spenser expresses the moral directly to the audience:

> So ought all faytours, that true knighthood shame,
> And armes dishonour with base villanie,
> From all brave knights be banisht with defame:
> For oft their lewdness blotteth good deserts with blame.
>
> (V.iii.38.6-9)

As in the proclamation of the Earl of Northumberland's degradation, we should notice the apparent independence of the 'armes' liable to dishonour in these lines. Spenser in fact reverses our normal expectations of the potential fate of the 'armes' and the 'good deserts'. The physical, material objects, the 'armes', have their abstract honour injured. But the 'good deserts' are 'blotted', as though they were physically corruptible (like Braggadocchio's 'blotted ... armes' [V.iii. 37.7]). The implications of such a reversal may be that the 'armes' do possess an abstract existence and that the pollution of the symbols of knighthood involves the pollution, through them, of the ideal itself. The return of these chivalric symbols at the spousals tournament represents the reversal of the corruption resulting from their usurpation by Braggadocchio, and thus may signal the regeneration of knighthood within the poem.

2. The 'Cingulum militare' and Florimell's Girdle

I

Perhaps the most prominent of the emblems of knighthood not yet alluded to is the military girdle, the *cingulum militare*. Although previous critics have never even hinted at its presence, I shall attempt to demonstrate that Spenser uses the *cingulum* as a symbol throughout *The Faerie Queene*: from Prince Arthur in Book One to Astraea in the 'Mutabilitie Cantos'. This symbolism also has a bearing on the fate and interpretation of Florimell's girdle.

I retain the Latin term because of the number of ways in which *cingulum* is translated, even within a single author's work. The chivalric writers frequently interchange 'belt' and 'girdle' as translations; and equally common is the rendering as 'baldric'. Both Selden and Segar appear to use all three as synonyms, and with reason:[11] during the coronation of Elizabeth I the ceremony of 'girding' was performed with a baldric;[12] that is to say, in the words of the *OED*, 'with a belt or girdle, usually of leather and richly ornamented, worn pendant from one shoulder across the breast and under the opposite arm'.[13] The *cingulum militare* and the baldric are explicitly related by Favyn, who discusses their common origins; and Ashmole, using a different etymology, states that the *cingulum militare* was called *baltheus* or *balteus*, hence baldric.[14]

However translated, the *cingulum militare* is often regarded as the principal emblem of knighthood, as William Segar writes:

> the girdle was the first Ensigne bestowed upon souldiers, and without it no man might accompt himselfe among the number of militarie men, nor claim the priviledges due unto souldiers. (p.6)

John Selden adds the essential buttress to such a claim by stressing the antiquity of the *cingulum*:

> by consent of *Romans, Grecians*, and other Nations the Belt ... was both the main part of Martiall acoultrement, and under it the whole was comprehended, so mongst our Northerns ... it specially succeeded into the room of that solemn taking Armes for a Knights outward ensign of Nobility. (p.311)

---

11 Selden, p.369; and Sir William Segar, *Honor, Military, and Civill, contained in foure Bookes* (1602), p.99.
12 Nichols, Vol.1, p.62: 'and ther was a sworde with a girdele putt over her and upon one of her shoulders and under the other: And soe the sword hangeing by her side'.
13 *OED* Baldric 1.
14 Favyn, p.58; and Ashmole, p.28.

According to Selden, not only is the *cingulum* the most important of the emblems of knighthood, but it also stands for all the others: it comprehends the significance of the lesser garments and weapons. Many other writers on chivalry give examples of the early Roman emperors' ceremony of making knights by the donation of a girdle. Favyn shows the reverse of this coin, confirming the significance of the *cingulum* in his description of imperial degradations, during which members of the equestrian order were expelled by the symbolic loss, not only of their eponymous horses, but also of their belts.[15] This brief survey of references to the *cingulum militare* may be concluded by noting that the association of a girdle with war is both ancient and literary. Selden notes that, in the *Iliad*, Agamemnon's appearance is characterized by his resemblance to a whole pantheon of gods, from each of whom he takes a distinguishing attribute: he is, as Selden says, ' "like *Mars* in his Girdle, belt," or indeed, as it interprets, "armor" ' (p. 311).

The common feature of all types of *cingulum*, whether worn as a belt or as a girdle, is that they are binding garments; and in this we see their relationship with the Garter. The author of the *Liber Niger* tells us that the 'orbicular Garter' symbolizes the 'Union and Band of Friendship' (p. 26); the word 'orbicular' links the garter with other circular, binding garments of the *cingulum* group.

Indeed the form of the insignia of the Order of the Garter is less stable than its name and present-day usage suggest. In the past it could take the more standard forms of the *cingulum*. The *Liber Niger* records that Edward III ordered the garter to be 'worn over one of their Shoulders, on the Leg and sometimes on the Thum' (p. 24). Furthermore the insignia of the Order includes a blue sash worn as a baldric, from which the George is now suspended; and this is the normal insignia of a Knight of the Garter. Related to this possible use of baldrics is the suggestion that, in the unclear development of this Order, influence upon its insignia was exerted by the Spanish Ordre de la Banda, the chief garment of which was a sash worn baldric-wise across the breast.[16] On the basis of these connections it may be suggested that Spenser's contemporaries did not view the Garter's eponymous emblem as standing apart from the *cingulum* group, but rather saw it as taking its place among them as *primus inter pares*.

As we have seen, the circular, binding quality of the *cingulum* gave rise to its being interpreted as indicative of the unity and integrity of

---

15 Favyn, p. 51.
16 See Richard Barber, *The Knight and Chivalry* (1970: Sphere, 1974), pp. 339-344. That this order and its attributes were known in Spenser's time, see Selden, pp. 369-370, and Segar, pp. 99-102.

the knight and of the institution of knighthood. More detailed allegorical explanations of the *cingulum* were sometimes given. For instance, John Ferne develops his out of the normal basic meaning:

> Very aptly is this girdle ... added to the ornament of a Knight, as a signe of his degree, since that it is expedient to a man, that taketh in hand any businesse of difficultie ... to gird his loines .... The girdle then is a signe of labor businesse, not of sloth and effeminate wantonnes.[17]

Ferne is clearly drawing additionally on the Christian symbolism of Ephesians, as commented upon in Chapter Four: his 'gird his loines recalls the Pauline injunction, 'your loines gird about with veritie'. Other interpretations remain predominantly unreligious; Segar derives his from secular scripture:

> the law Civill seemeth to note that the girdle signified administration or dignitie.   (p.61)

But although Ferne, Segar, and others embellish the basic meaning of the *cingulum*, they have no lasting effect on it. The *cingulum militare* remained in general a symbol of knighthood itself.

The one non-chivalric meaning that does persist is chastity. In Christine de Pisan's *Ordene de Chevalerie* Saladin is instructed,

> Sire, by that girdle is signified that your pure flesh, your loins, your whole body you must keep absolutely as in virginity.[18]

This tradition remained strong long after Spenser's day. The eighteenth-century herald John Anstis still interprets the *cingulum* thus in his essay on the origins of the Order of the Bath:

> His white Girdle or Belt, represents the Vertue of Chastity, not in Opposition to Marriage, but to impure and criminal Love, which Knights ought particularly to detest, as being the avow'd Guardians of female Vertue and Honour.[19]

And Jean de Carthenay gives some idea of the literary uses of the combination of the military girdle and the girdle of chastity in *The*

---

[17] *The Blazon of Gentrie* (1586), p.109.
[18] *L'Ordene de Chevalerie*, ed. F.S.Ellis (1893):
> Sire, par cheste chainturete,
> Est entendu que vo car nete,
> Vos rains, vos cors entierement
> Devez tenir tout firmement
> Aussi com en virginitie
[19] *Observations introductory to an Historical Essay upon the Knighthood of the Bath* (1725), p.80.

Wandering Knight. His misguided hero is initially armed with 'a Cinture ... termed Intemperance'. When he turns to God and repentance, he is re-equipped with 'the well-befitting and graceful Cinture of Chastity'.[20] In this example, the two traditions of the *cingulum* as an emblem of knighthood and the girdle as representing chastity are combined in a manner that foreshadows Spenser's usage.

II

Like Carthenay, Spenser uses the *cingulum militare* in *The Faerie Queene* in order to demonstrate the difference between good and evil. However, Spenser does not achieve this by physical substitutions but by playing on the word for *cingulum* and the various ways in which this garment can be worn. He divides the binding garments into two groups: baldrics and belts. Three knights or warriors wear the *cingulum* as a baldric, Prince Arthur, Britomart, and Belphoebe; and they are contrasted with three wearing belts.

The greatest baldric in the poem is, of course, that worn by Prince Arthur:

> Athwart his brest a bauldrick brave he ware,
> That shynd, like twinkling stars, with stons most pretious rare.
> (I.vii.29.8-9)

The position of this description within the first book is significant: it comes at the beginning of the second half, in canto seven, at just the moment when the adventure of the Dragon must recommence after St George's defeat at the hands of Orgoglio. Following this, Una, travelling with her champion's abandoned armour, meets Prince Arthur; and his armour, including the baldric, is then described. Thus placed, it parallels the description of the enchanter Archimago in the first canto, whom Una meets with the Red Cross Knight. Comparing the two descriptions, we notice that Archimago also wears a *cingulum*:

> At length they chaunst to meet upon the way
> An aged Sire, in long blacke weedes yclad,
> His feete all bare, his beard all hoarie gray,
> And by his belt his booke he hanging had;   (I.i.29.1-4)

---

[20] *The Wandering Knight: His Adventurous Journey*, tr. A.J.H[ammer] (1889), pp.14 and 222. This is a translation of a fuller edition (1572) than that used in the English translation of 1581, edited by Dorothy Atkinson Evans (see Chapter Four, notes 5 and 19).

Archimago's belt contrasts with Arthur's baldric. The contrast is heightened, and to some extent comes alive, when we consider the items suspended from each *cingulum*. From Arthur's baldric,

> his mortall blade full comely hong
> In yvory sheath, ycarv'd with curious slights;   (I.vii.30.6-7)

Prince Arthur's sword, as suggested in the third chapter, may be interpreted with St Paul as 'the sword of the Spirit, which is the worde of God' (Eph. 6.17). If Arthur possesses the Spirit, then it is only fitting that Archimago should have hanging at his side a 'booke'. From his *cingulum* is suspended the physically present Letter; and the distinction recalls St Paul's words, 'for the letter killeth but the Spirit giveth life' (2 Cor. 3.6). The contrast contributes to our perception of Prince Arthur as a Christ-like rescuer, superseding the deadly Old Law. The contrasts between the forms of *cingulum* worn by Archimago and Arthur, and the items suspended from them develop and express the opposition between these two figures.

The other two baldrics are presented less prominently, but are equally significant in establishing through costume oppositions between figures in the moral allegory of *The Faerie Queene*. The contrasts with the bearers of belts seem almost parodic, as in that between Belphoebe and Maleger. The virginal huntress, although not a knight, wears a baldric:

> at her backe a bow and quiver gay,
> Stuft with steele-headed darts, wherewith she queld
> The salvage beastes in her victorious play,
> Knit with a golden bauldricke, which forlay
> Athwart her snowy brest, and did divide
> Her daintie paps; which like young fruit in May
> Now little gan to swell, and being tide,
> Through her thin weed their places only signifide.   (II.iii.29.2-9)

Other meanings for the baldric are no doubt active here: as Alastair Fowler has pointed out, Valeriano allegorizes the *cingulum* as temperance, and its connections with chastity have already been mentioned.[21] Yet our interpretation should take into account Belphoebe's use of the baldric to support her weapons; and it may thus be counted a form of *cingulum militare*. The connection is strengthened by com parison with her opposite: the chief enemy of the temperate soul in Book Two is Maleger, the leader of the 'monstrous rablement' attacking the House of Alma. His description answers Belphoebe's in all points: he carries a 'bended bow' (II.xi.21.1) and has 'many arrowes

---

21 I am indebted to Professor Fowler for the reference to Valeriano, *Hiero-glyphica*, f.229v.

173

under his right side' (21.2). However his are headed with flint and dyed with blood. His clothing also recalls Belphoebe's:

> All in a canvas thin he was bedight   (II.xi.22.6)

Maleger's 'canvas thin' parodies Belphoebe's 'thin weed' of 'silken Camus'. But again a specific difference lies in the means by which they are girded: Belphoebe wears a 'golden bauldricke', whereas Maleger's rags are tied with 'a belt of twisted brake' (II.xi.22.7). Again, baldric and belt are contrasted, with the belt emerging as an attribute of evil. And we may note that in the battle before Alma's house, Maleger's adversary is the baldric-wearing Prince Arthur.

We can have no doubt that Britomart wears the *cingulum militare*; nor that Spenser is aware of the chivalric significance of this garment. The *cingulum* is part of the armour she purloins from King Ryence's church when she first assumes the role and costume of a knight. The first specified item she takes is the 'brave bauldrick' (III.iii.59.9); and although we have to wait two books before her adversary appears, our expectations of a contrasted *cingulum* are not disappointed. Radigund wears,

> her Cemitare ... tide,
> With an embrodered belt of mickell pride;   (V.v.3.4-5)

As with the moon symbol common to both these female warriors, the general similarity serves to draw our attention to crucial differences: Britomart's baldric, the *cingulum* she shares with Belphoebe and Prince Arthur, contrasts with Radigund's belt.

There is only one other use of the word 'baldric' in *The Faerie Queene*. When Astraea leaves the unjust Earth, she retires to 'heavens bright-shining baudricke' (V.i.11.7). Although distant from the oppositions listed above, there may be a faint but telling contrast later in the poem. In the 'Mutabilitie Cantos' Astraea walks with August in the procession of the months; and they are preceded by an ireful Jove bearing a sickle 'under his belt' (VII.vii.36.9). Astraea and August are associated with the Saturnine world of peace and plenty; July with the usurping Jove. The opposition of Astraea retiring to the baldric at the end of the Saturnine Age and July with his belt is faint, but it may be intended.

Excluding this last, highly tentative, example, we may conclude that Spenser uses the *cingulum militare* to convey the contrasts and oppositions between characters. In the cases of Arthur, Britomart, and Belphoebe the baldric is a prominent part of the overall contrast. In considering these examples we have noted all the baldrics and almost all the binding garments in *The Faerie Queene*; the most significant omission is that of Florimell's girdle.

174

At first sight Florimell's cestus seems to have little in common with either the exchanged emblems of knighthood or the *cingulum militare*. However, the events concerning the cestus follow the pattern established by the emblems of knighthood: it is appropriated by an unworthy imitation and is returned to its true owner at the spousals tournament. In this way its adventures recall those of Guyon's horse and spear, the shield used by Arthegall, and the armour Braggadocchio wears. And its relationship with these emblems of knighthood is cemented by the chivalric connotations it has gathered as a result of the circumstances in which it is lost, found, worn, and fought over. Sir Satyrane's wearing of the girdle, for instance, links it with the *cingulum militare*.

These latent chivalric connotations are rendered more active by the close resemblance between the cestus and the Garter. The garter-emblem, originally a purely personal possession like the cestus, is transformed by its context into a chivalric symbol of the highest honour and virtue. The sense of transformation is stressed in the accounts of the Order of the Garter's origins. Sir William Segar states that Edward III first wore the garter 'about his left legge for a favour', nothing more. But to quell laughter,

> smiling sayd, HONY SOIT QUI MAL Y PENSE. I will make of it yer it be long the most honourable Garter that ever was worne, and thereupon instituted the order of the Garter. (p.66)

John Speed is even more aware of the transformation being from a meaningless personal object to a recognizable symbol. He too tells the story of the Countess of Salisbury's garter:

> whereat the by-standers smiling, he [the king] gave the impresse to checke all evill conceits, and in golden letters embellished the Garter with this French poesie, HONI SOIT QUI MALY PENSE'[22]

For Speed, the conscious addition of the 'poesie' or verse turns the garter into the Garter; from a favour into something akin to an *impresa*. In *The Faerie Queene* Spenser uses the reference to the history of the Garter to indicate the transformation of Florimell's girdle from an attribute belonging to an individual into a chivalric symbol.

As with other binding garments, Spenser uses different words, apparently synonyms, to convey the moral status of the cestus depending on its wearer. Normally it is described as a 'girdle'. But

---

[22] *The Theater of ... Great Britain* (1611), p.27.

when the false Florimell is awarded it, the cestus becomes 'that gold-en belt' (IV.v.16.1); and belts are, as has been seen, associated with evil. The false Florimell is unable to tie the 'golden belt' securely; but when Amoret tries and succeeds, being chaste and thus worthy of it, it becomes a 'girdle' once more. (IV.v.19.3). However, at this

> [the false] *Florimell* exceedingly did fret,
> And snatching from her hand halfe angrily
> The belt againe, about her bodie gan it tie.   (IV.v.19.7-9)

As the snowy maiden seizes it, the cestus becomes 'the belt againe'. The rapid changes in nomenclature express the perversion and cor-ruption of the symbol as it leaves the hands of the chaste woman for those of the false Florimell.

The girdle thereafter remains a 'belt' while in the false Forimell's possession. It only regains its former name, and then permanently, in the course of Marinell's tournament; but the passage in which it does so may seem to undermine the play on names suggested. Arthegall returns the cestus to its true owner:

> But *Artegall* that golden belt uptooke,
> The which of all her spoyle was onely left;
> Which was not hers, as many it mistooke,
> But *Florimells* owne girdle   (V.iii.27.1-4)

Without close attention to Spenser's rhetorical forms here the terms 'belt' and 'girdle' might seem undifferentiated. But following the syntax reveals that there is a difference: as part of the imposter's spoil, the cestus is a 'belt'. But in the third line Spenser uses *epan-orthosis* to correct, and thus emphasize the need to correct, the notion that the cestus ever really belonged to the snowy maiden. And in correcting that notion, he also corrects the name, from 'belt' to 'girdle'. Puttenham's definition of *epanorthosis* (which he calls *'Metanoia* or the penitent') aptly applies to Spenser's play on these terms: 'we seem to call in our word again and to put in another fitter for the purpose'.[23] As Arthegall in the narrative returns the cestus to its true owner, Spenser 'calls in' the term 'belt' and restores the fitter name of 'girdle', assigning the cestus finally to that group of binding garments associated with good.

The prominence of the cestus and the *cingulum* garments in *The Faerie Queene* may be foreshadowed in one of the poem's puzzling inconsistencies. Satyrane's tournament, at which the cestus is raised to the status of a relic, is the last occasion on which we see the

---

[23] *Arte of English Poesie*, ed. Gladys Doidge Willcock and Alice Walker (Cam-bridge: Cambridge UP, 1936), p. 215.

knights-patron of Book Four, Cambell and Triamond. Or rather, Cambell and Telamond, for so the second knight is called on the title-page of the book. The meaning of the name Triamond is relatively clear, given his adventures; but a widely accepted meaning for Telamond has yet to be proposed. The most interesting and satisfying interpretation is that of T.P.Roche, who sees its derivation as *teleos* and *mundus*, with the meaning 'perfect world'.[24] This unfortunately involves a certain amount of letter-changing; and its macaronic nature is also slightly unsatisfactory. A simpler alternative is the Greek *telamon*, meaning the belt or baldric supporting a shield; and this is particularly apt for the cestus dominated events of the tournaments of Books Four and Five. In this interpretation, the title-page's version of the knight's name would announce the significance of the baldrics and the girdle; and, through the symbolism of the *cingulum militare*, of the chivalric theme running through these books.

3. Marinell's Tournament

I

The constitution and values of chivalry are explored throughout *The Faerie Queene*. But this theme is distilled and concentrated at the two tournaments, chivalric focal-points as in Elizabethan England. They present the discussion of knighthood in complementary halves: Satyrane's tournament demonstrates chivalry's flaws as perceived in the poem; and the way in which these must be corrected is presented at Marinell's.

The transfers of attributes described in the earlier sections of this chapter utterly dominate Marinell's tournament. The three days of fighting require a mere seven stanzas of description, in contrast with the thirty-one needed for combat of similar duration at the previous event. However, twenty-eight stanzas are devoted to the unmasking of Braggadocchio and the return of the emblems of knighthood. And it is in these actions that the resolution of the theme of chivalry in *The Faerie Queene* is expressed.

Satyrane's tournament is a concentration of questions inherent but unformulated in *The Faerie Queene* up to this point. At his event we are faced uncompromisingly with the knowledge that, although

[24] *The Kindly Flame*, pp.16-17.

the poem contains knights acting in the full spirit of theoretical chivalry, there are also those knights of dubious morality, if not worse, undermining the ideal: those whose conduct could be described, with Paridell's, as 'knighthood fowle defaced by a faithlesse knight' (III.ix.1.9). The shambles of Satyrane's tournament sweeps away any pretence that the chivalry of the 'heard', those knights who are not patrons of virtue, is founded upon the *summa perfectio*, the integration of the virtues.

Although the fighting at Satyrane's tournament is indecisive, the result of the cestus competition itself is only too clear. The various knights present their ladies to be judged: but the criterion for judgement is physical attractiveness alone, irrespective of virtue. From the contest the false Florimell emerges victorious; but Britomart, Cambell, and Triamond, the knights who have first choice of her by virtue of their success in battle, spurn the prize. Their disdain further distances these knights-patron from the others present: after they reject her, the knights of the 'heard' instantly erupt in passionate dispute over her possession, and this despite the sexual incontinence proclaimed in her inability to tie the cestus. The election of the false Florimell exemplifies the debased ideals of Satyrane's tournament, and of the chivalry espoused by most there: the knights of the 'heard' have fought, not for virtue or honour, but for an empty, easy facsimile, the fraudulence of which is barely cloaked by the basely acquired attributes of the more demanding reality.

Spenser reveals the unworthiness and the unfitness of such knights in the resolution of the dispute: the quarrels become so heated that the snowy maiden is allowed to select her own mate. Her chosen consort, logically, is none other than Braggadocchio, the entirely fraudulent knight. Now reunited, this pair is elevated to become the central, triumphant image of Satyrane's tournament, just as the boaster had set out to be in the opening procession. And in their ascendency they are representative of the fraudulent chivalry celebrated there: Braggadocchio strides forwards as the embodiment of the dishonest and superficial knighthood of the 'heard'; and his consort with the untieable belt perfectly symbolizes a chivalry to which the attributes and symbols of virtue are only relevant as ornamentation.

Satyrane's tournament is one 'of beautie and of might' (IV.iv.16.2); in other words, it is a chivalric celebration at which, paradoxically, the *summa perfectio* is irrelevant. The spurious honour gained there is justly awarded to Braggadocchio and the false Florimell because these two are pure imitations, possessing none of the inner substance of virtue.

II

Testimony to the seductive appearance of these imposters is supplied by the ecstatic reaction they provoke at Marinell's tournament: 'so feeble skill of perfect things the vulgar has' (V.iii.17.9). Here Braggadocchio reaches the zenith of his power, temporarily able to confront and confound the true Florimell and her spouse, Marinell. Arthegall's action, in revealing the boaster as a 'losell' (V.iii.20.6) and a fraud, provides a resolution for the discussion of chivalry: his judgement reasserts the interdependence of virtue and nobility, the basis of true knighthood.

As has been suggested, both tournaments are to be seen within the context of the courtly entertainments of Spenser's day: although neither is actually a 'balletic' tournament, both require that the same methods of interpretation should be employed by the reader to gain full understanding. And Marinell's tournament in particular benefits from association with contemporary pageants and masques. To a degree, this tournament is presented within the narrative as belonging to the tradition of courtly festivities: taking place to mark the spousals of Marinell and Florimell, it echoes the many similar wedding celebrations which included tilting.[25] And as well as the occasion, the details of Spenser's description recall the magnificent visual spectacles of the Elizabethan court: there are 'devicefull sights' (V.iii.3.2) and 'royall banquets' (3.5). What is more, the knights joust 'full rich aguiz'd, / As each one had his furnitures deviz'd' (4.4-5); that is, they enter the lists in the extravagent and fanciful costumes common in the entertainments of the time. Once more it is worth noting that Spenser does not dissipate his effects by extensive description of individual costumes, but rather uses this economical reference to achieve the necessary sense of richness and to suggest the connection with the courtly entertainments of his own day. Although this atmosphere of courtly game and festivity is disrupted by Braggadocchio's challenge, his banishment is followed by a return to 'pleasure and repast' (40.1).

For those involved there is no sense in which Braggadocchio's interruption can take its place in the otherwise orderly nature of the celebrations: the threat he poses seems real enough from within the poem; and his savage, egotistical rejection of Florimell does not follow any courteous scenario. But to the reader, the overall structure of the episode can be seen to possess parallels with the renaissance entertainment which go beyond superficial detail; and seen in this

[25] See Ivan L. Schulze, 'Reflections of Elizabethan Tournaments in *The Faerie Queene*, 4.4 and 5.3', *ELH* 5 (1938), pp. 278-284.

light the structure accommodates, and perhaps demands, Bragga-docchio's attack.

The analogy can best be understood by citation of two masques by Ben Jonson which post-date this section of *The Faerie Queene* by some years. Stephen Orgel sums up the purpose of the antimasquers in the *Masque of Queens* (1609) as 'to destroy the festivities and the world of the impending masque'.[26] Their 'ultimate threat ... is a return to chaos: as always to an Elizabethan the villain is disorder, misrule, Mutabilitie' (p.134). Orgel's definition of an antimasquer applies equally to Braggadocchio: the boaster is the focus, also the symbol, of discord and disorder at Satyrane's tournament; and carrying that discord with him, is nearly successful in disrupting the spousals. Orgel, in his reference to 'Mutabilitie', is clearly aware of the implicit connection with Spenser and the world of *The Faerie Queene*; but Braggadocchio reveals himself as more powerful than any Jonsonian antimasquer when, unlike them, he penetrates the masque-world, attacking its inhabitants and their values.

The precise nature of the boaster's attack and the source of his power are also elucidated by comparison with a Jonsonian villain. In *Love Restored* (1612) the principal antimasquer is Plutus. Having 'stol'n Love's ensigns', Plutus claims to be Cupid, the god of love; and his impersonation is leading to corruption in the manners of love and the institution of marriage.[27] Robin Goodfellow exposes the imposter before the masque itself can begin; and in doing so makes the same point as Spenser concerning the credulousness of the mob and its consequences:

'Tis you, mortalls, that are fooles; and worthie to be such, that worship him: for if you had wisdome, he had no godhead. (p.385)

Robin reprimands the audience because it has failed to distinguish the true god of love from an imposter merely decked in the other's accoutrements; and that mistake, he explains, dangerously endows a fraud with godhead. In this context it is significant that Robin chooses to use the term 'ensigns': his metaphor alludes to the chivalric world, in which visual symbolism occupies a fully recognized and crucial place. Like Plutus, Braggadocchio derives his power to deceive from the theft of other people's attributes; and from the 'feeble skill of perfect things the vulgar has'.

---

26 *The Jonsonian Masque* (Cambridge, Mass.: Harvard UP, 1965), p.137.
27 *Ben Jonson*, eds. C.H.Herford, Percy and Evelyn Simpson, 11 vols (Oxford: Clarendon Press, 1925-1952); vol.7, p.382.

Unlike the others present, including even the bridegroom Marinell, only the knight-patron of justice can perceive the falseness of Braggadocchio and his snowy maiden. Arthegall identifies the boaster as a 'losell', and thus shows himself as the first character in *The Faerie Queene* to gauge Braggadocchio as the author himself does (II.iii. 4.1).[28] But the speech in which Arthegall thus vilifies him contains more far-reaching judgements than this. As in the succeeding adventure of the two disputing brothers Bracidas and Amidas, Arthegall at the tournament is shown delivering a formal judgement: his speech outlines the legal and just basis of his decision; and the sentence designs the appropriate consequences.

The concern with chivalric signs, symbols, and their validity which I have suggested as being at the heart of Marinell's tournament is made explicit in Arthegall's speech and actions when he judges and dismisses the boaster. In his denunciation of Braggadocchio, Arthegall stresses both the physical indications of chivalry and martial activity, and their symbolic or significant quality and function. Questioning whether Braggadocchio is worthy of the honour and glory represented by the armour and weapons he bears, Arthegall challenges the boaster:

> That shield, which thou doest beare, was it indeed,
> Which this dayes honour sav'd to *Marinell*;
> But not that arme, nor thou the man I reed,
> Which didst that service unto *Florimell*.
> For proofe shew forth thy sword, and let it tell,
> What strokes, what dreadfull stoure it stird this day:
> Or shew the wounds, which unto thee befell;
> Or shew the sweat, with which thou diddest sway
> So sharpe a battell, that so many did dismay.
>
> But this the sword, which wrought those cruell stounds,
> And this the arme, the which that shield did beare,
> And these the signes, (so shewed forth his wounds)
> By which that glorie gotten doth appeare. (V.iii.21; 22.1-4)

This speech recognizes the issue of the emblematic appearance of the knight, bringing martial and chivalric symbolism to the forefront of our attention. Arthegall calls on Braggadocchio to show his notched sword as proof of his participation in the battle (in all his adventures the boaster, of course, never obtained a sword). But that practical,

---

[28] See A. C. Hamilton's note in his edition of *The Faerie Queene*, p. 546.

physical object is also explicitly called upon to act as a symbol of the bearer's worthiness: 'Let it *tell*, / What strokes, what dreadfull stoure it stird this day' (my italics). The repeated use of 'shew' in these lines emphasizes the visual nature of the signs Arthegall invokes; to claim victory for himself he 'shewed forth his wounds', and in doing so names them as symbolic: they are 'the *signes* ... By which that glorie gotten doth appeare' (my italics).

Arthegall's indictment of the boaster confirms the poem's attention to the chivalric meaning of the arms and emblems Braggadocchio has purloined:

> Thou losell base,
> Thou hast with borrowed plumes thy selfe endewed,
> And others worth with leasings doest deface,
> When they are all restor'd, thou shalt rest in disgrace.

> (V.iii.20.6-9)

The 'borrowed plumes' have a two-fold significance. They are, as Gough rightly noted, an allusion to Aesop's fable of the jackdaw 'adorned ... with peacock's feathers' (*Var* 5, p.189). But the circumstances render probable a second, complementary allusion: the 'borrowed plumes' are also those of a helmet and thus stand (as in Gower's *Confessio Amantis* 5.6044) for the arms and armour, the emblems of knighthood, which form the plumage this jackdaw has purloined. This second allusion is that which is taken up in the rest of Arthegall's sentence, and especially in the final line of the stanza. Arthegall predicts that when Braggadocchio's stolen goods are restored to their true owners, the boaster will be disgraced. Understood as a reference to knighthood, this is necessarily so, since the return of his plumage will enact the formal degradation of a knight.

The terms in which Arthegall condemns the boaster also indicate the nature of the latter's crime and thus explain its seriousness. The knight-patron of justice asserts that Braggadocchio's behaviour has undermined 'others worth'; and the truth of this assertion lies in the relationship between chivalry and its emblems as perceived in the poem. Modern scholarship has demonstrated the profound value accorded to symbolism by many in the Renaissance: rational or not, the sixteenth-century mind was capable of locating deep truth in apparently simple images, mottoes, and combinations of word and image. William Camden, himself keenly interested in emblems and *imprese* as well as the imagery of heraldry, raises his voice in condemnation of the excesses of such studies; and in his need to reprehend the credulous is a tribute to the seductions of such learned games.

But it was not just the credulous who accorded symbolism such status. E. H. Gombrich's essay *'Icones Symbolicae'* examines the relationship between the symbol and that symbolized in the Renaissance; and he demonstrates that in both Christian and Neoplatonic doctrine symbolism could be seen, not as a human and arbitrary association, but as a divine language or system of interrelationships, study and use of which could enable the mortal mind to perceive truth in ways otherwise inaccessible to reason. Citing Christophoro Giarda and the myth of the two pillars of wisdom, Gombrich states that in Christian terms 'the language of symbolism is as directly derived from God as is the language of the Scriptures'.[29] And according to the Neoplatonists,

> The Universe ... is a vast symphony of correspondences in which each level of existence points to the level above. It is by virtue of this interrelated harmony that one object can signify another and that by contemplating a visible thing we can gain insight into the invisible world.   (p.152)

The implication of both these approaches is that symbols possess a validity and an authority independent of the particular writer or artist employing them: their meaning is inherent and the artist, whether visual or verbal, discovers and uses, but does not create, it.

There is no need to suggest that Spenser consciously participated in these theories, although they have clear relevance for a writer of allegory. But awareness of the contemporary attitude to symbolism is necessary in our attempt to understand *The Faerie Queene* and in particular the two tournaments. At both Spenser shows us the attempted perversion of symbols of virtue and chivalry, which have been expropriated by evil characters. Given, in Gombrich's phrase, the blurred 'rational distinction between symbol and reality' (p.155), such perversions are of more than local or trivial significance; rather, they strike at the harmony and order of that 'vast symphony of correspondences' which is the universe of *The Faerie Queene*. The activities of Braggadocchio and the false Florimell are perceived by the poet as threatening more than the spousals; they constitute an attack on the underlying structure of Spenser's fictive world (and with it, his chosen poetic medium of allegory). This deeper significance explains why the return of the emblems of knighthood and virtue is so stressed at the tournaments; and why Arthegall's judgement on and Talus's degradation of Braggadocchio are accorded such prominence.

As was suggested at the beginning of the previous chapter, the institution of chivalry is in part an image of the perfect society. And as Spenser says in the *Letter to Raleigh*, his overall hero is 'the image of a brave knight, perfected in the twelve private morall vertues': the

---

[29] *Symbolic Images* (1972; second edition, Oxford: Phaidon Press, 1978), p.150.

perfect man in chivalric costume. Marinell's tournament shows the chivalric world of the poem under severe pressure; and, as in Robin Goodfellow's use of 'ensigns', the presentation of the attack on human perfection in chivalric terms enables Spenser to use the self-conscious symbolism of knighthood as a means of distillation and emphasis. So much of *The Faerie Queene* is concerned with hypocrisy, from Archimago onwards, that the perverting effects of the dishonest use of chivalric symbolism, the inversions of value threatened by Braggadocchio's deceit, concentrate powerfully the challenge both to chivalry and the wider ideal. This concentration is even more arresting since chivalric symbolism is not confined to literature or art, but exists and is employed in the world beyond the poem.

In the course of his career Braggadocchio develops into the supreme exemplar of the unworthy knight. From the outset he is a vehicle for satire on contemporary attitudes to chivalry and nobility: had Spenser been writing ten years later, the boaster would have been a baronet. When he acquires Guyon's arms he immediately sees the opportunities thus presented; and, once more agreeing with Robin Goodfellow's analysis, presented through the less than rigorous standards of those around him:

> He gan to hope, of men to be receiv'd
> For such, as he him thought, or faine would bee:
> But for in court gay portaunce he perceiv'd,
> And gallant shew to be in greatest gree,
> Eftsoones to court he cast t'avaunce his first degree. (II.iii.5.5-9)

From his entry Braggadocchio is associated with the chief danger for chivalry and the perfect society: the acceptance of outward show at the expense of inner virtue. At Marinell's tournament, in the popular acclaim he receives, in the substitution of the false for the true Florimell, and in the inability of all but Arthegall to confront him, Braggadocchio comes close to success in his attempt to become chivalry's preeminent representative. The result of his success would have been the destruction of true chivalry as it was remade in the boaster's image.

It is in the context of this larger perversion that we may understand Arthegall's accusation, while denouncing the 'losell base', that Braggadocchio 'defaces' the worth of others with his 'leasings' (V.iii. 20.8). By using the word 'deface' Arthegall continues the linking of a man's honour with his shield, his 'honours stile'. Yet it is initially difficult to see how Braggadocchio's 'leasings', his lies, can have this effect. However, Spenser may intend a pun in 'leasing'; the word has the alternative meaning of gleaning or the gathering up of scraps.[30] Taken in this sense, Arthegall's accusation develops his indictment of Braggadocchio for the damage caused by his impersonation of a knight: the armour, weapons, and emblems of knighthood he has gleaned along the way to the tournament, which have lent credence to his claims, have undermined both the institution of chivalry and those true knights within it.

Arthegall's speech can be seen as the moral sentence or explicative verse to the emblematic tournaments discussed in this and the preceding chapter. His words comment explicitly on the symbolic function of the equipment of a knight. Fittingly, this most explicit recognition of chivalric symbolism is followed by Braggadocchio's degradation, a fictional version of the most potent use of chivalric symbolism in the world beyond *The Faerie Queene*.

[30] *OED* Lease v1.1.

VII: THE ORDER OF THE GARTER AND 'THE FAERIE QUEENE'

I

In the earlier chapters of this book martial and chivalric symbolism was presented as one of the central means of expression employed in *The Faerie Queene*. The language of this symbolism is common in the literature of Spenser's day, being found prominently in works as different as the *New Arcadia* and the plays of Marlowe and Jonson. Such symbolism is also pervasive in the ceremonial forms used by the Elizabethan court to convey its authority and dramatize its higher qualities. In *The Faerie Queene*, martial and chivalric symbolism has been seen to be operative in crucial passages: the description of Prince Arthur's armour and the combat over Sir Guyon, for example. It has also led to the heart of some of the poem's central themes, such as the Christian knighthood of Book One; and, through allusions to her heraldic bearings, to the overall, complex relationship between the poem and its dedicatee, Queen Elizabeth.

These are general points concerning the use of martial and chivalric symbolism throughout the poem. The two preceding chapters, however, have contained discussions of the tournaments held by Satyrane and Marinell and have argued the existence of a specific and lasting concern with chivalry in *The Faerie Queene* and in particular with the institution of knighthood. Connections have also been suggested between Spenser's epic and the Order of the Garter.

Given the unfinished state of the poem, the ultimate importance of these specifically chivalric themes is unclear. Despite the air of finality at Marinell's tournament, many of the larger issues concerning chivalry remain open, with resolutions tantalizingly only indicated by unfulfilled structures and patterns within the first six books. Chiefly, the reformation of the Order of Maidenhead, shown decisively as corrupt during Satyrane's event, remains unachieved and Spenser leaves us with little certain information concerning the further development of his epic beyond the general comments found in the *Letter to Raleigh*. However, despite the difficulties involved, it is important in the context of the arguments advanced in this book to speculate cautiously concerning Spenser's intentions.

The Faerie Queene is, from the outset, an Arthurian epic. The

186

reasons for Spenser's selection of the Matter of Britain have been rehearsed sufficiently often for me to need do no more than mention them generally. The Tudors derived a specious aura of legitimacy and authenticity from the legend of King Arthur, from whom they claimed descent. But in the late sixteenth century this legendary history of England became valuable for other than purely dynastic reasons. With the Reformation and Henry VIII's rejection of Roman sovereignty, powerful nationalistic support for English independence of the Papacy and the Empire could be found in the stories of Arthur's conquests. Not only was he thought to have become emperor himself, and thus established the independence and *imperium* of the English crown; but the Once and Future king had also proved his religious supremacy in his supposed defeat of the Saracens. And this role as an early *fidei defensor* provided a popular counterpart to Matthew Parker's exaltation of the primitive English church over that of Rome, for instance. The value of the Arthurian legend to populist reformers, such as John Bale and John Foxe, can be seen in their hostility to the more rigorous historiography of such as Polydore Vergil, historiography clearly inimical to unquestioning acceptance of the Matter of Britain.

The Arthurian subject of *The Faerie Queene* is thus both nationalistic and, potentially, reformist in character. And, as C.B.Millican shows in *Spenser and the Table Round*, Spenser was far from alone in responding to the opportunities provided by this English heroic legend.[1] Milton's interest in an Arthurian epic is testimony to the attractiveness of the subject long after Spenser's death.

However, Millican goes further than merely pointing out the general context of Arthurian enthusiasm, seeing instead a greater and more specific parallel between Spenser's poem and the stories of the king. The quest motif of *The Faerie Queene* imitates that of Arthurian romance; and the poem's ultimate (but unfulfilled) structure may recall the Round Table:

> it is worth while to note that the magic number *twelve* was connected with Arthur in many ways. As early as Nennius, Arthur fought twelve Herculean battles against the Saxons, and this report ... was Arthur's one achievement that caught the imagination of the people. In Malory, Arthur slays twelve kings, and the Grail romances frequently refer to twelve knights of the Round Table. James Calfhill records in 1565 that Arthur 'had .xij. knightes of the rounde table,' and John Hardyng says that Galahad 'made

---

[1] Charles Bowie Millican, *Spenser and the Table Round: A Study in the Contemporaneous Background for Spenser's Use of the Arthurian Legend* [Harvard Studies in Comparative Literature, Volume 8] (Cambridge, Mass.: Harvard UP, 1932), especially Chapter Three.

> .xii. knightes of the order Of saynt Graall.' With Spenser's plan 'to frame the other part of polliticke vertues' in Prince Arthur's person in mind, it is interesting to observe that the number of knights whose names appear about the edge of the traditional Round Table at Winchester is twenty-four. Encircling the Tudor Double Rose in the centre is an inscription: 'This is the rownde Table of Kyng Arthur with XXIIII. of his namyd Knyghtes.'
>
> (pp.115-116)

Millican's theory has much to recommend it. The number twelve as a structuring element is certainly found in Arthurian legend as well as in classical epic; and the sum of the books of Spenser's two projected poems equals the number of seats, with the king's own, on the famous Winchester Round Table.

But in order to make full sense, Millican's theory must be taken further. The traditional Arthurian Round Table did not seat twenty-four knights: the number varied from Laȝamon's sixteen hundred, to one hundred and fifty in Malory, to twelve elsewhere. Nor was the traditional Table adorned with the Tudor Rose. The Winchester Round Table, anomalous in both these ways, was made probably in the fourteenth century but repainted in the early Tudor period; and its decoration is evidence of the appropriation of the Arthurian legend by the new dynasty. In particular, the number of places at the table, twenty-four, is evidence of the self-conscious association of King Arthur and his band of knights with the revived Order of the Garter.

The Order of the Garter is composed of the Sovereign, usually his heir, and twenty-four 'elected' knights, each of whom has his appointed stall in St George's Chapel, Windsor Castle; a number of other members, usually female or foreign royalty, are today regarded as supernumerary. The prestige of the order is founded upon its antiquity and its exclusiveness; unlike most other forms of knighthood, the Garter has remained small and select despite even James I's profligacy. In the sixteenth century, the Garter increased its prestige and also its authority by cultivating pre-existing links with Arthurian legend, asserting them in the *Liber Niger* and acting them out in pageant and ceremonial; had Henry VII's eldest son lived to accede to the throne as King Arthur, this Tudor development of the Order as a revived Round Table would no doubt have gone even further.

Despite the failure of this plan, the Garter and its Arthurian associations were at the heart of much Tudor political symbolism. And Spenser's poem, perhaps the greatest work of the period to explore and use the myths of England and the Tudors, deliberately evokes both the Arthurian legend and the Order of the Garter, marrying the two in the Order of Maidenhead and in the events of the two tournaments. If Millican's assumption that the number twenty-four is significant in Spenser's poem is correct, we must see it as alluding, not just to King Arthur, but also to the pseudo-Arthurian institution of the Order of the Garter.

II

In previous chapters I have confined myself to pointing out specific allusions to the Garter. But the possibility of a structural analogy with the composition of the Order suggests that the Garter may be more central to the poem than I have hitherto implied. Developing and qualifying Millican's purely Arthurian suggestion, we now recognise that the number of books in Spenser's projected double epic would have equalled the number of knights in the Order; and that, given the chivalric nature of the poem and the many incidental references to the Garter, this would have been clear to his original readers. The obviousness of the allusion is confirmed by the stress in the *Letter to Raleigh* on the 'Annuall feast' presided over by a Virgin Queen and stated to be the occasion at which each quest commences; a direct allusion to one of the central events in the ceremonial of Elizabeth's court, the Garter feasts held each year in celebration of (though rarely on) St George's day.[2]

Some corroboration for this theory may be found in the devices borne by the knights-patron of the first two books, as was suggested in the first chapter. It was remarked there that the device of the red cross, borne by St George, and that of the 'heavenly Mayd', borne by Sir Guyon, form also the two greatest badges of the Order of the Garter. The presence of St George himself as patron of the first book should perhaps be seen as an allusion to the Order, especially given Spenser's dedication of his poem to the Garter's sovereign, Queen Elizabeth. Moreover, St George's battle with the dragon, which dominates Book One from the outset, is precisely the subject represented on the Great George, the richly ornamented pendant worn by all Knights of the Garter. Taken together, it seems at least possible that Spenser is announcing a Garter-structure for his poem from the outset, indeed from the very first stanzas of Book One; and if this is correct, recognition of this structure is necessary to the meaning of the poem.

[2] See Ivan L. Schulze, 'Elizabethan Chivalry and the Faerie Queene's Annual Feast', *MLN* 50 (1935), pp.158-161. Schulze does not specify which of the ceremonial feasts of Elizabeth's court he considers *The Faerie Queene* to imitate and he states that 'obviously there are no direct parallels' (p.161) with any of them. With this I disagree.

Many more incidental correspondances could be adduced; but this theory (as well as Millican's more limited proposal of a solely Arthurian structure) is of little value unless the speculation can be shown to add to our understanding of the poem as we have it. In order, then, to explain the value of a possible allusion to the Garter, some further information concerning contemporary perception of its role and potential is necessary.

Frances Yates has shown that, late into the sixteenth century, it was still hoped that orders of chivalry might heal religious wounds and prevent both internecine and international strife.[3] The Order of the Garter had been used, since its inception, for diplomatic purposes, often as a means of binding together the rulers of opposing countries. As has been seen in many of the contemporary references to the Garter, the Order was regarded primarily as an instrument for promoting concord, both within the realm and between the various monarchs invited to become members. Even after the Reformation membership was accorded to Catholic, as well as Protestant, princes, and to rulers of France as well as those of the frequently opposed Habsburg dominions: in the more optimistic early part of her reign, Elizabeth's 'dalliance with religious reunion' was accompanied by the election to the Order of Charles IX of France in 1564 and the Emperor Maximilian II in 1567.[4] In Marcus Gheeraerts the Elder's etching of the Garter procession of 1576 Maximilian walks with Philip II of Spain, Henri III of France and such agressively Protestant English nobles as the Earl of Huntingdon; and the procession is only fictional in so far as not all were actually present, although all were members.[5]

But in the darker times of the next emperor, when religious compromise seemed hopeless, Henri III's election in 1585 occurs as part of a concerted, though ultimately fruitless, effort to achieve an alliance against the Spanish threat; the same year saw a mission to the German Protestant princes and the King of Denmark.[6] As the storm-clouds gathered, the Garter's diplomatic function became less idealistic and more geared to the protection of English interests, an orientation necessarily corresponding in the main to the religious alignments of the age. Although Elizabeth was ever cautious not to

3 *Astraea*, pp.208-210.
4 Strong, *Cult of Elizabeth*, p.177. Unfortunately Strong passes over the later elections of Protestant princes largely without comment.
5 See Hind, *Engraving in England …: Part I, The Tudor Period*, pp.107-121; and Strong, *Cult of Elizabeth*, pp.169-172.
6 On the mission to Denmark and the German princes, see Wallace T. MacCaffrey, *Queen Elizabeth and the Making of Policy 1572-1588* (Princeton: Princeton UP, 1981), pp.309-310.

commit herself (to have done so would have antagonized Spain and the Empire), her subjects, and among them some of her leading counsellors, wished to promote a league involving the reformed princes of Germany and the Protestant monarchs of northern Europe.[7] The queen blew hot and cold, using the German princes and the Low Countries in particular to fight her wars by proxy when these were unavoidable, reluctantly funding the armies of her allies rather than engaging her own.

There were many in England, however, who saw in this worsening of relations an opportunity for the queen and her country to assume the leadership of the anti-Catholic forces in Europe; and to these, the Garter appeared a valuable instrument. At times of particular crisis for the Protestant cause Elizabeth's ambassadors are found on the continent, seeking to cement the fractious princes of the reformed religion into some sort of defensive league; and these missions often take place in conjunction with, and perhaps concealed by, the investiture of a foreign prince as a Knight of the Garter. William Waad, one of Sir Francis Walsingham's correspondents, kept the minister informed in 1582 of the progress of the embassy delivering the Garter insignia to Frederick II of Denmark; and he reports that 'there have been who have borne the king in hand that my lord's coming is to tie him in some alliance for the defence of the Duke of Anjou in the Low Countries and so to embark him in some dangerous action'.[8] And such suspicions were not totally unjustified: Frederick II's secretary, Arnold Wittfeldt, wrote in the same year to Walsingham, as one godly monarch's minister to that of another, concerning the king's election to the Order; and although his comments initially seem to echo routine praise of the Garter, they ultimately reveal a sectarian and militant interpretation. Wittfeldt remarks that, 'its insignia are of great force in conciliating the minds of princes and will always remain the symbol of mutual amity'. But he goes on to stress that the alliance signalled by membership of the Garter is Protestant, not universal: the alliance is

---

7 On the Book of Concord and other attempts at a Protestant league, see Hajo Holborn, *A History of Modern Germany: The Reformation* (Eyre and Spottiswoode, 1965), p. 262. For the attitude of Elizabeth's councilors to this move, see Conyers Read, *Mr Secretary Walsingham and the Policy of Queen Elizabeth*, 3 vols (Oxford, 1925), vol. 1, pp. 299-302. A recent summary of the queen's relations with the Protestant princes, and of the vacilations on both sides, is found in the introduction to E. I. Kouri, *Elizabethan England and Europe: Forty Unprinted Letters from Elizabeth I to Protestant Powers* (University of London Institute of Historical Research, 1982).
8 *CSP Foreign May – December 1582* (HMSO, 1909), p. 216.

a joy to friends, a grief and envy to enemies and rivals. Therefore we, who are the ministers of princes that worship God aright, must work all the more zealously, that this friendship so honourbly confirmed between the King and the Queen may not only be lasting, but may increase from day to day.[9]

Wittfeldt's interpretation was shared by Casimir of the Palatinate, one of the principal proponents of a Protestant league and frequently Elizabeth's agent in negotiation with the German princes. Also in 1582, he writes to Walsingham concerning the progress of the re- formed faith in various kingdoms, informing the minister that James VI in Scotland is 'served by persons holding the right side', and predicting that 'God will bless the labours of those who are working at this task'. Casimir then discusses the Baltic monarchies:

> I was also very glad to hear that the King of Denmark, my good cousin and near kinsman, had received the honour of the most noble Order of the Garter, and had thus become my brother in arms, wherein I feel myself much honoured. But as for the King of Sweden, I fear that the news which I sent you of his change of religion are only too true, and that your advices were not so sure as mine.[10]

It is clear that Casimir regards the Garter as a device for unifying the princes of the reformed faith for future action against the Roman Catholics. He had himself received the Garter in 1578, during the period when Elizabeth was most keen on a Protestant league;[11] furthermore, it is probably not coincidence that 1578 was also the year in which Walsingham, the most radically Protestant of Elizabeth's chief ministers and a keen proponent of league with the German princes, became Chancellor of the Order. Throughout Casimir's many years of involvement and correspondence with Elizabeth, both referred to his membership of the Garter in connection with the mirage of a Protestant league: on 23 July 1591 he wrote that he was,

> bound to her service by the Order with which she had honoured him and whose motto was included in his arms .... And she wished, he would write to some of the Princes Protestant, especially the Elector of Saxony with whom he was now in close union, to remind them of her goodwill.[12]

---

9 *CSP Foreign May -- December 1582*, p.253.
10 *CSP Foreign May — December 1582*, p.466.
11 See Walsingham's letter to Dr Daniel Rogers of 31 October 1577 concerning the queen's anger at the failure of proposals for a league: *CSP Foreign 1577- 78*, p.294.
12 *List and Analysis of State Papers, Foreign June 1591 — April 1592* (HMSO, 1980), pp.467-68.

Although the idea of a Protestant league was probably anachronistic by the 1570s, that did not prevent its being taken seriously both by politicians and poets until long after. In 1577 Casimir and William, Landgrave of Hesse, both wrote to the queen welcoming the mission of Sir Philip Sidney to further plans for a league.[13] Sidney and the militantly Protestant group to which he belonged did not give up the idea of a pan-European alliance of reformed states; and this alliance possessed in their minds an heroic, chivalric aura.

III

It is in this light that Spenser's treatment of chivalry and its institutions in *The Faerie Queene* becomes most interesting. The disgrace of the Order of Maidenhead, and through it of the corrupt version of chivalry espoused by Braggadocchio and his like, may only be the first stage in the creation of a new order modelled on the ideal of the Garter which is militant, virtuous, and Protestant. The creation of that order would be enacted by the poem's structure, in its resemblance to that of the Garter: gathering in the twenty-four knights-patron as the poems progress, Prince, later King Arthur will eventually lead a reformed and reforming order, dedicated to the *summa perfectio* of theoretical chivalry and presided over by Gloriana herself.

Spenser's close ties to the Earl of Leicester and the Dudley/Sidney circle make this possibility more credible. Leicester's opposition to the Catholic, Alençon marriage was shared by his followers, including his nephew Philip Sidney, who endangered his career by writing outspokenly to the queen. And Paul E. McLane's discussion of the political allegory of the *Shepheardes Calendar* makes powerful claims for Spenser's poetic involvement in opposition to those of her actions which seemed to proclaim religious compromise.[14] While Leicester's fears may have been inspired partially by personal reflections on the power he would lose if the queen married, there is no denying the commitment of such as Sidney and Spenser to the Protestant cause or the honesty of their belief in Elizabeth as the potential protector and patron of true religion, of 'true Holinesse',

---

[13] *CSP Foreign 1575-77*, pp. 575 and 580 respectively. Sidney's involvement in missions to the Protestant princes is considered in Andrew D. Weiner, *Sir Philip Sidney and the Poetics of Protestantism: A Study of Contexts* (Minneapolis: University of Minnesota Press, 1978), especially pp. 18-28.

[14] *Spenser's Shepheardes Calendar: A Study in Elizabethan Allegory* (Notre Dame, Indiana: University of Notre Dame Press, 1961).

not only in England but throughout Europe. But while the November Eclogue of the *Shepheardes Calendar* is, according to McLane, 'designed to embody the prophetic fears of the group around Leicester who were strongly opposing the French marriage' (p.60), *The Faerie Queene* can be seen almost as an attempt to persuade England and England's monarch into virtue and reform through the epic and mythic prophesy of their success. In this the chivalric theme is of paramount significance: as Rosemond Tuve judges, 'Spenser's choice of genre [is] a masterly stroke'.[15]

But Tuve's explanation of the poet's achievement seems ultimately limiting because she regards chivalry as purely metaphoric: Spenser,

> is able to use a knight-errant-romance form so that we grasp not only man's struggle for attainable excellence but see an image of his quest for unattainable perfection. (p.356)

Through the allusion to the Order of the Garter, however, Spenser achieves more than this: the Order acts as a focal point, at which the fictional, legendary world of heroic and triumphant Arthurianism intersects with the Elizabethan world, and through which the qualities of the one can be attributed prophetically to the other. Unlike Tuve's medieval examples, which 'leave this world for another', Spenser's poem embraces its Elizabethan context. As was suggested of the *Letter to Raleigh*'s explanation of the figure of Prince Arthur, chivalry in *The Faerie Queene* has peculiar power here in that it is both vehicle and tenor in this metaphor, both allegorical and that which is allegorized. The projected chivalric order of the poem, replacing the disgraced Knights of Maidenhead, contains both the contemporary Order of the Garter and a prophesy of what that Order could and should be.

Without more of the poem to confirm or invalidate this theory, it must remain speculation. However, one incident in Book Five can be interpreted as participating in the theme I have suggested, of a political and religious chivalry centred on the Garter. When Sir Burbon surrenders his shield in the fight for Flourdelis and is reprehended by Arthegall, Spenser stresses the device on the shield and its origin. Burbon explains,

> True is, that I at first was dubbed knight
> By a good knight, the knight of the *Redcrosse*;
> Who when he gave me armes, in field to fight,
> Gave me a shield, in which he did endosse
> His deare Redeemers badge upon the bosse:
> The same longwhile I bore, and therewithall

---

[15] *Allegorical Imagery*, p.356.

> Fought many battels without wound or losse;
> Therewith *Grandtorto* selfe I did appall,
> And made him oftentimes in field before me fall.　　(V.xi.53)

It is clear that the reference is to Henri IV of France and his politic conversion to Catholicism in 1593, a stunning desertion of the Protestant cause, represented here in the abandonment of the shield of the true faith. But that desertion becomes even more acute if one takes the badge of the red cross to be that of the Order of the Garter. Henri IV had been admitted to the Order in 1590, the year of his accession to the French throne; to Spenser and the more militant Protestants his change of religion must have represented a betrayal of the chivalric ideal of reform, the ideal of the Garter. Such an interpretation is supported by the fact that it is St George, the patron-saint of the Order, who 'dubbed [him] knight' and by whom the device had been conferred. Burbon's willing surrender of the device given him by the Red Cross Knight is, as Sir Arthegall goes on to say, a repudiation of true knighthood; but Burbon rejects, perhaps, not just the shield and knighthood in general, but also the new, re-formed order to which the virtuous knights-patron of *The Faerie Queene* will belong and which is to be revealed in triumph at the end of the poem.

BIBLIOGRAPHY

Place of publication, unless otherwise stated, is London.

Ackerman, Robert W. 'Armor and Weapons in the Middle English Romances'. *State College of Washington Research Studies*, 7 (1939), 104-118.

Adam-Even, Paul. 'Études d'Héraldique Mediéval'. *Archives Héraldiques Suisses*, 62 (1948), 1-10.

Adam-Even, Paul. 'Les Usages Héraldiques au Milieu du XIIe Siècle d'Après *Le Roman de Troie* de Benoit de Sainte Maure et la Littérature Contemporaine'. *Archivum Heraldicum*, 77 (1963), 18-29.

Alciati, Andrea. *Emblemata cum commentariis (Padua, 1621)* in *The Renaissance and the Gods*, edited by Stephen Orgel, vol.25. New York: Garland, 1976.

Allen, Don Cameron. 'Arthur's Diamond Shield in *The Faerie Queene*'. *JEGP*, 36 (1937), 234-243.

Allen, Don Cameron. *Image and Meaning: Metaphoric Traditions in Renaissance Poetry*. Baltimore: Johns Hopkins Press, 1960.

Allen, Don Cameron. *Mysteriously Meant: The Rediscovery of Pagan Symbolism and Allegorical Interpretation in the Renaissance*. Baltimore: Johns Hopkins Press, 1970.

Alpers, Paul. *The Poetry of 'The Faerie Queene'*. Princeton: PUP, 1967.

Anglo, Sydney. 'The London Pageants for the Reception of Katherine of Aragon: November 1501'. *JWCI*, 26 (1963), 53-89.

Anon. 'MS Notes to Spenser's *Faerie Queene*'. *N & Q*, 202 (1957), 509-515.

Anstis, John. *Observations Introductory to an Historical Essay, upon the Knighthood of the Bath.* (1725).

Aptekar, Jane. *Icons of Justice: Iconography and Thematic Imagery in Book V of 'The Faerie Queene'*. New York: Columbia UP, 1969.

Arthos, John. *On the Poetry of Spenser and the Form of Romances*. Allen and Unwin, 1956.

Arthurian Romances, the Vulgate Version of the. Edited by H.Oskar Sommer. 8 vols. Washington, 1908-1916.

Ashmole, Elias. *The Institution, Laws and Ceremonies of the most Noble Order of the Garter*. 2 vols. 1672.

Atkinson, Dorothy F. 'A Note on Spenser and Painting'. *MLN*, 58 (1943), 57-58.

Atkinson, Dorothy F. '*The Wandering Knight*, the Red Cross Knight and "Miles Dei"'. *HLQ*, 7 (1944), 109-134.

Augustine, St. *Augustine: Later Works*. Translated by John Burnaby. S.C.M. Press, 1955.

Axton, Marie. 'Robert Dudley and the Inner Temple Revels'. *Historical Journal*, 13 (1970), 365-378.

Bachiler, Samuel. *Miles Christianus.* Amsterdam, 1625.

Barber, Richard. *The Knight and Chivalry.* 1970; reprinted, Sphere, 1974.

Barclay, Alexander. *The Life of St George.* Edited by William Nelson [EETS. OS. 230] . OUP, 1955.

Barret, Henry. *The Armyng of a Christen Warrier.* 1549.

Bateson, F.W. *English Poetry and the English Language.* 1934; third edition, revised, Oxford: Clarendon Press, 1973.

Bayne, Paul. *The Spirituall Armour.* 1620.

Bayrav, Suheyla. *Symbolisme Mediévale.* Paris: Presses Universitaires de France, 1957.

Bennett, Josephine Waters. *The Evolution of 'The Faerie Queene'.* Chicago: Chicago UP, 1942.

Benoit de Sainte Maure. *Le Roman de Troie.* Edited by Léopold Constans. 6 vols. Paris, 1904-1912.

Berger, Harry, Jnr. *The Allegorical Temper: Vision and Reality in Book II of Spenser's 'Faerie Queene'.* New Haven, Connecticut: Yale UP, 1957.

Bergeron, David M. *English Civic Pageantry 1558-1642.* Arnold, 1971.

The Geneva Bible: A Facsimile of the 1560 Edition. Edited by Lloyd E. Berry. Madison, Milwaukee: Wisconsin UP, 1969.

Birch, Walter de Gray. *Catalogue of Seals in the Department of Manuscripts in the British Museum.* 6 vols. 1887-1900.

A Book of Masques: In Honour of Allardyce Nicoll. Edited by T.J.B. Spencer and S.W. Wells. Cambridge: Cambridge UP, 1967.

Bossewell, John. *Workes of Armorie.* 1572; facsimile reprint, Amsterdam: Theatrum Orbis Terrarum, 1969.

Boutell's Heraldry. Revised by J.P. Brooke-Little. Warne, 1978.

Bradbrook, M.C. *John Webster: Citizen and Dramatist.* Weidenfeld, 1980.

Brault, Gerard J. *Early Blazon: Heraldic Terminology in the Twelfth and Thirteenth Centuries, with Special Reference to Arthurian Literature.* Oxford: Clarendon Press, 1972.

Briggs, Geoffrey. *Civic and Corporate Heraldry: A Dictionary of Impersonal Arms of England, Wales, and Northern Ireland.* Heraldry Today, 1971.

BL Harley MS 6085: Sir William Segar's Book of Royal Arms and Badges. 1604.

BL Harley MS 6064: An Heraldic Book in Folio. Article 15: Instrument for Degrading Thomas Earl of Westmorland and Thomas Duke of Norfolk. 1569.

British Heraldry: From its Origins to c.1800. Edited by Richard Marks and Ann Payne. British Museum Publications, 1978.

Bush, Douglas. *Mythology and the Renaissance Tradition in English Poetry.* Minneapolis: Minnesota UP, 1932.

Calendar of State Papers, Foreign Series 1575-1577. HMSO, 1909.

Calendar of State Papers, Foreign Series 1577-78. HMSO, 1901.

Calendar of State Papers, Foreign Series May – December 1582. HMSO, 1909.

Calvin, Jean. *Sermons de Jean Calvin sur l'Epistre S. Paul Apostre aux Ephesiens.* Geneva, 1562.

Camden, William. *Britain.* Translated by Philemon Holland. 1610.

Camden, William. *Remaines of a Greater Worke, Concerning Britaine.* 1605.

Camden, William. *Remaines of a Greater Worke, Concerning Britaine.* 1614.

Cartigny [or Carthenay] , Jean de. *The Wandering Knight: His Adventurous Journey.* Translated by A.J.H[anmer]. 1889.

Cartigny [or Carthenay], Jean de. *The Wandering Knight.* Edited by Dorothy Atkinson Evans. Seattle: Washington UP, 1951.

Chaucer, Geoffrey. *The Works of Geoffrey Chaucer.* Edited by F.N.Robinson. 1933; second edition, OUP, 1957.

Chew, Samuel. *The Pilgrimage of Life.* New Haven, Connecticut: Yale UP, 1962.

Chew, Samuel. *The Virtues Reconciled: An Iconographic Study.* Toronto: Toronto UP, 1947.

Chrysostom, St John. *Commentary on the Epistle to the Galations and Homilies on the Epistle to the Ephesians.* 1838; revised edition, 1879.

Chrysostom, St John. *The Homilies of St John Chrysostom on the Epistle of S. Paul to the Romans.* 1838; revised edition, 1887.

Collinson, Patrick. *Archbishop Grindal (1519-1583): The Struggle for a Reformed Church.* Cape, 1979.

Comes, Natalis [or Natali Conti]. *Mythologiae, sive explicationum fabularum libri decem.* Paris, 1583.

Corbett, Margery, and Ronald Lightbrown. *The Comely Frontispiece: The Emblematic Title-Page in England 1550-1660.* Routledge and Kegan Paul, 1979.

Corrozet, Gilles. *Hecatomgraphie.* 1540; facsimile reprint, Ilkley: Scolar Press, 1974.

C[otton], R[oger]. *An Armor of Proofe.* 1596.

Coulman, D. ' "Spotted to be Known" '. *JWCI*, 20 (1957), 179-180.

Covarrubias Orozco, Sebastian de. *Emblemas Morales.* 1610; facsimile reprint, Menston: Scolar Press, 1973.

Crawford, John W. 'The Fire from Spenser's Dragon: *The Faerie Queene* I.xi'. *South Central Bulletin*, 30 (1970), 176-178.

Cullen, Patrick. 'Guyon *microchristus*: The Cave of Mammon Reexamined'. *ELH*, 37 (1970), 153-174.

Cullen, Patrick. *Infernal Triad: The Flesh, the World, and the Devil in Spenser and Milton.* Princeton: PUP, 1974.

Dante Alighieri. *The Divine Comedy.* Edited and translated by John D.Sinclair. 3 vols. 1939-1946; revised edition, OUP, 1975.

Dante Alighieri. *Dante con l'espositione di Christoforo Landino, et di Alessandro Vellutello.* Venice, 1564.

La Devise des Armes des Chevaliers de la Table Ronde. Paris, [?] 1520.

Duncan-Jones, Katherine. 'Nashe and Sidney: The Tournament in *The Unfortunate Traveller*'. *MLR*, 63 (1968), 3-6.

Duncan-Jones, Katherine. 'Sidney's Personal *Imprese*'. *JWCI*, 33 (1970), 321-324.

Dundas, J. 'The Rhetorical Basis of Spenser's Imagery'. *SEL*, 8 (1968), 59-75.

Dunseath, T.K. *Spenser's Allegory of Justice in Book Five of 'The Faerie Queene'.* Princeton: PUP, 1968.

Dust, Philip. 'Another Source for Spenser's *Faerie Queene* 1.v.26, 27'. *English Miscellany*, 23 (1972), 15-19.

Dwyer, R.A. 'The Heraldry of Hector and its Antiquity'. *JWCI*, 34 (1971), 325-326.

Edwards, Philip. *Threshold of a Nation: A Study of English and Irish Drama.* Cambridge: Cambridge UP, 1979.

Ellrodt, Robert. *Neoplatonism in the Poetry of Spenser.* Geneva: Drox, 1960.

Elton, G.R. *England under the Tudors.* 1955; second edition, Methuen, 1974.

198

English Drama: Forms and Development. Essays in Honour of Muriel Clara Bradbrook, eds Marie Axton and Raymond Williams. Cambridge: Cambridge UP, 1977.

Entertainments for Elizabeth I, ed. Jean Wilson. [Studies in Elizabethan and Renaissance Culture II]. Woodbridge: D.S.Brewer, 1980.

Erasmus, Desiderus. *A Booke Called in Latyn Enchiridion Militis Christiani.* 1533; facsimile reprint, Amsterdam: Theatrum Orbis Terrarum, 1969.

Ericson, Eston Everett. ' "Reaving the Dead" in the Age of Chivlary'. *MLN*, 52 (1937), 353-355.

Evans, Maurice. 'The Fall of Guyon'. *ELH*, 28 (1961), 215-224.

Evans, Maurice. *Spenser's Anatomy of Heroism: A Commentary on 'The Faerie Queene'.* Cambridge: Cambridge UP, 1970.

Favyn, Andrew. *The Theater of Honour and Knight-Hood.* 2 vols. 1623.

Ferguson, Arthur B. *The Indian Summer of English Chivalry: Studies in the Decline and Transformation of Chivalric Idealism.* Durham, North Carolina: Duke UP, 1960.

Ferne, John. *The Blazon of Gentrie.* 1586.

Fillastre, Guillaume. *Le Premier [– Second] Volume de la Toison d'Or.* Paris, 1516.

Fletcher, Angus. *Allegory: The Theory of a Symbolic Mode.* Ithaca, New York: Cornell UP, 1964.

Fletcher, Angus. *The Prophetic Moment: An Essay on Spenser.* Chicago: Chicago UP, 1971.

Four Supplications 1529-1553 AD. Edited by Frederick J.Furnivall and J.Meadows Cowper [EETS. ES. 13]. 1871.

Four Visitations of Berkshire, ed. W.Harry Rylands. Harleian Society Vols LVI and LVII (1907, 1908).

Fowler, Alastair. *Conceitful Thought.* Edinburgh: Edinburgh UP, 1975.

Fowler, Alastair. *Edmund Spenser.* British Council-Longmans, 1977.

Fowler, Alastair. 'Emblems of Temperance in *The Faerie Queene*, Book II'. *RES*, N.S. 11 (1960), 143-149.

Fowler, Alastair. 'The Image of Mortality: *The Faerie Queene*, II, i-ii'. *HLQ*, 24 (1961), 91-110.

Fowler, Alastair. 'Oxford and London Marginalia to *The Faerie Queene*'. *N & Q*, 206 (1961), 416-419.

Fowler, Alastair. 'The River Guyon'. *MLN*, 75 (1960), 289-292.

Fowler, Alastair. *Spenser and the Numbers of Time.* Routledge and Kegan Paul, 1964.

Fowler, Alastair. *Triumphal Forms: Structural Patterns in Elizabethan Poetry.* Cambridge: Cambridge UP, 1970.

Fowler, Alastair, and Michael Leslie. 'Drummond's Copy of *The Faerie Queene*'. TLS, 17 July 1981, pp.821-822.

Fox, Robert C. 'Temperance and the Seven Deadly Sins in *The Faerie Queene*, Book II'. *RES*, N.S. 12 (1961), 1-6.

Friedman, Lionel J. 'Gradus Amoris'. *Romance Philology*, 19 (1966), 167-177.

Fulgentius, Fabius Plancidiades. *Fabi Plancidiadis Fulgentii V. C. Liber de Expositione Virgilianae Continentiae.* Heidelberg, 1589.

The Blue Garter No More a Sign of Honesty than a Gilded Bush is of Good Wine. 1713.

Gautier, Leon. *Chivalry*. Edited by J.Levron, translated by D.C.Dunning. Phoenix House, 1965.

Gawdy, Philip. *The Letters of Philip Gawdy*. Edited by Isaac Herbert Jeayes. [Roxburghe Club], 1906.

Geoffrey of Monmouth. *History of the Kings of Britain*. Translated by Sebastian Evans. 1912; revised edition, Dent, 1963.

Giamatti, A.Bartlett. *The Earthly Paradise and the Renaissance Epic*. Princeton: PUP, 1966.

Giamatti, A.Bartlett. *Play of Double Senses: Spenser's 'Faerie Queene'*. Englewood Cliffs: Prentice-Hall, 1975.

Gilbert, Allan H. 'The Ladder of Lechery, *The Faerie Queene* III, i, 45'. *MLN*, 56 (1941), 594-597.

Gilbert, Allan H. 'Spenserian Armor'. *PMLA*, 57 (1942), 981-987.

Giles, C.Wilfred Scott-. *Civic Heraldry in England and Wales*. 1933; revised edition, Dent, 1953.

Godfrey, Walter H. and Sir Anthony Wagner. *The College of Arms, Victoria Street*. London Scrutiny Committee, 1963.

Gombrich, Ernst H. *Symbolic Images*. 1972; second edition, Oxford: Phaidon Press, 1978.

Grabes, Herbert. *The Mutable Glass: Mirror Imagery in Titles and Texts of the Middle Ages and the English Renaissance*. Cambridge: Cambridge UP, 1982.

Graziani, René. 'Philip II's *impresa* and Spenser's Souldan'. *JWCI*, 27 (1964), 322-324.

The Great Chronicle of London. Edited by A.H.Thomas and I.D.Thornley. City of London, 1938.

Greaves, Margaret. *The Blazon of Honour: A Study in Renaissance Magnanimity*. Methuen, 1964.

Green, William. *Shakespeare's 'Merry Wives of Windsor'*. Princeton: PUP, 1962.

Greenlaw, E. *Studies in Spenser's Historical Allegory*. 1932; reprinted, Cass, 1967.

Griffin, Jasper. *Homer*. OUP, 1980.

Grueber, H.A. *Coins of the Roman Empire in the British Museum*. 3 vols. 1910.

Guillim, John. *A Display of Heraldry*. 1610; 7th edition, 1724.

Gurewich, Vladimir. 'Observations on the Iconography of the Wound in Christ's Side, with Special Reference to its Position'. *JWCI*, 20 (1957), 358-362.

Hall, James. *Dictionary of Subjects and Symbols in Art*. John Murray, 1974.

Hamilton, A.C. ' "Like Race to Run": The Parallel Structure of *The Faerie Queene*, Books I and II'. *PMLA*, 73 (1958), 327-334.

Hamilton, A.C. *The Structure of Allegory in 'The Faerie Queene'*. Oxford: Clarendon Press, 1961.

Hanford, James Holly and Sara Ruth Watson. 'Personal Allegory in the *Arcadia*: Philisides and Lelius'. *MP*, 32 (1934-1935), 1-10.

Hankins, John Erskine. *Source and Meaning in Spenser's Allegory: A Study of 'The Faerie Queene'*. Oxford: Clarendon Press, 1971.

Hardison, O.B. *The Enduring Monument: A Study of the Idea of Praise in Renaissance Literary Theory and Practice*. Chapel Hill: North Carolina UP, 1962.

Henkel, A. and A.Schone. *Emblemata*. Stuttgart: J.B.Metlersche Verlagsbuchhandlung, [1967].

Hieatt, A.Kent. *Short Time's Endless Monument: The Symbolism of the Numbers in Edmund Spenser's 'Epithalamion'.* 1960; reprinted, Port Washington, New York: Kennikat, 1972.

Hill, John N. 'Braggadocchio and Spenser's Golden World Concept'. *ELH*, 37 (1970), 315-324.

Hind, A.M. *Engraving in England in the Sixteenth and Seventeenth Centuries. Part I: The Tudor Period.* Cambridge: Cambridge UP, 1952.

Hind, A.M. *Engraving in England in the Sixteenth and Seventeenth Centuries. Part II: The Reign of James I.* Cambridge: Cambridge UP, 1955.

Hoccleve, Thomas. *Works.* Edited by F.L.Furnivall and Sir I.Gollancz. 3 vols. [EETS. ES. 61, 72] 1897-1925.

Holborn, Hajo. *A History of Modern Germany: The Reformation.* Eyre and Spottiswoode, 1965.

Holdsworth, W.S. *A History of English Law.* 17 vols. Methuen, 1903-1972.

Homer. *The Iliad.* Edited and translated by A.T.Murray. 2 vols. [Loeb Classics] 1924; reprinted, Heinemann, 1978.

Howell, Roger. *Sir Philip Sidney: The Shepherd Knight.* Hutchinson, 1968.

Hughes, Merritt Yerkes. *Virgil and Spenser.* Berkeley, California, 1929.

Huizinga, J. *The Waning of the Middle Ages.* Translated by F.Hopman. 1924; reissued, Harmondsworth: Penguin, 1979.

Huston, J.Dennis. 'The Function of the Mock Hero in Spenser's *Faerie Queene'.* *MP*, 66 (1969), 212-217.

Hutton, James. 'Spenser and the "Cinq Points en Amours"'. *MLN*, 57 (1942), 657-661.

Jenkinson, Hilary. 'The Great Seal of England: Deputed or Departmental Seals'. *Archaeologia*, 85 (1935), 293-340.

Jones, C.Meredith. 'The Conventional Saracen of the Songs of Geste'. *Speculum*, 17 (1942), 201-225.

Jones, Inigo. *Inigo Jones: The Theatre of the Jacobean Court.* Edited by Stephen Orgel and Roy Strong. 2 vols. Sotheby Parke Bernet, 1973.

Jonson, Ben. *The Works of Ben Jonson.* Edited by C.H.Herford, Percy and Evelyn Simpson. 11 vols. Oxford: Clarendon Press, 1925-1952.

Junius Hadrianus. *Emblemata.* 1565; facsimile edition, Menston: Scolar Press, 1972.

Kaske, Carol V. 'The Dragon's Spark and Sting and the Structure of Red Cross's Dragon-Flight: *The Faerie Queene*, 1.xi-xii'. *SP*, 66 (1969), 609-638.

Katzenellenbogen, Adolf. *Allegories of the Virtues and Vices in Medieaval Art.* Warburg Institute, 1939.

Kemp, Martin. *Leonardo da Vinci: The Marvellous Works of Nature and Man.* Dent, 1981.

Kendrick, T.D. *British Antiquity.* Methuen, 1950.

Kermode, Frank. 'The Cave of Mammon'. *Stratford-on-Avon Studies*, 2 (1960), 151-173.

Kermode, Frank. *Shakespeare, Spenser, Donne.* Routledge and Kegan Paul, 1971.

Kinsley, J. 'Dryden and the Art of Praise'. *English Studies*, 34 (1953), 57-64.

Kipling, Gordon. *The Triumph of Honour: Burgundian Origins of the Elizabethan Renaissance.* The Hague: Leiden UP, 1977.

Kirkpatrick, Robin. 'Appearances of the Red Cross Knight in Book Two of

Spenser's *Faerie Queene*. *JWCI*, 34 (1971), 338-350.

Kouri, E.I. *Elizabethan England and Europe: Forty Unpublished Letters from Elizabeth I to Protestant Powers*. University of London Institute of Historical Research, 1982.

Laking, G.F. *A Record of European Armour and Arms*. 5 vols. 1920-1922.

Lauretus, Hieronymus. *Sylva allegoriarum totius sacrae scripturae*. 2 vols. Venice, 1575.

Legh, Gerard. *The Accedens of Armory*. 1562.

Legh, Gerard. *The Accedens of Armorie*. 1576.

Leonard, H.H. 'Knights and Knighthood in Tudor England'. Unpublished Ph.D. dissertation, University of London, 1970.

Levy, Bernard S. 'Gawain's Spiritual Journey: Imitatio Christi in *Sir Gawain and the Green Knight*'. *Annuale Medievale*, 6 (1965), 65-106.

Lewalski, B.K. *Donne's 'Anniversaries' and the Poetry of Praise*. Princeton: PUP, 1973.

Lewis, C.S. *The Allegory of Love*. Oxford: Clarendon Press, 1936.

Lewis, C.S. *English Literature in the Sixteenth Century Excluding Drama*. Oxford: Clarendon Press, 1954.

Lewis, C.S. 'Neoplatonism in the Poetry of Spenser'. *Etudes Anglaises*, 14 (1961), 107-116.

Lewis, C.S. *Spenser's Images of Life*. Edited by Alastair Fowler. Cambridge: Cambridge UP, 1967.

Lewis, C.S. *Studies in Medieval and Renaissance Literature*. Cambridge: Cambridge UP, 1966.

[*Liber Niger*] *The Register of the most noble Order of the Garter, from its cover in black velvet, usually called the Black Book*. Edited and translated by John Anstis. 2 vols. 1724.

The Library of Drummond of Hawthornden. Edited by Robert H.MacDonald. Edinburgh: Edinburgh UP, 1971.

Liceti, Fortunii. *Hieroglyphica sive antiqua schemata*. Padua, 1653.

Linn, Irving. 'The Arming of Sir Thopas'. *MLN*, 51 (1936), 300-311.

List and Analysis of State Papers, Foreign Series June 1591– April 1592. HMSO, 1980.

Locke, Frederick W. *The Quest for the Holy Grail: A Literary Study of a Thirteenth-Century French Romance*. Stanford, California: Stanford UP, 1960.

London, H.Stanford. 'The Greyhound as a Royal Beast'. *Archaeologia*, 97 (1959), 139-163.

London, H.Stanford. *Royal Beasts*. East Knoyle: Heraldry Society, 1956.

Loomis, R.S. 'The Heraldry of Hector or Confusion Worse Confounded'. *Speculum*, 42 (1967), 32-35.

Lotspeich, H.G. *Classical Mythology in the Poetry of Edmund Spenser*. Princeton: PUP, 1932.

Lull, Ramon. *The Book of the Ordre of Chyvalry*. Translated by William Caxton. Edited by Alfred T.P.Byles. [EETS. OS. 168], 1926.

Lycophron. *The Alexandra of Lycophron*. Edited and translated by George W. Mooney. 1921.

Lydgate, John. *The Pilgrimage of the Life of Man*. Edited by F.L.Furnivall. 3 vols. [EETS. ES. 77, 83, 92], 1889-1904.

MacCaffrey, Wallace T. *Queen Elizabeth and the Making of Policy, 1572-1588.* Princeton: PUP, 1981.

MacIntyre, Jean. 'Arthegall's Sword and the Mutabilitie Cantos'. *ELH*, 33 (1966), 405-414.

McLane, Paul E. *Spenser's Shepheardes Calendar: A Study in Elizabethan Allegory.* Notre Dame, Indiana: University of Notre Dame Press, 1961.

McNeir, Waldo F. 'The Behavior of Brigadore: *The Faerie Queene*, V, 3, 33-34'. *N & Q*, 199 (1954), 103-104.

Major, John M. '*Paradise Regained* and Spenser's Legend of Holiness'. *Renaissance Quarterly*, 20 (1967), 465-470.

Malory, Sir Thomas. *The Works of Sir Thomas Malory.* Edited by Eugene Vinaver. 3 vols. 1947; revised edition, Oxford: Clarendon Press, 1967.

Millican, Charles Bowie. *Spenser and the Table Round.* Cambridge, Massachusetts: Harvard UP, 1932.

Minor Elizabethan Tragedies. Edited by T.W.Craik. Dent, 1974.

Murrin, Michael. *The Veil of Allegory: Some Notes toward a Theory of Allegorical Rhetoric in the English Renaissance.* Chicago: Chicago UP, 1969.

Nashe, Thomas. *The Works of Thomas Nashe.* Edited by R.B.McKerrow, revised by F.P.Wilson. 5 vols. Oxford: Blackwell, 1958.

Nearing, Homer, Jnr. 'Caeser's Sword (*Faerie Queene* II.x.49; *Love's Labour's Lost* V.ii.615)'. *MLN*, 63 (1948), 403-405.

Nelson, William. 'Queen Elizabeth, Spenser's Mercilla, and a Rusty Sword'. *Renaissance News*, 18 (1965), 113-117.

Nennius. *The Works of Gildas and Nennius.* Translated by J.A.Giles, 1841.

Nichols, John. *The Progresses and Public Processions of Queen Elizabeth.* 3 vols. 1788-1805; second edition, 1823.

Nohrnberg, James. *The Analogy of 'The Faerie Queene'.* Princeton: PUP, 1976.

Northrop, Douglas A. 'Mercilla's Court as Parliament'. *HLQ*, 36 (1972-1973), 153-158.

Northrop, Douglas A. 'Spenser's Defence of Elizabeth'. *UTQ*, 38 (1969), 272-294.

O'Connell, Michael. 'History and the Poet's Golden World: The Epic Catalogues in *The Faerie Queene*'. *ELR*, 4 (1974), 241-267.

O'Connell, Michael. *Mirror and Veil: The Historical Dimension of Spenser's 'Faerie Queene'.* Chapel Hill: North Carolina UP, 1977.

Official Guide to Reading. Gloucester: British Printing Corporation, 1977.

Orgel, Stephen. *The Illusion of Power: Political Theater in the English Renaissance.* Berkeley: California UP, 1975.

Orgel, Stephen. *The Jonsonian Masque.* Cambridge, Massachusetts: Harvard UP, 1965.

Ortunez de Calahorra, Diego. *The Mirrour of Princely Deeds and Knighthood, Part One.* Translated by M[argaret] T[yler]. 1578.

Ovid. *Metamorphoses.* Edited and translated by Frank Justus Miller, revised by G.P.Gould. 2 vols. [Loeb Classics] 1916; third edition, Heinemann, 1977.

Ovide Moralisé: Poeme du Commencement du Quatorzième Siècle, publie d'après tous les manuscrits connus. Edited by C. de Boer. 5 vols. Amsterdam, 1915-36.

Panofsky, Erwin. *Hercules am Scheideweg und andere Bildstoffe in der Neueren Kunst.* Leipzig: Teubner, 1930.

Panofsky, Erwin. *Studies in Iconology: Humanistic Themes in the Art of the Renaissance*. 1939; reprinted, New York: Icon Editions, 1972.

Partridge, Eric. *A Dictionary of Slang and Unconventional English*. 2 vols. 1937-1938; fifth edition, Routledge and Kegan Paul, 1961.

Peele, George. *The Life and Works of George Peele*. General editor, C.T.Prouty. 3 vols. New Haven: Yale UP, 1952-1970.

Petrarch, Francesco. *Lord Morley's 'Tryumphes of Fraunces Pertrarcke'*. Edited by D.D.Carnicelli. Cambridge, Massachusetts: Harvard UP, 1971.

Petrarch, Francesco. *Rime e Trionfi*. Edited by Ferdinando Neri. Turin: Unione Tipografico, 1966.

Pincinelli, D.Philippo. *Mundus Symbolicus*. 1681.

Piggott, Stuart. *Ruins in a Landscape: Essays in Antiquarianism*. Edinburgh: Edinburgh UP, 1976.

Pisan, Christine de. *L'Ordene de Chevalerie*. Edited by F.S.Ellis. 1893.

Plato. *The Dialogues of Plato*. Translated by Benjamin Jowett. 4 vols. 1868-1871; fourth edition, corrected reissue, OUP, 1964.

Popham, A.E. 'An Etching by Marcus Gheerhaerts'. *Print Collectors Quarterly*, 16 (1929), 253-257.

Puttenham, George. *The Arte of English Poesie*. Edited by Gladys Doidge Willcock and Alice Walker. Cambridge: Cambridge UP, 1936.

Read, Conyers. *Mr Secretary Walsingham and the Policy of Queen Elizabeth*. 3 vols. Oxford, 1925.

Robinson, J.A.T. *The Body: A Study in Pauline Theology*. S.C.M. Press, 1952.

Roche, T.P. *The Kindly Flame: A Study of the Third and Fourth Books of Spenser's 'Faerie Queene'*. Princeton: PUP, 1964.

Ruskin, John. *Stones of Venice*. 3 vols. 1851-1853.

Sachs, Arieh. 'Religious Despair in Medieval Literature and Art'. *Medieval Studies*, 26 (1964), 231-256.

Scherer, Margaret R. *The Legends of Troy in Art and Literature*. New York: Phaidon Press, 1963.

Schiller, Gertrude. *The Iconography of Christian Art*. Translated by Janet Seligman. Lund Humphries, 1972-.

Schofield, W.H. *Chivalry in English Literature*. Cambridge, Massachusetts, 1912.

Schulze, Ivan L. 'Elizabethan Chivalry and the Faerie Queene's Annual Feast'. *MLN*, 50 (1935), 158-161.

Schulze, Ivan L. 'Notes on Elizabethan Chivalry and *The Faerie Queene*'. *SP*, 30 (1933), 148-159.

Schulze, Ivan L. 'Reflections of Elizabethan Tournaments in *The Faerie Queene*, 4.4 and 5.3'. *ELH*, 5 (1938), 278-284.

Segar, Sir William. *The Booke of Honor and Armes*. 1590.

Segar, Sir William. *Honor, Military and Civill, contained in Foure Bookes*. 1602.

Selden, John. *Titles of Honor*. 1614.

Sidney, Sir Philip. *An Apology for Poetry*. Edited by G.Shepherd. 1965; reprinted, Manchester: Manchester UP, 1973.

Sidney, Sir Philip. *The Countess of Pembroke's Arcadia*. Edited by Maurice Evans. Harmondsworth: Penguin, 1977.

Sidney, Sir Philip. *Miscellaneous Prose*. Edited by Katherine Duncan-Jones and Jan van Dorsten. Oxford: Clarendon Press, 1973.

Sidney, Sir Philip. *The Psalms of David Translated by Sir Philip Sidney and the Countess of Pembroke.* 1823.

Smith, Roland M. 'Origines Arthurianae: The Two Crosses of Spenser's Red Cross Knight'. *JEGP*, 54 (1955), 670-683.

Speed, John. *The Theatre of the Empire of Great Britaine.* 1611.

Spenser, Edmund. *The Works of Edmund Spenser: A Variorum Edition.* Edited by Edwin Greenlaw *et al.* 11 vols. 1932-1949; reprinted Baltimore: Johns Hopkins Press, 1966.

Spenser, Edmund. *The Poetical Works.* Edited by J.C.Smith and E.de Selincourt. 3 vols. Oxford, 1909-1910.

Spenser, Edmund. *The Poetical Works.* Edited by J.C.Smith and E.de Selincourt. 1912; reprinted OUP, 1970.

Spenser, Edmund. *Spenser's 'Faerie Queene': A New Edition with a Glossary, and Notes Explanatory and Critical.* Edited by John Upton. 2 vols. 1758.

Spenser, Edmund. *The Faerie Queene.* Edited by A.C.Hamilton. Longman, 1977.

Spenser, Edmund. *The Faerie Queene.* Edited by T.P.Roche with C.Patrick O'Donnell, Jnr. Harmondsworth: Penguin, 1978.

Spenser, Edmund. *Books One and Two of 'The Faerie Queene': The Mutability Cantos and Selections from the Minor Poetry.* Edited by R.Kellogg and O.Steele. New York: Odyssey Press, 1965.

Staveren, Augustinus van. *Auctores Mythographi Latini.* Leiden, 1742.

Steadman, J.M. 'Una and the Clergy: The Ass Symbol in *The Faerie Queene*'. *JWCI*, 21 (1958), 134-137.

Sterne, Laurence. *The Life and Opinions of Tristram Shandy, Gentleman.* Edited by G.Petrie. Harmondsworth: Penguin, 1967.

Stokstad, Marilyn, and Jerry Stannard, eds. *Gardens of the Middle Ages.* Lawrence, Kansas: Spencer Museum of Art, 1983.

Strong, Roy. *The Cult of Elizabeth.* Thames and Hudson, 1977.

Strong, Roy. *The English Icon: Elizabethan and Jacobean Portraiture.* Paul Mellon Foundation—Routledge and Kegan Paul, 1969.

Strong, Roy. *Portraits of Queen Elizabeth I.* Oxford: Clarendon Press, 1963.

Strong, Roy. 'Queen Elizabeth I and the Order of the Garter'. *Archaeological Journal*, 119 (1964 [for 1962]), 245-269.

Strong, Roy. *Tudor and Jacobean Portraits.* 2 vols. Her Majesty's Stationery Office, 1969.

Sutcliffe, Matthew. *The Practice, Proceedings, and Lawes of Armes.* 1593.

Tasso, Torquato. *Poesie.* Edited by Francesco Flora. Milan: Ricciardi, [1952].

Tervarent, Guy de. *Attributs et Symboles dans l'Art Profane 1450-1600: Dictionnaire d'un Langage Perdu.* 3 vols. Geneva: Droz, 1958-1964.

A Theatre for Spenserians. Edited by Judith M.Kennedy and James A.Reither. Toronto: Toronto UP, 1973.

Thompson, Edward Maude. 'The Revision of the Statutes of the Order of the Garter by King Edward the Sixth'. *Archaeologia*, LIV (1894), 173-198.

Tilley, Morris Palmer. *A Dictionary of the Proverbs in England in the Sixteenth and Seventeenth Centuries.* Ann Arbor: Michigan UP, 1950.

Tonkin, Humphry. *Spenser's Courteous Pastoral: Book VI of the 'Faerie Queene'.* Oxford: Clarendon Press, 1972.

Tosello, Matthew I.M.C. 'Spenser's Silence about Dante'. *SEL*, 17 (1977), 59-66.

Tuve, Rosemond. *Allegorical Imagery: Some Medieaval Books and their Posterity.* Edited by T.P.Roche. Princeton: PUP, 1966.

Tuve, Rosemond. *Elizabethan and Metaphysical Imagery: Renaissance Poetic and Twentieth-Century Critics.* Chicago: Chicago UP, 1947.

Tuve, Rosemond. *Seasons and Months.* Paris: Librarie Universitaire, 1933.

Vaivre, Jean-Bernard de. 'L'Héraldique et l'Histoire de l'Art au Moyen Age'. *Gazette des Beaux Arts*, 93 (1979), 99-108.

Valeriano Bolzoni, J.P. *Hieroglyphica sive de sacris aegyptiorum literis commentarii.* Basel, 1556.

Valeriano Bolzoni, J.P. *Hieroglyphica sive de sacris aegyptiorum literis commentarii.* Basel, 1575.

Van Marle, R. *Iconographie de l'Art Profane au Moyen-Age à la Renaissance.* 2 vols. La Haye: Martinus Nijhoff, 1931-32.

Virgil. *The Aeneid of Virgil.* Edited by R.D.Williams. 2 vols. Macmillan, 1972-1973.

Virgil. Edited and translated by H.Rushton Fairclough. [Loeb Classics], 1916; revised edition, Heinemann, 1978.

Voltaire. *Romans et Contes.* Edited by Rene Groos. Paris: Gallimard, 1954.

Voragine, Jacobus de. *The Golden Legend.* Translated by William Caxton, edited by F.S.Ellis. 1892.

Wagner, Sir Anthony. *Heralds of England: A History of the Office and College of Arms.* College of Arms, 1967.

Wagner, Sir Anthony. *Records and Collections of the College of Arms.* Burke's Peerage, 1952.

Walker, David M. *The Oxford Companion to Law.* Oxford: Clarendon Press, 1980.

The Warfare of Christians. Translated by Arthur Golding. 1576.

Warton, Thomas. *Observations on the 'Faerie Queene' of Spenser.* 2 vols. 1754; second edition, enlarged, 1762.

Watson, Thomas. *Poems.* Edited by Edward Arber. 1870.

Weiner, Andrew D. *Sir Philip Sidney and the Poetics of Protestantism: A Study of Contexts.* Minneapolis: University of Minnesota Press, 1978.

Welsford, Enid. *The Court Masque.* Cambridge, 1927.

West, Michael. 'Spenser and the Renaissance Ideal of Christian Heroism'. *PMLA*, 88 (1973), 1013-1032.

Whiting, Bartlett Jere with Helen Wescott Whiting. *Proverbs, Sentences, and Proverbial Phrases from English Writings Mainly before 1500.* Cambridge, Massachusetts: Harvard UP, 1968.

Whitaker, V.K. *The Religious Basis of Spenser's Thought.* Stanford: Stanford UP, 1950.

Williams, Kathleen. *Spenser's 'Faerie Queene': The World of Glass.* Routledge and Kegan Paul, 1966.

Wilson, D.B. *Descriptive Poetry in France from Blason to Baroque.* Manchester: Manchester UP, 1967.

Wind, Edgar. *Pagan Mysteries in the Renaissance.* 1958; second edition, Harmondsworth: Penguin, 1967.

Wittkower, R. 'Transformations of Minerva in Renaissance Imagery'. *JWCI*, 2 (1938-1939), 194-205.

Yates, Frances A. *Astraea: The Imperial Theme in the Sixteenth Century*. Routledge, 1975.

Yates, Frances A. *The Valois Tapestries*. Warburg Institute, 1959.

Zitner, S.P. 'Spenser's Diction and Classical Precedent'. *PQ*, 45 (1966), 360-371.

INDEX

Cartigny, Jean, 102, 119, 120, 171-72
Casimir of the Palatinate, 192-93
Catherine of Aragon, 51
Caxton, 102, 136
Cecil, William, 151
cestus, 77, 153, 155, 156, 159, 175-77
Chapman, George, 55
chastity, 23, 28-32, 41-45, 75-84,
    144, 173, 171-72
Charles IX, 190
Chaucer, 38, 122, 123, 133
checklaton, 38
Chitting, Henry, 141
chivalry, 5-7, 132-38, 186-195
Christ, 17-18, 21, 56, 61-62, 99, 101,
    102, 106, 107, 108, 113, 114-15,
    116, 125-26, 128-131, 173
Chrysostom, St John, 101-102, 107,
    117, 125-26
Church, Ralph, 33
cingulum militare, 169-177
Claude of Brittany, 32
clubs, 77
College of Arms, 8, 141
Collinson, Patrick, 152n
Comes, Natalis, 20, 98
Common Pleas, Court of, 66-68
concupiscence, 96-98
Cotton, Sir Robert, 9
'couch', 54
Coulman, D., 13n
courtesy, 46-48
Crayer, Gaspar de, 43
crests, 52-56, 63-68 (Arthur's); 57-
    68 (Arthegall's)
Crusaders, 102, 127
crux invicta, 55, 130-31
Cullen, Patrick, 21-22
Cupid, 20

Danae, 21
Daniel, Samuel, 27n
Dante, 57-62
degradation, 160-65, 168, 170
Deguileville, 124-25
despair, 122-25
diamond, 15-20, 24, 36, 90
Diogenes, 99-100

disarming, 40-49
dragon, 30, 52-56, 63-66
dragon-crest, 23 (Arthur's), 52-56,
    63
Drayton, Michael, 9
Drummond, William, of Hawthornden,
    62n
Dugdale, Sir William, 8-9
Duncan-Jones, Katherine, 13n
Dunseath, T.K., 4, 27-28, 30, 35, 65,
    84, 146, 153-54
Dwyer, R.A., 33n

Ecclesia, 130
Eden, Garden of, 114
Edward III, 6, 140, 144, 148, 170, 175
Edward IV, 134
Edward VI, 6, 142, 151-52
Elizabeth I, 6-7, 11, 22-23, 25, 31-32,
    36-37, 63-68, 124, 142, 144, 145,
    149, 152, 169, 186, 190-94
Elizabeth of York, 36
Elton, G.R., 66n
emblems, 7
epanorthosis, 176
equestrian order, 167
Erasmus, 102
ermine, 27-29, 31-32, 63
Ermine, Order of the, 32
'Ermine Portrait' (Hatfield House),
    31-32
Essex, Earl of, 145
Evans, Maurice, 49, 54n
Evelake, King, 24
Excalibur, 53, 85

faith, 90, 111, 113-14, 119, 120-21,
    127, 195
fame, 87
fantasy houses, 7
Favyn, Andrew, 136, 164-65, 166,
    169, 170
Ferguson, Arthur B., 132-34
Ferne, John, 171
Fillastre, Guillaume, 136, 138
'finesse', 158
fire, 81, 86
Fletcher, Angus, 138-39

209